Praise for *Blackhorse Riders*

"Philip Keith has written a riveting account of one of the most extraordinary and courageous rescues in U.S. military history. *Blackhorse Riders* is written with enough detail to satisfy even the most particular of military historians, yet Keith's compelling storytelling breathes life into the personalities involved, so that minute by minute, following both rescuers and rescued, you keep turning pages to find out who lives and who dies."

—Karl Marlantes, *New York Times* bestselling author of *Matterhorn* and *What It Is Like to Go to War*

"One of the finest and best-told combat stories to come out of Vietnam. *Blackhorse Riders* is a portrait of men at war, reluctant soldiers in an unpopular conflict whose actions on a single day rose to the level of extraordinary heroism, courage, and sacrifice. For those of us who were there, this is the kind of book we would be proud to pass on to our children."   —Nelson DeMille

"This gripping, vividly detailed narrative finally tells a story that was overlooked for far too long, a story of nail-biting action and *Band of Brothers*–like courage. Many men are alive today because of the bravery of Alpha Troop, the officers and their men who would not turn their back on comrades in mortal danger in the jungles of South Vietnam. *Blackhorse Riders* is a bold tale, well told, of heroism, rescue, and, finally, recognition."

—Bob Drury and Tom Clavin, *New York Times* bestselling authors of *Halsey's Typhoon* and *The Last Stand of Fox Company*

"This riveting true story of young American soldiers fighting in Vietnam paints a gut-wrenching picture of combat rarely described in print. It is told by the soldiers who fought the battle, received the wounds, and suffered the loss of friends. Forty years after the battle, the survivors are brought together at the White House to be rec-

ognized for their heroism with the Presidential Unit Citation. The emotion of the 'old soldiers' is truly extraordinary and perfectly captured in this book."　　　　　　　　　　　—John C. "Doc" Bahnsen,
Brigadier General, U.S. Army (Ret.),
former Squadron Commander of 1st Squadron,
11th Armored Cavalry, the "Blackhorse Regiment"

"A masterful and compelling narrative that focuses on individuals relating their experiences of heroism, sacrifice, teamwork, and extraordinary feats under the harshest conditions. This chronological tale superbly describes in significant detail the challenges faced on an almost daily basis by American units serving in Vietnam. Phil Keith has written a very readable, extremely well-researched, difficult-to-put-down narrative that leaves the reader at once informed, saddened by the inevitable casualties enumerated, but also very proud of U.S. citizen-soldiers performing their duties."
　　　　　　　—Mike Conrad, Major General, U.S. Army (Ret.)

"A riveting account of tragedy and death in Vietnam—and of wrongs ultimately righted."　　　　　　　　　　　—*The Washington Times*

"A fine, precisely detailed record of an obscure but nasty battle in Vietnam in which heroism was forgotten even more quickly than the war itself . . . Keith provides an engrossing, almost minute-by-minute account of the preliminaries and the battle itself."
　　　　　　　　　　　　　　　　　　　—*Kirkus Reviews*

"A definite must-read."　　　　　　　　　　　　　　　—*Booklist*

BLACKHORSE RIDERS

A **Desperate** Last Stand,
An **Extraordinary** Rescue Mission,
And the **Vietnam Battle** America Forgot

Philip Keith

 St. Martin's Griffin ❧ New York

www.stmartins.com

Design by Phil Mazzone

The Library of Congress has cataloged the hardcover edition as follows:

Keith, Philip A.
    Blackhorse riders : a desperate last stand, an extraordinary rescue mission, and the Vietnam battle America forgot / Philip Keith.
        p. cm.
    Includes bibliographical references and index.
    ISBN 978-0-312-68192-0 (hardcover)
    ISBN 978-1-4299-4095-5 (e-book)
    1. Vietnam War, 1961–1975—Campaigns—Vietnam—Tay
Ninh.   2. United States. Army. Armored Cavalry Regiment, 11th—
History.   3. United States. Army. Cavalry Regiment, 8th. Charlie
Company.   4. Vietnam War, 1961–1975—Jungle warfare.   5. Vietnam War,
1961–1975—Regimental histories—United States.   I. Title.   II. Title:
Vietnam battle America forgot.
    DS558.4.T39K45 2012
    959.704'342—dc23

                                                                2011033223

ISBN 978-1-250-02122-9 (trade paperback)

First St. Martin's Griffin Edition: February 2013

10 9 8 7 6 5 4 3 2 1

To all the valiant men of Alpha Troop, 1st Squadron,
11th Armored Cavalry Regiment,
who were present and ready for duty,
March 26, 1970,
and
all Vietnam Veterans everywhere,
plus, if I may,
to my wonderful Muse . . . she believed . . .

CONTENTS

AUTHOR'S NOTE

The chronicle of events in this book is based on information provided by the men who were directly involved. The material comes from their written statements or from my conversations with the men themselves, sometimes both. All interviews, some requiring many sessions, took place in person, by phone, or via the Internet; on occasion, all three. The vast majority of all that appears on these pages is the thoughts, interpretations, true statements, and reactions of the soldiers who were there, on the ground, fighting for their lives. This is their story, not mine, and as such I have made every effort to tell it as they saw and experienced it.

I have provided some background, at the outset, on the actual tactical and physical environment that surrounded these men at the time of the actions detailed. All the events central to the story take place within an area of the former Republic of Vietnam called War Zone C, a vast tract of land north of Saigon and the actual operating locale of the 11th Armored Cavalry during early 1970. The backdrop material is included to offer some perspective and context. This book is not a discourse on the Vietnam War. Many eminent authors have already tackled that project. *Blackhorse Riders* is a book about a discrete series of proceedings that took place during a few days of that war.

In the same fashion, and for the same reason, I have included a few details on the arms and equipment these men used, principally the cavalry vehicles that are such an important part of the overall narrative. I wanted the reader to have a sense of the power, the effectiveness, and even the vulnerability of the weapons employed in the total framework of this combat setting.

I also felt it was important to provide a fairly robust glossary. (It is positioned immediately before the bibliography.) Readers unfamiliar with the military terms and common soldier slang of the day will have reference to the acronyms and bits of jargon used in the text. I have also defined each unique term or bit of vernacular the first time it is used in the text, hoping this will help orient the non-military reader.

In addition to the interviews and contacts I made with these remarkable warriors, I conducted extensive research in the National Archives and other official army records. I was also allowed to read a number of personal journals, a few diaries, and some letters written by the men. Several former soldiers also favored me with caches of their contemporary photographs.

The actions that form the bulk of this account occurred under conditions that could only be described as extreme. There was immense emotional and mental duress. The surrounding environment was debilitating, and almost all the participants were engaged in constant combat. Many of the memories shared here are as vivid to these veterans as if the events had happened yesterday. Other recollections have been diffused through a forty-year-old prism. Some reminiscences have shifted entirely as the decades have passed, as we might expect. Certain details have been forgotten, or even repressed completely.

As the author—narrator, really—I have made every effort to duplicate the actual sequence of events, but there were occasional differences from one soldier's account to another's. In cases where memories clashed, I tried as much as possible to triangulate the recollections; that is, to make sure at least two other reminiscences corroborated the memory under discussion. I have done my best to relate the version of the events that seemed the most consistent. Happily, the conflicts were few. What results, I hope, is a free-flowing story line that tries to do justice to the incredible acts of bravery that occurred in this compressed period of time. The bottom line to this recounting is that these "average Joes" took deep breaths, ignored the dangers, and did what they thought was right. They decided they had to at least try to help out a group of fellow soldiers who had run out of options and found themselves in deep, serious, life-threatening trouble. We could hardly ask for more from the American fighting men—and, today, the fighting women—who guard the front lines of freedom.

There were certainly bigger and more important battles during the Vietnam War than the one these men fought on March 26, 1970. In fact, some of these same men would become involved in a more horrific encounter six days later, on April 1, at a hellhole called Fire Support Base Illingworth. Most of these men would participate in the Cambodian Incursion that would begin six weeks hence. The battle of March 26 does not even have an official name to this day, but it does have an importance far outstripped by its lack of documentation and size. Here's why:

Had these men not tackled the rescue, an entire company of infantry, over eighty men, would have been killed or captured. This would have been one of the worst single-unit, single-day losses for the American military in Vietnam. There was even a time during this "anonymous battle" when the brave commander of the infantry unit that became surrounded by the NVA actually contemplated becoming the "George Armstrong Custer of Vietnam."

There's more, though: The tale of Team Alpha's derring-do in 1970 is not the whole story. Beyond the fight itself, there is the subsequent saga of recognition initially denied and lost valor finally redeemed. I first read the story of these men within the pages of the *New York Times*, on October 1, 2009. In a national news piece, I learned about Alpha Troop* and their pending date at the White House for their investiture with the prestigious Presidential Unit Citation. The article detailed the heroics that earned them this award, but it also documented the incredible forty-year wait for recognition and the long, hard slog their former commander, John Poindexter, had endured to get them their rightful place in history. Instantly, I knew this was a tale that deserved a bigger audience.

Here, then, is the story of what these men still call "the Anonymous Battle" and a chronicle of the saga of their lives after Vietnam. I daresay these brave and deserving Americans will be anonymous no more.

—PHIL KEITH
Southampton, New York
January 2012

---

* The PUC was awarded to Alpha Troop, 1st Squadron, 11th Armored Cavalry, which was half of what this book describes as "Team Alpha." The other half of the team was Company A, 2nd Battalion, 8th Cavalry. Company A, unfortunately, did not participate in the ceremonies at the White House. The reasons why will be explained within the text.

DRAMATIS PERSONAE

Each individual is listed with his rank and assignment as of March 1970.

ALPHA TROOP, 1ST SQUADRON, 11TH ARMORED CAVALRY REGIMENT

Captain John B. Poindexter, Commanding Officer

First Lieutenant Paul Baerman, Executive Officer

First Lieutenant Mike Healey, Platoon Leader, 2nd Platoon

First Lieutenant Robert "Robin" Henderson, Platoon Leader, 3rd Platoon

Master Sergeant Jerry Holloman, First Sergeant

Sergeant First Class Robert Foreman, Platoon Sergeant, 3rd Platoon, Tank Commander, A-37

Sergeant First Class William McNew, Acting Platoon Leader, 1st Platoon

Staff Sergeant Peter Cavieux, Acting Sheridan Tank Commander, A-18

Staff Sergeant Dennis Cedarquist, ACAV Commander, A-14

Staff Sergeant Pasqual Gutierrez, Platoon Sergeant, 2nd Platoon, Tank Commander, A-27

Staff Sergeant "JC" Hughes, Tank Commander, A-18
Staff Sergeant Curtis Sorenson, Tank Commander, A-38
Sergeant Ronald Bench, Mortar Section NCO
Sergeant Donnie Colwell, Medic Track Commander, A-81
Sergeant James Crew, Tank Commander, A-39
Sergeant William Daniels, Tank Gunner, A-37
Sergeant Dennis Jabbusch, Track Commander, A-66
Sergeant Francis "Bud" Smolich, Mortar Section Chief
Sergeant Greg Steege, Senior Radio Operator, A-66
Sergeant Ronald Vaughan, Track Commander, A-33
Sergeant Joe Wakefield, Mortarman
SP5 Walter "Chip" Andrews, Mortarman, A-86
SP5 Rod Lorenz, Tank Driver, A-37
SP5 Gary McCubbin, Track Commander, A-23
SP5 Craig Wright, Medic
SP4 John Biggs, Tank Gunner, A-27
SP4 George Burks, Tank Gunner, A-19
SP4 James Cadotte, M-60 Gunner, A-34
SP4 Floyd Clark, M-60 Gunner, A-34
SP4 Floyd Coates, Mortarman
SP4 Bryan Cupp, Track Driver, A-26
SP4 Donald Dush, M-60 Gunner, A-66
SP4 Robert K. "Kenny" Euge, Track Driver, A-10
SP4 Gary Felthager, Medic
SP4 Don Grayson, Tank Loader, A-38
SP4 Jerry Guenthardt, M-60 Gunner, A-14
SP4 Burl "Topper" Hart, M-60 Gunner, A-66
SP4 Larry King, M-60 Gunner, A-21
SP4 Ray Moreno, M-60 Gunner, A-26
SP4 Angel Pagan, M-60 Gunner, A-13
SP4 Fred Pimental, M-60 Gunner, A-26
SP4 Larry Roberts, Track Commander, A-13
SP4 Irwin Rutchik, M-60 Gunner, A-10
SP4 Raymond Tarr, Tank Loader, A-38

SP4 Larry Toole, Tank Gunner, A-17

SP4 Lowell Walburn, Tank Gunner, A-39

PFC Stanley Carter, Tank Loader, A-27

PFC Thomas Hudspeth, M-60 Gunner, A-10

PFC Romeo Martin, M-60 Gunner, A-21

PFC August Whitlock, Field Cook

COMPANY A, 2ND BATTALION, 8TH CAVALRY, 1ST CAVALRY DIVISION

Captain Ray Armer, Commanding Officer, Company A

SP4 Fred Harrison, Machine Gunner, 3rd Platoon

COMPANY C, 2ND BATTALION, 8TH CAVALRY, 1ST CAVALRY DIVISION

Captain George Hobson, Commanding Officer

Staff Sergeant Preston Dawson, Acting Platoon Leader

SP4 Dave Nicholson, Point Man

SP4 Richard Hokenson, Sniper

PFC Paul Evans, Rifleman

PFC Ken "Mississippi" Woodward, Rifleman and Radio Telephone
Operator (RTO)

FIRST SQUADRON, 11TH ARMORED CAVALRY

Lieutenant Colonel John Norton, Squadron Commander

2ND BATTALION, 8TH CAVALRY, 1ST CAVALRY DIVISION

Lieutenant Colonel Michael Conrad, Battalion Commander

1ST CAVALRY DIVISION

Brigadier General George Casey Sr., Assistant Division Commander

FOREWORD

*B**lackhorse Riders* is a Soldier's story of ordinary men who voluntarily undertook an extraordinary mission. The narrative is riveting, powerful, and inspirational. It is also a timeless story that represents the best of what we have come to expect of our men and women fighting along the front lines of freedom.

As a young man coming of age into the United States Army at the end of the Vietnam War, I began my forty-one years of service as these Soldiers, like my father, were winding up an unpopular conflict. I have always felt that their legacy was undervalued and that we have too often been left with the fractiousness caused by that war and not the valor and recognition that these brave men and women deserve.

Blackhorse Riders is only one account of the many thousands of engagements of the Vietnam War, but one that can help reverse an unpopular image of the Vietnam War that we have carried for far too long. Here is a chronicle of unparalleled courage focusing on a daring rescue pulled off by common Soldiers who would not abandon a group of their peers who were in desperate trouble. It is a Vietnam story with a happy ending, for once, that will resonate with not only Veterans of that conflict but with the public at large.

I am extraordinarily proud of my father's role in this action. I knew my dad best in the context of our family surroundings, and he was an incredible role model for me. I also knew him by his reputation among his men. The fact that he, even as a general officer and assistant division commander, would jump into his own helicopter and ride to the assistance of some of his men who had become trapped behind enemy lines does not surprise me. It was just the kind of thing he did—caring for his men, just as he did for his family. It was, in fact, on a mission of care and concern, only four months after the actions described in this book, that we lost him in a tragic helicopter crash in the Vietnam highlands.

I have spent a good portion of my career in the 1st Cavalry Division, and I have always had a soft spot in my heart for the role of the cavalry in our history. I was, therefore, thrilled by the description of how this brave troop from the 1st Squadron of the 11th Armored Cavalry Regiment charged through the dense jungles to come to the aid of a company of infantry surrounded and cut off by an overwhelming enemy force. I was also fascinated by the account of how some of their brave deeds had been overlooked and then ultimately recognized by a grateful nation when Alpha Troop was awarded their well-deserved Presidential Unit Citation.

As President Obama said in his remarks at the PUC ceremony, "After all these years, why honor this heroism now? The answer is simple: because we must." The recognition may have come a bit late, but as I learned over my four decades of service, the U.S. Army tries very hard to take care of its own and by rendering these brave men these honors, we are fulfilling a pledge to them as well as to all Vietnam Veterans.

I highly recommend *Blackhorse Riders* to anyone in search of a positive and compelling story about the resiliency and dedication of the American Soldier.

—General (Ret.) George W. Casey Jr.

BLACKHORSE RIDERS

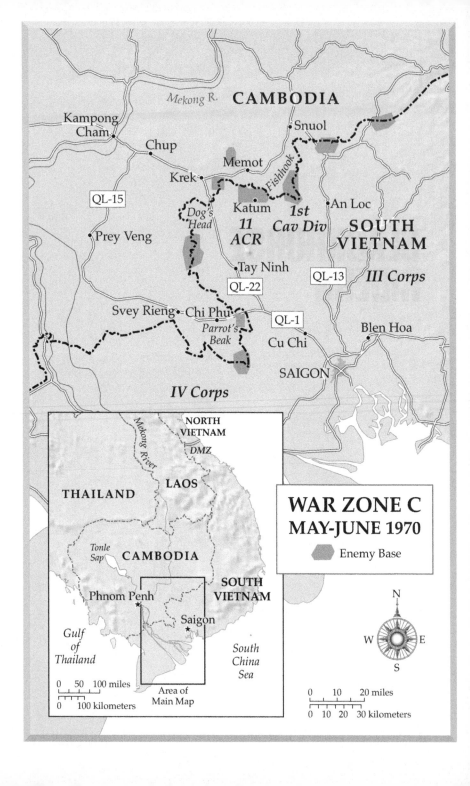

INTRODUCTION

OCTOBER 20, 2009, THE ROSE GARDEN,
THE WHITE HOUSE, WASHINGTON, DC

It was a glorious fall morning, crisp and clean, burnished by a late October sun. It was just warm enough that sweaters and topcoats would not be required. By 8:00 A.M., electricians from the White House Press Office were busily stringing cable and electrical cords from a junction box hidden behind the fading roses. Two men carefully lifted the presidential podium and walked it to the spot just off the portico steps where the president would deliver his remarks. Masking-tape Xs were placed on the temporary decking to mark locations where the special guests would stand behind the president. Other technicians began to install the teleprompters this president loved to use with such effect. More workers began diligently unloading piles of folding chairs and started placing them in evenly spaced rows. It was a ballet that had been performed a thousand times before, all of it choreographed for evening news stories where serious announcers would dramatically intone, "Today, in a special ceremony in the Rose Garden of the White House, the president . . ."

This day's preparations heralded a landmark: the first time for Barack Obama, as commander in chief, to bestow the prestigious Presidential Unit Citation, commonly called the PUC, on a military unit singled out for "extraordinary heroism." In its proper precedence among United States military decorations the PUC is equivalent to the army's Distinguished Service Cross, the Navy Cross, or the Air Force Cross, medals designated for individual acts of great bravery under fire. The PUC, by contrast, is granted to an entire unit and all the service members attached to the unit at the time of the underlying action. The PUC is highly prized among all the military's branches. Since its inception in 1942, and over the course of World War II, Korea, Vietnam, Panama, Grenada, Gulf One, Iraq, and Afghanistan, the PUC had been awarded less than one hundred seventy times.

The actual ceremony and the president's remarks were scheduled to begin shortly after noon, but the honorees and their guests were being escorted to the Rose Garden well in advance. A good thing, too, since there were a few canes, a couple of wheelchairs, and several metal walkers among the 119 veterans and other attendees who would be squeezed into the confines of this famous patch of flowers and lush green grass.

Extra time to get to their assigned seats would be appreciated by more than a few. Honorable wounds or injuries received while in uniform certainly accounted for some of the assistance items in use, but most of those who filed into the garden were simply a little older, a little grayer, a little slower of step than some. This ceremony may have been the new commander in chief's first, but it was not, as might have been surmised, a recognition event to mark the heroics of some worthy unit recently tested in the deserts of Iraq or the mountains of Afghanistan. No, this was an awards program that would stretch back almost forty years, to thick and steamy jungles, in a forbidding place called War Zone C, deep in the heart of Vietnam.

This PUC was being awarded to Alpha Troop, 1st Squadron, 11th Armored Cavalry, the famed Blackhorse Regiment, for an action that occurred on March 26, 1970, when the men gathering around the president were nineteen- and twenty-year-old soldiers. The president, by contrast, had only been a boy of eight. Now in their late fifties and early sixties, these same men were finally going to get their due. They might look a bit older, they might move a tad slower, but their faces would still beam with pride in their long-ago accomplishments.

The story of the battle these men fought is remarkable in and of itself, but so, as it turns out, was the campaign to achieve its recognition. It started this way: In March 1970, Alpha Troop was staged far out in what the men then called "the boonies" (i.e., the middle of nowhere). The unit was a specialized armored cavalry outfit equipped with tanks and armored cavalry assault vehicles. Late in the morning of the 26th, they began hearing plaintive radio calls from an infantry unit that had run across a hidden North Vietnamese Army stronghold. Outnumbered by seven or eight to one,* the eighty-odd Americans were quickly surrounded, pinned down, and fighting for their very lives. Rescue seemed impossible. Helicopters could not penetrate the dense jungle to land, drop supplies, or extract the men. Artillery and air support could not be targeted effectively without the possibility of killing friendlies as well as the enemy. It seemed the company was fated to be worn down, outgunned, and eventually all killed or captured.

By chance, Alpha Troop was then staged about four klicks (slang for "kilometers") away, in a formation called an NDP (night defensive position). The commander of Alpha Troop, twenty-five-year-old Capt. John Poindexter, weighed the options. It became apparent

---

* Estimates of the enemy ran from a low of "four to one" to a high of "nine to one." The truth is that no exact count was ever determined, but it was at least "five to one" based on the author's research and more probably "seven or eight to one."

to him that his outfit was the only hope for the trapped company. Might it be possible for his mechanized unit to smash through enough jungle by nightfall to reach them? Not making the attempt was deemed unacceptable, so he ordered his men to "saddle up." With the grit, guts, and determination that often make legends out of ordinary men, they made it. They shoved their way through the jungle, effected a daring rescue, fought a pitched battle, and managed to pull everyone out. Many brave deeds were done that day, and Captain Poindexter tried to make sure his men were recognized for their heroics. However, in this particular instance, for reasons never discovered, the recommendations for some of the medals and, indeed, even the record of the battle itself were either lost or misplaced in a haze of army paperwork.

Thirty years later, and quite by accident, the very same John Poindexter was made aware that these papers had somehow gone missing. Thus began the second phase of this remarkable story: another six-year-long "battle" to restore the awards gone astray and get his brave men recognized for what they had accomplished. Long-forgotten details needed to be resurrected; faded paperwork had to be tracked down; new witness statements were required to be produced; and reluctant minds had to be convinced. Thankfully, after Herculean efforts and great cost—most of the financial burden borne by John Poindexter himself—the past is recovered and honor is restored.

The full circle is completed as President Obama finally steps to that podium on October 20, 2009, and begins his remarks with "Good afternoon, everybody, and welcome to the White House. And welcome to a moment nearly forty years in the making . . ."

A complete copy of the president's remarks is contained in appendix 1.

1

ALPHA TROOP: MEN OF IRON, STEEDS OF STEEL

1200, MARCH 26, 1970, ALPHA TROOP'S NDP,
WAR ZONE C, REPUBLIC OF VIETNAM

*S*omebody's in serious trouble, Capt. John Poindexter
told himself as he sat, sweltering, in the stifling heat. The long, tall
Texan, twenty-five, was trying to steal a few minutes of downtime
after a horrible night of pain, terror, and numbing death among the
members of his cavalry troop.

It was well over a hundred degrees, even under the cover of the
canvas tent-top that extended from the rear of Poindexter's M-577
(a specialized ACAV, or armored cavalry assault vehicle). Seconds
before, the battalion radio inside the baking command vehicle behind him had crackled to life. Racer Two-Nine was calling Stone
Mountain Two-Nine and insistently asking for help.

Poindexter perked up and cocked an ear to listen. He knew Stone
Mountain Two-Nine was his current boss, Lt. Col. Mike Conrad,
battalion commander of the 2nd Battalion, 8th Cavalry. It took him
a few more seconds to recall that Racer Two-Nine was that fellow

Hobson, the commander of Charlie Company, also part of Conrad's battalion. Poindexter had worked with Hobson's company, but that was before Hobson had taken over a couple of weeks back. Poindexter's men were soldiering with Alpha Company, a brother company to Charlie, currently under the command of Capt. Ray Armer. Armer was, in fact, sitting just a few feet away from Poindexter, suffering in the same heat and also intently interested in what the radio was pumping out.

From the semigarbled back-and-forth it eventually became clear that Hobson was in a real shit sandwich (a very bad tactical situation). His company of infantry, about eighty men, had inadvertently walked into the middle of a large, concealed, heavily fortified North Vietnamese Army (NVA) supply base. Worse, the complex seemed to be populated by frontline regular soldiers, possibly as many as a battalion. If the NVA were even at moderate strength, Hobson was outnumbered at least seven or eight to one, maybe more. Even worse news: The NVA were entrenched in bunkers. This meant they were safely behind stout dirt-and-log barricades and Hobson and his men were out in the open, or at best ducking down behind much less substantial jungle foliage, fallen timbers, or whatever cover they could find. They had already taken boo-koo (bastardization of the French *beaucoup*, many) casualties and were getting dangerously low on ammunition.

Poindexter got up wearily and stepped into the back of the M-577. He found a map of the local operations area. He didn't know exactly where Hobson was, but by the sound of the gunfire that was growing in volume he guessed he and his men had to be somewhere off to the northwest about four klicks away (approximately two and a half miles). He tossed the chart down on the table and went back outside, sinking into his grime-and-grease-stained canvas chair once more.

Four Cobra gunships and two U.S. Air Force F-4 Phantom jets streaked overhead, racing to where Poindexter figured Hobson was bogged down. Artillery rounds, from Fire Support Base Illingworth, a few klicks behind them, arced overhead, trying to reach out to the NVA and cover the stranded Americans. The distant crash and boom ratcheted up and up, the crescendo building, indicating an all-out firefight was under way.

Ray Armer stared at Poindexter and quietly said, "Sounds like they need help."

Both officers knew that their small command of approximately two hundred soldiers, Sheridan tanks, and ACAVs were the only ground forces within miles that could come to Charlie Company's aid. They were way out in the boonies, far in advance of the main force, but Charlie was out even farther, probably very close to the Cambodian border.

Both men also knew that the jungle nearby was virtually impenetrable from the air. Unless Charlie had somehow located or manufactured an LZ (landing zone) before they were jumped (not very likely) it would be impossible to send in a rescue force by air or attempt any kind of vertical extraction. If Charlie Company couldn't fight their way out, and the radio traffic clearly indicated they were surrounded, their only hope was a rescue column of some sort. The only conceivable "column" was hunkered down in the middle of a dry lake bed, licking its own wounds, and separated from Charlie by a couple of miles of dense, choking jungle.

The choices were few and ugly: Do nothing until ordered, in which case the men of Charlie Company would continue to suffer and die without hope; or mount up and charge off into the jungle with every prospect of either getting ambushed along the way or being chopped up in the same meat grinder that was chewing through the ranks of Charlie.

The sweat rolled off Poindexter's brow, but it was no longer only because of the heat of the day.

The subsequent decisions made by John Poindexter and the resultant actions of the men of Team Alpha are the main focus of this

book. Before we learn more about what happened to this re-
doubtable band, it is important to describe their organization, their
capabilities, and how they came to be sitting in that dust-choked
depression in the middle of War Zone C, deep in enemy territory.

ALPHA TROOP, THE MECHANIZED COMPONENT The 11th Armored Cavalry
Regiment (see appendix 2) traces its roots back to the 11th Cavalry,
a much-decorated unit that began operations in 1901 at Fort Myer,
Virginia. It was all about the horses at first, but the real provenance
of the 11th begins after the flesh-and-blood mounts were traded in
for steeds of steel. Reorganized first as a tank battalion at the beginning of World War II, and then converted into a true armored
cavalry regiment, the 11th served steadfastly in France and Germany, including the D-day landings and the Battle of the Bulge.
After the end of World War II, the 11th, like many similar units,
was caught up in a rapid and extensive demobilization effort intended to take the army back to much smaller and more traditional
peacetime levels. The 11th was ultimately deactivated completely
on November 30, 1948.

No one knew the Korean War was coming, of course, so when
that conflict erupted in 1950, the army planners reversed course
and reactivated the proud old unit, this time as the 11th Armored
Cavalry Regiment, and stationed it at Camp Carson, Colorado. The
regiment had to be rebuilt from scratch, except for its motto, which
remained, "Allons" ("Let's go," in French) and its "Blackhorse" logo.

Once the 11th was back on line, it was moved again, to Fort
Knox, Kentucky, and the unit was given the task of training re-
servists. They relocated yet again in 1957 to Germany, where the
men took up duties of guarding the German-Czechoslovakian border. The regiment's overseas duties ended in 1964 and the entire
command, now supporting an aviation company, was shipped back
to Fort Meade, Maryland. The 11th would remain at Fort Meade
until its deployment to Vietnam in September 1966.

The 11th would stay in Vietnam almost six years. The last men out would not return until March of 1972. In that long stretch of time, the regiment would engage in many actions, such as the one that is the subject of this book; be led by nine different commanders, including Col. George Patton Jr., son of the legendary General Patton of World War II; and three of its members would receive the Medal of Honor.

In March 1970, the 11th Armored had three squadrons with four troops in each. Troops are akin to company-sized units but slightly larger, about 160 men per troop. Alpha Troop, in 1st Squadron, was commanded by Capt. John Poindexter and had an official allowance of thirty-one "tracks": nine M-551 Sheridan tanks, fifteen M-113 ACAVs, three mortar tracks (modified M-113s), and four armored command and admin vehicles.

On March 26, Alpha Troop was short one M-113. ACAV A-13 had been disabled by a land mine a few days earlier. Their roster had "somewhere around" 110 or 115 men present for duty. Exact lists were hard to maintain. Squad and platoon leaders could generally keep a precise count or a mental list of all the men for whom they were responsible; then again, they might not all be present. A few were always on R&R (rest and relaxation); some were detailed to rear echelon duties helping the XO (executive officer—second in command) with supplies, rearmament, the squadron kitchen, and the like. There were always broken bones, wounds, and a myriad of illnesses to deal with, all of which constantly kept at least a few men in the hospital.

COMPANY A, THE INFANTRY COMPONENT Soldiering along with Alpha Troop was Company A, 2nd Battalion, 8th Cavalry, 1st Cavalry Division (Airmobile). Company A numbered about a hundred men (keeping track here, too, was not an exact science for the same reasons stated above) and was a straight-leg, nonmechanized infantry company of regular grunts (what the men called themselves, a modern-day equivalent to "GI").

Together, the two units were designated Team Alpha. To grasp the tactical logic that had thrown these two normally incompatible units together, it is essential to further understand the military objectives for War Zone C.

THE TACTICAL ENVIRONMENT War Zone C, in 1970, was an area of roughly 1,000 square kilometers, much of it thick jungle, containing the all-but-deserted town of Katum and the more active Tay Ninh City. In the rainy season (May to September), the area was a swamp. In the dry season (the balance of the year), it was often a choking, ovenlike dust bowl. The western boundary was the north-south Highway 15; the eastern boundary ran parallel to the north-south Highway 13 from Loc Ninh to Saigon; the southern boundary ran east-west from Highway 13 to Highway 15; the northern boundary was the Cambodian border itself. The entire zone was located northwest of Saigon, and the rough contours of the upper sector, when viewed on a chart, resembled the outline of a canine's profile; thus, it became known as "the Dog's Head."

In more peaceful times, a portion of the area had been a moderately populated region of rice-producing families. For the past two decades, however, it had been a free-fire zone containing all the warring factions attempting to control Vietnam. By 1970, the district was almost totally depopulated.

The old French colonial government had built a roadway through the region to connect the area towns with Cambodia and Saigon, but that highway had been completely reclaimed by the jungle. The roadbed was still in reasonable shape, however, and it became the reason why Alpha Troop found itself stuck in War Zone C. For reasons that were completely unfathomable to the troopers, they had been assigned to protect a group of South Vietnamese and American engineers who had been tasked with clearing the old road. It seemed to make no sense: The thoroughfare went straight into the dense forest and up to the Cambodian border, and then it stopped. Why did the army want a "road to nowhere" through a tract peppered with enemy troops? The reasons would only become apparent as the same men rolled along that road, two months later, headed to the currently planned but still secret invasion of Cambodia.

Once the roadbed had been secured and cleared, Alpha Troop was reassigned to serve under the commander of an infantry battalion, the 2nd Battalion, 8th Cavalry. This repositioning was puzzling: The squadron commander, Lt. Col. John Norton, had been told to send one of his troops to work with the infantry. The reasons were hazy, at best, but apparently someone wanted to know if the two disparate branches could work together effectively at the company/troop level in the jungle. Norton selected Poindexter, knowing that his gung ho young troop commander could probably figure out how best to handle the situation.

Poindexter dutifully reported to Lt. Col. Mike Conrad, the commander of the 2nd Battalion, who promptly announced, "Well, I've got you, but I have no idea what to do with you." Poindexter told Conrad not to worry; he asked to be loaned a company of Conrad's men. His suggestion was that they patrol together and see how it might work out. Conrad said, "OK," and indicated he'd assign companies, on a rotating basis, to work with Alpha Troop. He told Poindexter, "Keep me informed."

The hybrid unit's new duties morphed into making the rounds of the area along the cleared highway and probing for enemy activity. This unorthodox combination of cavalry and infantry did not feel comfortable, at first, to the men of either outfit, but as the weeks wore on, the men got used to it, and their joint operations proved to be highly effective.

The infantry provided extra patrol and search capabilities for the crews of the armored vehicles; the cavalry offered transport and thereby increased speed and reaction times for the infantry. It allowed the team to cover more territory, but it also got them into more firefights. Enemy body counts increased in Team Alpha's AO (area of operations), but so did fatigue and friendly casualties.

The main weapon in the arsenal of Alpha Troop was the M-551 Sheridan tank (see appendix 3 for a more complete description of the Sheridan and its history). The troopers assigned to Sheridan crews in Vietnam tended to be equally divided between those who loved the Sheridan and those who hated it with a passion.

On the negative side, the Sheridan had been designed, in part, to be "air drop capable," that is, deployable by parachuting it into hostile environments. This proved to be a particularly useless design characteristic in the jungles of Southeast Asia. It also meant that the Sheridan had to be much lighter than its predecessors (the hedgerow-smashing main battle tanks of World War II) so it could be hauled around by air. The turrets would still be made of steel, but the hulls were made of aluminum and could, unfortunately, be penetrated by mines, rocket-launched grenades, and heavy-caliber machine-gun bullets.

The Sheridan fired caseless ammunition which meant "without solid brass casings." If a round was roughly handled, the projectile could easily separate from the pelletlike explosive used to fire it, which meant that there were many instances when highly flammable bags of explosive particles would be rolling around in the bottom of the tank. This was not at all desirable in a hostile warfare environment where sparks and flame were ever present.

The Sheridan's diesel engine was quite reliable and could run all day at top speeds of over 40 mph, but there weren't many roads in the bush, and the Sheridan had a frustrating tendency to overheat quickly when it was asked to bust jungle (smash down or roll over trees and foliage). The Sheridan was cramped for a crew of four and, of course, had no air-conditioning: Temperatures inside the hull often exceeded 100°F.

There were some design aspects to love: The Sheridan rarely threw track; that is, the mechanical treads so critical to its locomotion rarely came off, even in the jungle. It had a really big main gun: a whopping 152 mm cannon. This gun fired either a high-explosive artillery-type round or the very popular "beehive" round. The beehive was filled with ten thousand tiny aluminum-alloy darts that could shred wide swaths of foliage or, unfortunately for the NVA, large groups of men. Last but not least, the Sheridan was relatively easy to maintain, from a mechanical standpoint: a very valuable characteristic in the middle of the jungle, where there were no handy repair shops.

The troopers could love the Sheridan or hate it but, as they themselves were fond of saying, "and there it is."

The other main vehicle in Alpha Troop's inventory was the ubiquitous M-113 ACAV, or all-purpose track. (See appendix 4 for a more complete description and a brief history of the M-113 in Vietnam.) The M-113 was used for just about every motorized function imaginable: troop transport (its original design), light tank (it mounted a .50 cal and two M-60 machine guns), roving minimedical ward, mobile mortar platform, repair vehicle, tow truck, and so on.

In Alpha Troop, the ACAV was a mainstay and provided a light, mobile, and spirited gun platform. It could also haul a squad of infantry to wherever troops were needed. It had a crew of four: a driver, two M-60 machine-gunners, and a track commander (TC). The TC operated the .50 caliber machine gun from a rotatable cupola atop the ACAV.

Like the Sheridans, M-113s were mostly made of aluminum. Also like their big brothers, they didn't provide complete protection, but they could deflect small-arms fire and generally withstood RPGs (rocket-propelled grenades) unless the aim was dead-on. The M-113s proved to be nimble and reliable, but compared to the Sheridans, they threw track more often—especially in swamps or bomb craters.

The infantry derisively called the M-113s "buckets," but that was probably more out of pride in their own role as the "Queen of Battle" (an old reference to the queen in chess, which, like the infantry, is the most versatile piece on the board). The cavalrymen scoffed at that. They rather liked the M-113, at least more than running around on a battlefield with nothing more between them and eternity than a steel pot (helmet) and a fatigue jacket.

1800, MARCH 25, 1970, TEAM ALPHA NDP

As Team Alpha set up their NDP on the night of March 25, they found themselves in an open area about the size of two football fields. They would be very exposed, but so would any enemy that might try to creep up on the troop at night. They were just west of the nearly deserted town of Katum. It had been another long day of exhausting patrols and fruitless searches for an elusive foe.

Spirited horses and canvas-topped prairie schooners were only ghostly memories to these modern-day cavalrymen, but some old habits died hard. As they settled in for the night, the troop "circled their wagons" as a precaution against an adversary with a penchant for nighttime attacks. The Sheridans and stubby ACAVs were placed in a huge circle at 10-meter intervals, all guns facing outward toward the black wall of jungle. The command, mortar, medic, maintenance, and FO (forward observer) tracks were centered in the middle of this laager. The infantrymen, as their forebears had done since conflicts immemorial, dug in and tried to find comfort in shallow foxholes between the tracks.

The commander of each track rigged a claymore mine about 50 feet in front of his vehicle. This small, directional antipersonnel device would blast steel balls, shotgun-style, at any enemy seeking to storm the NDP. The claymore was tethered to a thin detonating cord that the soldier on watch in the track would keep handy. Out beyond the claymores, the troopers often set out trip flares. These illumination rounds were wire-triggered and intended to expose anyone sneaking up on the laager during darkness. Then, on top of these precautions, each Sheridan main gun was loaded with a canister round. Vigilance and preparation were paramount to survival in "Indian country."

By 2300, the NDP was pretty well buttoned down. Every vehicle had been rearmed and refueled, with maintenance conducted where it was necessary. The men had cleaned, oiled, and reloaded their machine guns and all their personal weapons. A hot meal had been flown in by Shit-hook (what the men called the CH-47 Chinook helicopter), and there was fresh coffee, cold sodas, and innumerable cigarettes.

2300, MARCH 25, 1970, TEAM ALPHA NDP

Capt. John Poindexter was making one last circuit of his defensive perimeter before trying to turn in for the night. Poindexter was a third-generation Texan. He had received a BS in business administration, with honors, from the University of Arkansas in 1966. He accepted a job at Western Electric in New York City right after graduation. It was the first step in an as yet undefined career path that would eventually lead to Wall Street. Within a year, the war in Southeast Asia was reaching its fevered apex, and he realized it would be wise to address his military obligation. He had been preselected for officer training in college, so he volunteered for Army OCS (Officer Candidate School) and reported to Fort Knox, Kentucky. He did very well at OCS, becoming president of his class and head of the Student Brigade. After graduation he was commissioned a second lieutenant in the armor branch. A tour with the 3rd Armored Cavalry in Germany followed, as did promotion to first lieutenant and command of a troop. Poindexter completed Airborne and Ranger training and volunteered for Vietnam. Upon arrival "in country" he was assigned to the 11th Armored Cavalry. Promotion to captain followed almost immediately, and he was given command of 1st Squadron's Headquarters Troop by none other than the legendary Maj. John C. "Doc" Bahnsen Jr. (see chapter 20 and the epilogue).

The Headquarters Troop normally surrounded the workings of the squadron staff with direct protection and provided support to the other three troops. The aggressive captain found his new command to be highly capable in terms of support, maintenance, feeding the men, general supply, and necessary paper pushing but woefully underutilized in its fighting capabilities. Combat is not the Headquarters Troop's main function, but if the entire squadron ended up in a general engagement it would be nice if the cooks and supply sergeants could drop their pots and paperwork, jump in an ACAV, and be effective. Poindexter set about to make it so, and he did.

Poindexter's leadership performance was so effective, in fact, that when command of a line troop, in this case Alpha, became available it was offered to him. This was highly unusual for two reasons. First, command opportunities at this level for young captains were rare. To be given two chances in one tour was almost unheard of. Second, Poindexter was a reserve officer, not a holder of a regular commission, and not a West Pointer either. Poindexter would barely have sufficient time remaining on his Vietnam deployment to take on the additional responsibility, but he leaped at it when it was offered.

He was known for being unemotional, distant, tough, and a bit of a "cowboy," but also fair. He demanded a lot of his men, but he was not a martinet. Most of all, he was a realist. He and his men were in a tough war that very few believed in, yet his sense of duty and honor remained steadfast. It was an underappreciated task they had been handed, but they would do it nonetheless. He would see to that and also try to get them through it.

Poindexter took up the reins of Alpha Troop quickly, and within a very short period Alpha had the top maintenance record in the squadron, which meant their equipment was in the best shape and most ready for action. On-the-job training was conducted constantly, and Poindexter kept the troop moving: They never spent two consecutive nights in the same NDP. To stand still in this environment meant to become big, fat targets for the NVA.

In early March, the squadron commander of 1st Squadron,

Lt. Col. John Norton, came to Captain Poindexter with an odd request. Someone "up the line" had directed that the 1st Squadron detach one of its troops to be temporarily assigned to an infantry unit, in this case the 2nd Battalion, 8th Cavalry, 1st Cavalry Division (Airmobile). This same someone had also decided, apparently, that this combination of otherwise incompatible arms would be an experiment in the disparate branches working together in the harsh jungle environment. The aims were not terribly clear to the on-scene commanders, but there it was. Would Poindexter be interested in taking his troop deep into War Zone C and giving it a try? Given his reputation for spirited participation, Poindexter could hardly refuse.

Thus began a series of hookups and engagements between Alpha Troop and one company or another of the 2nd of the 8th, usually Company A or the soon to be prominent Charlie Company. This combined arms team was directed to conduct tactical sweeps in War Zone C.

Poindexter had three platoons under his direct command. The 1st Platoon was being temporarily led by SFC William McNew, a twenty-year regular army veteran. On the cusp of being too old for this sort of arduous field duty, McNew had been pressed into service as a platoon leader in the absence of an available commissioned officer. Perpetually pink from too much Southeast Asian sun and partly balding, McNew was an old-school NCO (noncommissioned officer): army proud, profane, hard-drinking, tough on his men, but not afraid of a fight.

The 2nd Platoon was led by 1st Lt. Mike Healey, twenty-four, from Flint, Michigan. Healey was the senior platoon leader, but not by much. At least he had a few firefights under his belt and was known to be solid, dependable, and fearless. He had attended New Mexico Military Institute, then the University of South Carolina, where he graduated in 1967. His ambition was to go to law school, but he was certain he was going to be drafted, so he enlisted instead, hoping to get a slot in OCS. He made it and was commissioned a 2nd lieutenant in 1968. After one year stationed at Fort Hood,

Texas, he was issued orders to Vietnam. He got off the transport plane in Cam Ranh Bay in October 1969 and was sent immediately to the 11th ACR.

The 3rd Platoon belonged to 1st Lt. Robert Henderson Jr., twenty-four, from Oklahoma City. Henderson, who had gone by the nickname "Robin" since childhood, had graduated from the University of Oklahoma in 1968. He did a year toward an MBA before finally accepting the 2nd lieutenant's commission he had started working toward as an ROTC cadet at Oklahoma. He was following in his father's footsteps. Robert senior had also gone through ROTC and served four years in the Army Air Corps, mostly in the Pacific, during World War II. Robin wasn't sure the army was his life's work. He was giving serious consideration to going back to Oklahoma and stepping into the successful oil and real estate businesses his father had started. In the interim, he would serve his country. A friend once asked him why he didn't simply leave, maybe go to Canada and avoid the war. With a shrug he responded, "Hell, I've been trained. If I stepped away some other poor bastard would just be called up to take my place."

Henderson was a newbie (a new guy—inexperienced in combat) in March 1970. He had yet to be in a significant firefight. He had a good deal to learn about jungle combat, but fortunately he was backed up by an exceptional platoon sergeant, SFC Robert Foreman. Foreman was another old hand from the regular army. Foreman knew his way around armored cavalry, and he'd keep Henderson—and the platoon—out of trouble. He was unique in another way, too. He was African American, and in an army that was still afflicted by deep-seated prejudice and class conflict, he had managed to stay above it all. He was respected not only by the men of his platoon but by nearly all the men in Alpha Troop. He knew how to keep a lid on the boiling pot of racism, train his men properly, fight his Sheridan expertly, and give good, soldierly advice when it was needed. When the men of Alpha Troop looked at Foreman they didn't see a "black man." They saw a professional soldier, through and through.

The senior enlisted soldier, the first sergeant of Alpha Troop, was Jerry Holloman. Holloman was also regular army, another twenty-year veteran, and as straight and true a soldier as the army ever produced. In the coming battle he would be the one Poindexter would trust as the commander of those elements of the troop that would remain behind to guard the NDP.

The NCO in charge of the three-track mortar section was twenty-eight-year-old Sgt. Francis "Bud" Smolich from Chaney, Illinois. Older than most of the men in the troop, including all the officers, he had taken a long time to be drafted, but once he was, he proved to be a steady and capable soldier. He was certainly the most well trained of anyone in the troop in regard to mortars.

The platoon sergeant for 2nd Platoon was S. Sgt. Pasqual "Gus" Gutierrez, twenty, from East Los Angeles. Although fairly senior in terms of his enlisted rank (E-6), Gutierrez had actually been in the army for only a year. He was a "shake 'n' bake," or instant sergeant. The wartime demands—and casualties—of the army had created a shocking number of vacancies for senior and midlevel NCOs. The army's answer to the need for enlisted leaders was to take high-scoring draftees of great aptitude, like Gutierrez, and shove them to the head of the line. It was hoped that what these men might lack in experience they would make up for quickly via their innate intelligence. Gutierrez did, indeed, graduate first in his class from the NCO Academy at Fort Knox. He went from E-1 to E-6 almost overnight. He was shipped off to Vietnam in short order, and upon arrival in country he was assigned to the 11th Cavalry as a tank commander and a platoon sergeant.

One of the specialized tracks, a converted M-113 designated A-81, was reconfigured as a medic track. The TC of this track was Sgt. Donnie Colwell, twenty, from Distant, Pennsylvania. ("It was pretty far from anywhere," Colwell states, "and way out in the western Pennsylvania woods, therefore 'distant.'") Colwell and his medic sidekick, SP4 Gary Felthager, would play crucial roles in the lives of Alpha Troop in the hours ahead, but they could not know that yet, of course. On this particular evening, Colwell and Felthager were just trying to square things away and get ready for another miserable day in the boonies.

These men formed the leadership core for Alpha Troop. Depending on them were another hundred-odd loaders, gunners, drivers, radiomen, mortarmen, medics, mechanics, machine gunners, and field cooks. Actually, most of them were barely men at all. The average age was just over twenty. There they were, half a world away from home, and about to be embroiled in what might become the most significant twenty-four hours of their lives. Sadly, for a few, it would be their last hours, period.

2

COMPANY A, 2ND BATTALION, 8TH CAVALRY

*C*ompany A, 2nd Battalion, 8th Cavalry, 1st Cavalry *Division (Airmobile)* was Alpha 2/8's official moniker, yet despite all the mention of cavalry, Company A was a pure, straight-leg infantry outfit. Tanks, ACAVs, or mechanized vehicles of any shape or kind were not part of their schema, not one iota. Why, then, was Company A in the cavalry?

In the army's somewhat arcane and convoluted structuring process, several different types of brigades or regiments can be combined to form a division, which typically consists of ten thousand to fifteen thousand troops and is commanded by a major general. The modern division is the smallest army field organization that can be labeled as capable of "independent operations," that is, being self-sufficient in the field. The principal combat arm of the division carries its primary designation. The 1st Cavalry was an infantry division that *rode* to battle in helicopters (versus walking), with mechanized units and artillery as support elements. Company A's division was thus designated the 1st *Cavalry* Division *Airmobile.*

The "1st Cav," or, by its own motto, the "First Team," had an extraordinarily distinguished combat record stretching back to hard fighting in the Philippines during World War II, fending off waves of Chinese attackers in Korea, and then Vietnam. Elements of the division had been in country since 1965, and unlike most American forces in Vietnam in early 1970, it had not been given any orders to withdraw or stand down.

The 8th Cavalry Regiment, part of the 1st Cav, had also garnered a glorious history, this one stretching back to the Indian Wars of the nineteenth century. By 1963 the regiment, whose motto is "Honor and Courage," was reorganized as an airmobile unit, and it was packed off to Vietnam two years later. Finally, drilling down in the structure to the 2nd Battalion of the 8th Cavalry, a unit of several companies, we find Alpha Company, about a hundred men, all infantry.

"Vietnamization" of the war was in full swing. This war was no longer going to be "won"—it could only be lost or handed off to the Vietnamese, and the entire military command structure, from the Pentagon on down, knew it. The current and final objective was to disengage as rapidly as possible, minimize U.S. casualties, and pass the responsibility for all military operations to the South Vietnamese military and its government.

The 2nd of the 8th and another eighty battalions and regiments (330,000 men and women) were still in Vietnam, along with 55,000 U.S. Marines. Most of these units had orders to rotate out—to finally go home—but not one of the 1st Cav battalions was in that lucky chain. Neither the 2nd of the 8th nor the 11th ACR, the main units on which this story is centered, would be going "back to the World" (the United States) anytime soon.

Everyone certainly wanted to go home, but most still wanted to do so with as much honor and face-saving as possible. Many of the senior American officers were convinced that the only way the

ARVN could possibly be successful in taking on the responsibility for their own defense would be if the NVA strongholds scattered along the Cambodian border, and mostly on the Cambodian side, were eradicated. These substantial caches of supplies and munitions were daggers poised at the throat of Saigon and at the heart of Vietnam itself. If the remaining U.S. forces, which were still considerable, could be used alongside their ARVN allies to seek out and destroy these staging areas, then maybe, just maybe, the South Vietnamese military might stand a chance of succeeding.

The first task, then, became one of interrupting the movement of the enemy through the northern regions of War Zone C. By so doing, the locations of many of the enemy's supply bases would be uncovered. This was what Alpha Company and other similar outfits (including Charlie Company, whom we will meet shortly) were doing during the first months of 1970. It was not an assignment, as they had been given before, of "search and destroy." It was "find, fix, and clear." Infantry companies like Company A would find them, then the fire support bases, armored cavalry, and air assets would fix and clear them. That was the plan, anyway.

JANUARY 1970, HEADQUARTERS, 2ND BATTALION, 8TH CAVALRY

"So, sir, what's it gonna take?" 1st Lt. Ray Armer held his breath. He was trying very hard to be cool and objective, but his gut was churning. This was the moment of decision, the instant he would know if his thirteen-year quest was going to pay off: Would he get his treasured command?

The battalion commander looked at the squared-away former sergeant standing in front of him. Armer was "good people." He had come up the hard way. The kid from St. Louis, Missouri, had dropped out of high school early, restless and anxious to get on with his life. The army would be his ticket out of boredom and uncertainty and into the wider world of adventure. There was just one problem: He was immediately classified 4-F, "unqualified," for vision problems he never knew he had. That didn't stop Ray Armer, however. If the regular army wouldn't take him, the reserves would. In 1957, the army reserves would enroll just about anyone with a pulse, and Ray Armer had more than a pulse: He had heart and enough ambition and determination to drive himself forward, even if he wasn't exactly sure what road map he needed to follow.

When his reserve unit went on its annual summer exercises in '58, that ACDUTRA (active duty for training) became Armer's window of opportunity. Once he was "in," and had at least donned the uniform and shown he could do more than breathe, he had a chance to jump across ranks and into the regular army, using his vantage point in the reserves. This time, he made it. He was initially assigned to the Engineers, then transferred to the Signal Corps. A four-year tour in Italy followed, after which Armer felt somewhat stymied. He was not getting the rank, pay, or adventure he craved. He decided to take another tack. He got out, went back home, and enlisted in the Missouri Air National Guard. He traded army green for air force blue—a whole new set of uniforms. Unfortunately, the E-4 specialist designation he had earned in the army had to be traded for E-3 airman's status in the National Guard. Not a good deal, as it turned out, and Armer was frustrated once more, but events would soon intervene on his behalf again.

Fortunately for Ray Armer, the army, by 1967, was in a forgiving mood—and desperate for experienced help. The war in Vietnam was moving into high gear. His previous stints in the army and air force were advantages he could put in play. Ray boldly upped the ante: He would ask for nothing less than a commission, lieutenant's bars. He would get them, but only after being shunted off to Korea for six months, then back to OCS at Fort Benning. Second Lieutenant Armer received his commission, as an officer of infantry, in February 1968. He immediately volunteered for the place where the army needed new lieutenants the most: the war in Southeast Asia. After Jungle Training School in Panama, Ray Armer finally got to Vietnam in November 1968.

Unlike many of his contemporaries, Ray Armer loved the infantry role in Vietnam. This was what he had been born to do, and he was finally getting the chance. As a former enlisted man, he could identify with the men underneath him and understand what they were feeling and going through. As a natural leader and infantry specialist, he was in his element. Scorching sun, monsoon rain, leeches, dust, dirt, shitty rations, crummy assignments, it made no difference to Ray Armer. Here was a job that needed doing, and he was the man to do it.

By February 1969, Ray Armer, newly promoted to first lieutenant, was leading a platoon from Alpha Company, 2nd Battalion, 8th Cavalry. In June his company commander came down with some sort of mysterious disease and was rotated out. Ray Armer, as senior lieutenant, was placed in temporary command of the company. He was ecstatic, but the euphoria wouldn't last. A little over a month later, a captain was rotated in to take over. Alpha Company, after all, was a captain's assignment. Armer dropped back to XO (second in command).

Armer knew, however, that in Vietnam, company commander assignments were of relatively short duration. The captain appointed over him would be there about six months, so Armer bided his time. Sure enough, in November 1969, Armer's CO received his orders. Alpha Company might finally be his, but there was one problem: Armer's tour was just about up, too. That's how Ray Armer found himself standing in front of his battalion commander asking, "What's it gonna take?"

What it would take was a voluntary extension of duty in Vietnam, which Ray Armer was happy to accept and the army all too happy to grant. Armer knew that at age thirty-one, with the war starting to wind down, there wouldn't be many more chances for a combat command. So in January 1970, 1st Lt. Ray Armer achieved his dream: company commander of Alpha 2/8.

FEBRUARY 1, 1970, TAY NINH PROVINCE, COMPANY A

Company A, as it turned out, was a pretty good outfit. Unlike most line companies detailed to War Zone C at the time, it had nearly a full complement of officers and NCOs. The company had been together for several months and had trained and soldiered well. Two of the platoon leaders Ray Armer inherited were West Pointers. Illegal drugs, which were decimating some less-squared-away units, were not tolerated, but Armer was a realist. He knew that temptation was always close at hand, even out in the bush. Armer had a very simple and yet effective caution for all of his men, "If your buddy's high, *you* are the one who's gonna get killed." He repeated this mantra over and over, and his men got it. Did it completely stamp out the challenges? No—but Armer had another dictum: Prior to going out on a mission, the entire unit lined up for a "shakedown." Before his platoon leaders and NCOs carefully checked each man for readiness, the grunts were given a chance to toss away anything that might be found during inspection that shouldn't be part of any soldier's gear. Armer and his officers turned their backs until the company was ready. When Alpha Company finally pulled out for the mission, the field where they had been standing was often littered with miscellaneous drug paraphernalia and canteens full of reefers.

FEBRUARY 11, 1970, TAY NINH PROVINCE, COMPANY A

On February 11, 1970, Brig. Gen. George Casey, assistant division commander of the 1st Cavalry, showed up to personally pin on Ray Armer's captain's bars. On the very same day, Division assigned Company A to work with Alpha Troop, 1st Squadron, 11th Armored Cavalry, to form Team Alpha. Combining the two combat arms— infantry and armor—into one mobile unit was a radical concept as far as Captain Armer was concerned, but good soldier that he was, he saluted and carried on.

Infantry in Vietnam was all about stealth: ranging the countryside to uncover NVA assets, rooting them out, and hopefully neutralizing them, mano a mano. The armor branch was all about noise: clanking tracks, diesel exhaust, and blasting away at anything and anyone foolish enough to cross paths with roving cannons and high-caliber machine guns. The two types were not completely incompatible, but the combination of two company-sized units like Company A and Alpha Troop was, to say the least, unconventional.

So, then, what are we supposed to do? Armer wondered. As usual, not all the intricacies of the overall strategy were leaching down to the ranks where it would be applied.

What Armer and his counterparts didn't know, of course, was that the invasion of Cambodia was imminent. This big push to interdict NVA supply routes and communications facilities was three months away, and it was a future where the army's leaders and their planners were envisioning groups of armor and infantry surging ahead together in coordinated surgical strikes. Everything that was happening then, in War Zone C, was becoming a rehearsal for the main event, but the lowly company-level participants were totally oblivious to these schemes.

The net result, in February 1970, was that Captain Poindexter found himself with an extra company of grunts and Captain Armer and his men had rides. The cavalrymen gained raw manpower with associated weaponry, and the infantrymen picked up the advantages of speed and mobility. Was it the right combination? Would it work in an actual confrontation with this enemy? Poindexter and Armer didn't really know, but they were sure going to give it a try.

FEBRUARY 25, 1970, TAY NINH PROVINCE, ALONG THE "ROAD TO NOWHERE"

Near the end of February, Team Alpha was riding herd on several squads of engineers who were trying to clear an ancient French roadbed with their bulldozers. The old highway, completely re-claimed by the relentless jungle, stretched from the area of Tay Ninh City to the ghost town of Katum, and then on out into . . . what? It seemed to the troopers that the road led nowhere. The rumor was that it went right up to the Cambodian border, then stopped. What good would it do to clear a road to the border of a neutral country that ended in more jungle? It was a head-scratcher, to be sure, but it wouldn't be the first time—nor the last—that incomprehensible directives were issued from on high.

On February 25, in an experience that would eerily foreshadow events a month hence, the jungle that the engineers had been try-ing to carve out and shove away suddenly started to shove back. The dozer drivers dove for the dirt as AK-47 rounds (the standard-issue NVA semiautomatic rifle) started to ping off the giant blades and pockmark the sides of their huge scraping machines.

Team Alpha, who had been shepherding the engineers as they did their work, sprang into action. Captain Poindexter urged his tracks forward. They muscled up in between the dozers and im-mediately provided covering fire. The .50 cals chattered into the foli-age on all sides, slashing away at greenery that was just yards away from the ends of their muzzles. The main tank guns unleashed round after round of canister, each one carving a wide, cylindrical hole in the vegetation ahead.

Captain Armer pushed his men forward, too. As the brutish tanks and ACAVs blazed away, creating wholesale mayhem, Arm-er's infantry carefully picked their way across the terrain between the armored vehicles, searching for whatever individual targets might have been left behind. In another, less harsh environment, it would be Ray Armer's gleaners sweeping up what was left by John Poin-dexter's grim reapers.

The engineers had unexpectedly pushed into a concealed NVA bunker complex set astride the road they were trying to reopen. It was as if an armadillo had knocked over an angry anthill. The "ants" fought back against the "armored" intruder but, realizing they were outgunned, grudgingly started to slip away through an intricate series of tunnels, bunkers, and hidden jungle trails. Before long, the enemy would be safely behind another set of concealed fortifications, maybe even across the border itself.

Team Alpha's blood was up: They pushed forward in an unflinching assault that they hoped would root out a major enemy force. As the cannon fire cleared the way, bunkers were revealed, one by one. Individual tracked vehicles picked their targets, and the fight devolved into a series of one-on-one actions, bunker by bunker. What the tanks and ACAVs couldn't blast away they tried to pulverize by driving directly over the soil-and-log fortifications. An unknown number of NVA were crushed and buried under the tons of dirt and wood flattened by the tracks.

Some bunkers were taken on by the infantry. Captain Armer's men would creep up to a newly exposed fortification, toss a few grenades into the entrance to clear it, then jump into the tunnels to ferret out any survivors. It was a nasty and dangerous business.

Captain Poindexter's command ACAV, A-66, rolled over a bunker that had been mauled and shot up extensively. In the wake of its mechanized treads, as if it had been some giant, burrowing beast, the ACAV churned up two battered NVA soldiers, half buried in the dirt and rendered senseless. They were weeds to be plucked, but in this case Poindexter wanted them alive—to be questioned. A little raw intelligence could be very valuable. Poindexter yelled and waved frantically to Armer, pointing at the potential captives. With the noise of battle drowning out everything intelligible, Armer couldn't hear what Poindexter was shouting, but he saw what he was gesturing toward. Armer nodded in recognition, then rushed toward the dazed enemy, hollering, *"Chieu hoi! Chieu hoi!"*—the Vietnamese phrase for "Surrender!"

Several of Armer's grunts saw the NVA soldiers half hanging out of the hole and brought their guns up, ready to blast the enemy troops to oblivion. Captain Armer was trying to shout his own men down, desperate to have live POWs and not just another duo of dead dinks (slang for NVA). Before any of them could finish reacting, however, an RPG flew by A-66 and slammed into the rear of another ACAV just a few yards away. The concussion knocked down everyone nearby. The injured ACAV teetered perilously on the lip of a huge pile of vegetation that it had pushed up, ripe for a second and probably fatal blast from the NVA grenadier who had disabled the track.

Poindexter shouted to his driver to push ahead. They would get between the crippled ACAV and the grenadier and distract him before he could reload and fire a second round. A-66 plunged into the thicket of bamboo shielding the NVA grenadier. The ACAV's momentum carried it up and over the compressed vegetation like some elephantine surfer riding the crest of a wave made of sticks. As A-66 slid down the other side of the crushed mountain of crackling, splitting wood, it suddenly stopped. A-66 was pinioned on a pile of vegetation and as helpless as the track it was trying to shield. Making matters even worse, sitting in a foxhole beneath a shattered thorn tree, only five feet away, was the enemy grenadier, locked and loaded.

A-66's left-side gunner was instantly on the target, but his frantic exertions would be fruitless: He couldn't depress the muzzle of his gun low enough to put the grenadier in his sights. The grenadier slowly swung the barrel of his shoulder-fired weapon to his left, placing the harpooned A-66 squarely in his view. At this range it would be a sure and deadly shot. The thin aluminum skin would not be able to absorb the powerful warhead. Yet it was probably that very closeness that caused the rocketeer to hesitate—for just a second. He was most likely considering whether he himself would survive the proximity of his own blast. It was just that fraction of time that Poindexter needed to untangle himself from the jostling track, point his .45 over the side of the ACAV, and pump two rounds squarely into the man's chest. The launcher tumbled from the NVA's hands.

In back of A-66, a hand grenade exploded, splattering hot steel fragments against the skin of the ACAV. AK-47 fire erupted from behind, too. Other NVA soldiers who had been trapped in the collapsing tunnel popped from their dirt prison and began firing at both the ACAV and Ray Armer's onrushing grunts. The two potential POWs were dead-center in the crossfire and instantly obliterated. So much for fresh intel.

The infantry quickly overwhelmed the NVA survivors and finished them off by rolling grenade after grenade into their defensive burrows, which, instead of escape tunnels, became death traps.

The wounded ACAV and A-66 both managed to back off the mounds of vegetation. Then, as abruptly as it had started, the firing ended.

One of Poindexter's men retrieved the RPG launcher that had nearly finished them. Upon closer inspection it was discovered that the trigger mechanism had been depressed, but for some reason the firing mechanism had failed to ignite the rocket. Whether it was shoddy Russian workmanship or the gods of war playing games, no one was willing to guess.

One of the men assigned to Captain Armer's Company A that day was a tall, young private first class by the name of John J. "Jack" Illingworth, from New Haven, Connecticut. He had just turned twenty, and he had been in Vietnam for barely six weeks. He was a dog handler and had been detailed to Armer's company with his canine companion. His job was to get the well-trained German shepherd to sniff out hidden enemy emplacements. Some said he was a model soldier, destined for a bright future in the army, if he chose to stay in, but the fortunes of war would not be so kind to Jack Illingworth. In less than three weeks he would be dead, shot down in a surrender ruse perfectly executed by the NVA.

It was at this time that the 1st Cav was scattering FSBs (fire support bases) all around War Zone C. Heretofore, they had been named quixotically, after someone's girlfriend (FSB Barbara) or perhaps in mocking testimony to the environment (FSB Danger). As things got a little more serious, the FSBs were named in honor of soldiers who had fallen. Thus it was that on March 17, three days after his death, a fire support base would be carved out of the jungle in Tay Ninh Province and named for Illingworth. Soon thereafter, in a couple of macabre twists, the new FSB Illingworth would figure prominently in the fate of Charlie Company, and Alpha Company, where Private Illingworth had fought and died, would become a critical element in the rescue of Charlie Company.

3

COMPANY C, 2ND BATTALION, 8TH CAVALRY

Company C, 2nd Battalion, 8th Cavalry, was a brother company to Alpha 2/8 (as were the battalion's two other infantry companies, Bravo and Delta). On the battalion's organization chart Charlie was a square box where the name of a captain, four lieutenants, platoon sergeants, and squad leaders were grouped, all supported by the ninety-odd other lower ranks that make up a typical company of grunts. In reality, however, by March 1, 1970, Charlie Company was no longer a neatly organized box. It had turned into a sieve, riddled with holes and pouring out the blood of its constantly changing personnel. Because of deaths, woundings, disease, and normal rotations, the officers, NCOs, and men were being swapped as rapidly as tires at the Indy 500. The wheels had, in fact, come off the company in terms of its cohesiveness.

FEBRUARY 14, 1970, TAY NINH PROVINCE

Once known in the battalion as "Lucky Charlie" (they seemed to get all the easy patrols and only light casualties), Charlie Company began its descent into pure hell on Valentine's Day 1970. On that February 14, the word came down for Charlie to hook up with C Troop, 11th ACR (Capt. George Patch, commanding) and chase down the NVA's 95th Rocket Battalion, which was supposed to be hiding in a copse of trees and jungle near Tay Ninh City. The 95th had been shelling FSB Carolyn with impunity, and battalion leadership wanted them stopped.

SP4 Dave Nicholson was actually eager to go. The twenty-five-year-old Vermonter was an exception to the normal brand of grunt in a frontline infantry company. He had a bachelor's degree from Middlebury College, and two years ago his whole life had been ahead of him—with just one challenge: the draft. It finally caught up with Nicholson in early 1968, and unlike many of his college contemporaries he decided, "What the hell?" As soon as his draft notice arrived he went down to the local recruiting office and enlisted. It seemed to make more sense to go ahead and volunteer than blithely succumb to the inevitable.

Born with amblyopia, Nicholson was functionally blind in one eye as a child. Many years of corrective measures and eyestrain had finally gotten him to the point where he could be classified as "fit for limited service" but restricted to noncombat duty—in this case, finance clerk. Once Nicholson was in, though, he wanted nothing less than orders to Vietnam. When asked why, Nicholson told whoever asked that it was because he believed it was his duty.

"It seemed to me that the burden of the war was falling disproportionately on poor, nonwhite minorities. I wanted to prove that the better-off 'white boys' could step up, too. But in truth, I think I really craved what I perceived to be a great adventure more than anything else."

The scrappy young payroll clerk pleaded, cajoled, and finally went to the Pentagon itself to convince someone he was serious about volunteering for Vietnam and changing his MOS (military occupational specialty) to "Infantry." With barely enough time remaining in his enlistment, but with the army losing thousands of lower-ranking enlisted soldiers to the rigors of constant combat, Nicholson finally got his wish: orders to Vietnam—carrying a rifle instead of a ledger.

A giant C-141 Cargomaster disgorged Nicholson and about 250 other GIs onto the tarmac at Cam Ranh Bay, Vietnam, on November 29, 1969. Three days later Nicholson was assigned to the 1st Cavalry and carted off to its huge headquarters base at Phouc Vinh, about 20 miles north of Saigon. Four days of intense training for cherries (slang for replacements or new-in-country soldiers) followed. Five days after that, he was out in the boonies searching for the enemy.

Nicholson was also unusual in that his favorite position was point man. This was normally an onerous and extremely hazardous assignment that rotated among the members of any given platoon. The point man was always out front and, by definition, usually the first to encounter the enemy. Point men were the tip of the spear and usually the first to need a medevac. Nicholson, for reasons he still doesn't understand, gravitated toward the potential danger.

Not much happened over the weeks that closed out 1969 and began 1970, at least for "Lucky Charlie." While other outfits were getting hammered, Charlie Company, solely through the luck of the draw, had gotten benign patrols, little enemy interaction, and long hikes through quiet areas of the jungle. That would soon change, however, as the inevitable odds finally caught up to Charlie Company and handed them more than their fair share of the quota of carnage.

So there they were: "Lucky Charlie," Point Man Dave, and the forward elements of the 11th ACR, Valentine's Day 1970, standing in an open field facing the suspected jungle enclave of a determined and well-hidden NVA regiment. The enemy's position was within a peninsula of trees and jungle sticking out into an open plain. Captain Patch and Capt. Joe Gesker, the commander of Charlie Company at that time, decided that the armored cavalry, with the advantages of speed and mobility, would quickly slip around to the far side of the jungle peninsula and take up blocking positions on the other side. They would take two platoons of Charlie with them; 3rd Platoon (Dave Nicholson's "Lonely Platoon") would stalk into the jungle from the front, acting like a large group of beaters attempting to flush an elusive quarry from its forested hideaway and into the path of the guns of the waiting Americans.

Sounded like a plan, and to the new men in Charlie, it seemed perfectly reasonable. To the NVA, however, who were highly experienced fighters, it was a perfect setup—to punish the Americans. Using an old tactic that had worked well against the French, the NVA commander sent a squad of his men racing to Lonely's side of the woods, where they promptly opened fire. C Troop, and the other platoons of Charlie, dropped the C-rats they were trying to eat and charged back to where they had left 3rd Platoon, hoping to help them out, but the NVA sent RPG grenadiers to blast away at C Troop when they were only halfway around the peninsula. The infantry jumped off the tracks and hit the dirt. The cavalry stopped and started shooting. This caught Lonely in a potentially deadly friendly-fire situation.

Struggling through the other side of the woods, 3rd Platoon was suddenly taking fire from another direction—and it didn't sound like AK-47 chatter. In fact, it wasn't. In addition to the fire from the NVA, the Lonely guys were on the receiving end of hundreds of .50 caliber rounds being fired by their cavalry buddies. Fortunately, the first volleys were a touch too high, and most of the lethal slugs zipped over the heads of Nicholson and his pals. Luckily, in seconds, their faces were in the dirt, too.

In the confusion, the NVA split into two sections. One group sprinted down the throat of the wooded peninsula to take on C Troop and two-thirds of Charlie Company. The second section poured more fire into Lonely, pinning them down completely. The element of surprise was gone, confusion reigned, and GIs started to go down all along both lines. The NVA were firing in two directions and had complete control of their cleverly concealed trails in the center of the outcropping.

A Loach (OH-6 light observation helicopter) was circling directly overhead. Its job was to spot the NVA and call in its big brother, the Cobra attack helicopter.

The Loach pilot saw men running through the woods. He dropped a red flare slightly ahead of them. The Cobra that was standing off nearby swooped in and fired off a rocket—practically on top of Lonely. Thirteen men were hit. Fortunately, none were killed, but several were wounded seriously.

By the end of the day, after all the fighting had ceased, the grim total reached eight dead and thirty-six wounded. Valentine's Day was turning into a red-letter day for Lucky Charlie, all right, but the letters were etched in blood, not hearts and flowers.

FEBRUARY 15, 1970, SITE OF THE
PREVIOUS DAY'S BATTLE

The violence continued right into the next day, but the Americans got a little smarter. What they had discovered on the 14th was that the NVA were there, all right, but it was not a simple rocket-firing formation. It was yet another sophisticated and deeply anchored bunker complex. The eradication of this well-hidden position would require a concerted effort and a better-coordinated attack. Then there was the job of extracting the GIs who had remained on the field at the end of the previous day's fighting. At least one tank and one ACAV had been left behind when darkness had foreclosed on yesterday's actions, and two men were missing. If they hadn't been dragged away as POWs, they were probably dead, and the army was bound and determined to leave no man behind, dead or alive. Charlie

Company was ordered into the van of the day's operations. They would find the abandoned cavalry equipment and the missing men, if it was humanly possible to do so.

This time, the attack would be carried out as a joint exercise with the infantry and cavalry operating together—and on the same side of the forested peninsula. Specialist Nicholson, a temporary squad leader at that moment, got the throat-drying, sphincter-tightening assignment to go in first. Forty yards of open space stretched ahead of Nicholson and his squadmates. The gap seemed more like a mile. If there were any enemy soldiers in there, and surely there were, they would be concealed just inside the woods and already sighting down their gun barrels at the hapless targets creeping slowly toward them.

The day was already sweltering, and rivers of salty perspiration sheeted off Nicholson and his men—not all of it, of course, caused by the oppressive heat. The foot-tall blades of grass swished off their boots and jungle trousers as they warily advanced. Bird cries could be heard echoing from the forest ahead, and then something out of place but oddly familiar: the low rumbling of an idling engine. Nicholson and his partners exchanged curious glances. A grunt named Tracy, who was nearest to Nicholson, simply shrugged, his handlebar mustache twitching with nervous energy.

They closed the distance by half, and they were still vertical when gunfire erupted. Machine gun! All five men turned and ran as fast as possible back to the tracks. Every one of them expected to be skewered in the back by at least one spine-shattering round. Miraculously, they all made it, only to discover that the firing had come from one of the tanks. A nervous machine gunner thought he had seen movement in the tree line and opened up. Some of the other tanks and ACAVs reflexively followed suit. False alarm.

Nicholson and his squad had to start all over again. If, in fact, there were any NVA opposing them, they were surely wide awake and ready by then. Nicholson felt these 40-odd yards were the longest he would ever walk. He expected to be drilled with each forward step. The flash of an SKS (a semiautomatic rifle similar to the

AK-47) would be his last living memory. It was equally likely, he thought grimly, that a .50 cal bullet might slam into him from behind. *If there ever was a shit sandwich, this is it*, he thought ruefully.

Mercifully, the jungle ahead stayed silent and motionless. The squad reached the woods intact and stepped into the foliage just slightly to the right of the smashed vegetation trail left by yesterday's cavalry charge. Ten yards into the jungle they halted—and took a deep breath. Their lieutenant raced up behind them and into the safety of the jungle. They could all hear that damn engine again, wherever it was, doing nothing but idling.

The L-T (slang for "lieutenant") directed his men to move forward. They cautiously skirted the area of jungle flattened by the cavalry. They had moved about 30 yards when Nicholson spied the remains of a collapsed enemy bunker directly ahead. It appeared to be unoccupied. Nicholson was bending close to the lieutenant's ear to quietly advise him on the bunker's apparent status when the loud *snap* of a breaking twig froze them all in place. Nicholson whirled around and fired on full automatic, directly into the bunker. The rest of the men came alive and did the same. The lieutenant plucked a frag (hand grenade) off his vest, pulled the pin, and while gently falling forward rolled the munition like a perfectly aimed bowling ball right into the mouth of the smoking shelter. All of them dove for cover a second before the ordnance roared to life, spraying dirt, dust, and shrapnel in all directions. Whoever or whatever had snapped that twig was gone or vaporized but, in any case, no longer a threat.

The squad arose once more, brushing away debris and patting newly acquired detritus from uniforms that were far beyond hope of ever passing an inspection. Fifty more yards ahead they found two more bunkers. This time they did not wait. Tracy pulled two frags out of his pockets, and while Nicholson covered him he pitched one grenade into the maw of each opening. They blew with satisfying *whumps*. Better yet, they produced no return fire. As the explosions died away, the mysterious idling engine noise seemed to grow louder. Whatever it was, it was very close by.

Less than 10 additional yards ahead, the jungle opened into a small clearing. The patrol stepped into it cautiously. What they discovered there both startled and amazed them. Sitting directly in front of them were the two missing vehicles. One was an empty Sheridan tank, seemingly unscathed, its engine still running. It had been sitting there spewing diesel exhaust, all cylinders firing, since yesterday. That was a head-shaker. The other was an ACAV that had not been so lucky. It had been blown apart, as if someone had popped the top and peeled back all four of its sides. There were no personnel in sight, living or dead, enemy or friendly. Out of the corner of his eye Nicholson suddenly picked out the contours of yet another bunker, this one facing right into the clearing and directly at the abandoned vehicles. It wasn't hard to imagine that the enemy in that bunker had probably been the men that had dispatched the ACAV and caused the Sheridan crew to *di di mau* (Vietnamese for "run away").

Nicholson decided it was his turn to have some fun with a grenade. He had been carrying three: two in his pockets and one on his web belt. Like thousands of other jungle-smart GIs, Nicholson had learned that fumbling for a grenade when you really needed one could be the difference between life and death; thus, the old hands had cultivated a habit of hanging one on their web belts. There was a little trick to this: The snarky tendrils of jungle foliage could snag exposed grenades and prematurely pull them off a belt. This could cause some nasty and unintended consequences, and apparently had. To keep this from happening, the grunts learned to bend the long retaining handle on the grenade up and under the edge of the belt each day; then, at the end of the day, bend it back. A simple trick of the trade.

Nicholson handed his M-16 to Tracy, tugged the grenade from his web belt, and started jogging toward the bunker, doing his best Audie Murphy imitation. He pulled the safety pin. The frag was then armed, but it would not go off until five seconds after he let go of the handle as he tossed the grenade. Except this time. Upon reflection, Nicholson realized that his daily bending of the handle must have weakened the metal just enough so that by the time he needed to use this grenade, the handle was ready to snap. He heard the sickening *ping* of the fracturing handle. As Nicholson later wrote:

> Five seconds is what you get, no mulligans or do-overs, and I had used up two of those precious seconds—perhaps even two and one-half of them—before my brain got the message. Time didn't quite stop, but it slowed eerily—everything was a little out of focus, as if I were looking through water. I felt that my body was too heavy and operating in slow motion as well. I knew what I had to do but wasn't sure I could accomplish the necessary tasks quickly enough.

He cocked his arm and pulled out every muscle memory from his Little League pitching days and hurled the deadly projectile toward the bunker. It exploded exactly one second later, before it could land in the dirt. Nicholson was on the ground and quaking like a leaf. His buddy Tracy was standing over him grinning like a cat and blissfully unaware of just how close they had come to being shredded. Nicholson got up, rendered his best "piece of cake" nonchalant shrug, and moved away from the smoking bunker. Nicholson never told Tracy, either.

The squad maneuvered closer to the vehicles. It was hard to imagine the force of the explosion that had been required to completely demolish the stout little ACAV. Nicholson mused that it must have been a lucky shot, probably an RPG that had somehow penetrated the interior and blown up inside, setting off secondary explosions. Then, to his amazement, he realized that just the day before he himself had jauntily posed for a picture right next to this very ACAV: *Cong Crusher*. The stenciled lettering was still visible on one of the crumpled metal side plates.

Then they saw them: two dead soldiers lying faceup, close to the back of the obliterated ACAV. Nicholson thought they were surprisingly intact, almost—except for their waxen faces and obvious rigor—as if they were resting and would get up and rejoin the fight at any moment. There were no bloody remnants, no gaping wounds, no torn or missing limbs. They were just—dead. One man had wrapped his own hands around his throat as if he couldn't breathe. His mouth was open as if gasping for air. What had killed these men? Speculation centered on dramatic concussion. Apparently, these grunts had been walking behind the ACAV when it had been hit by—whatever—and blown apart. These men had apparently been dispatched by the explosive blowback of supercompressed air from the detonations. Their lungs, hearts, and brains literally flattened inside their own bodies. They died choking and gagging, unable to breathe—their hearts stopped cold. It was a terrible way to die.

Since there was no obvious enemy activity in the immediate area, a recovery crew was called up. The bodies were tagged and bagged and hauled off by ACAV. A tank crew was found to drive the idling Sheridan back to the American lines. The *Cong Crusher* was a total loss. It is probably still there to this day, rusting away in the jungle, if it hasn't been turned into imported razor blades or aluminum cans.

FEBRUARY 16, 1970, THE TAY NINH BATTLEFIELD

On the 16th, Nicholson and his squadmates were treated to an "only in the army" moment. Nicholson and the rest of newly dubbed "Not-So-Lucky Charlie" were reunited at the same jungle clearing where they had started the last two days. Thankfully, it was quiet. The NVA had long since fled. The dead and wounded had been taken care of, and any usable equipment had been salvaged. The men of Charlie were lounging around, smoking, making small talk, and telling bad jokes. Two army clerks suddenly appeared and set up a card table in the middle of the clearing. A couple of Loaches flew in and disgorged several officers. The officers fanned out over the field, approaching each small group of soldiers. A cleaned-and-pressed lieutenant came over to where Nicholson and several of his buddies were sitting. The men stood and came to attention. The young lieutenant set them at ease. Would any of the group like to reenlist for six more years? They could do it right then, and he pointed to the clerks and the card table. Bonuses were available, too—as much as five thousand dollars, depending on the individual's specialty. Most of the men in Nicholson's group, including Nicholson, had either been drafted or had enlisted for the minimum two years of active duty—730 days. They were counting down the days remaining—most had under 200—not contemplating another 2,190 days of army crap. Several men laughed outright. A couple more snickered. The lieutenant was not surprised, but he had a velvet hammer at his disposal and he pulled it out then and there: "Just walk over to that table, sign on the dotted line, and you are off the line, done with combat duty immediately. You'll get on one of those Loaches and fly home—today."

An hour later Charlie Company had six fewer men—all winging out of the jungle and going home. They would, of course, be paying the army back with seventy-two more months of their lives, but Nicholson had to stop and wonder: *Six more years of army shit or maybe six more minutes to live?* Had he made the right choice?

MARCH 1, 1970, THE "GREAT RICE CAPER"

As the old retort says, "What's that got to do with the price of rice?" On this day, the price of rice turned out to be four dead grunts, fifty wounded, and two slicks (army slang for a UH-1 Huey transport helicopter without gun mounts hanging from its sides, thus clean and slick).

After the Valentine's week adventures, C Troop took Charlie Company to FSB Carolyn, where a memorial service for the eight men killed during the previous week was held on February 18.

Charlie stayed at Carolyn until the 25th, when they were airlifted to another bomb-crated field a few klicks away to begin building FSB Annie. On March 1, with the digging at Annie still under way, Charlie received an interesting call.

It seemed that a few days earlier, a routine Cobra gunship patrol in War Zone C had been blasting away at suspected enemy tin-roofed hooches (slang for a native home or hut). When the roofs were blown off, something looked funny. The walls of the huts turned out to be made of bags of rice—over a quarter million pounds of rice in all, stuffed into 50-pound bags. This was estimated to be enough rice to feed an NVA regiment for two months, and the U.S. Army wanted to deny the enemy the use of it.

More practical minds would probably have sent in a couple of F-4 Phantoms (high-power, twin-engine fighter jets) with six napalm canisters each, and it would have been fried rice. Not the army. There was propaganda value here, and it was decided to send in a company of grunts (guess who?), load the rice out on Chinooks, and fly it someplace where it could be photographed, written about in *Stars & Stripes* (the military newspaper), and then turned over to the South Vietnamese ARVN (Army of the Republic of Vietnam).

Charlie Company fought their way into the area (where they accumulated the casualties mentioned above), sweated and strained to load up the rice, then sat and waited for their next orders, which wouldn't be long in coming. When the last bag of rice was safely aboard the last Chinook, Specialist Nicholson wrote in his notes:

> By the time we had gotten that cursed rice all out, we had rolled in it, thrown it at each other, pissed in it, slept in it, dreamt about it, and gotten it in all of our orifices. It never occurred to us to take some, boil it in water, and actually eat it. After all, rice doesn't really taste like much, anyway.

Still, the cost was pretty high, and the Great Rice Caper was the trigger mechanism that got Charlie Company back into War Zone

C, into the Tay Ninh area, and in position for the terrible events ahead.

MARCH 7 AND 8, 1970, TAY NINH PROVINCE

On March 7, just before nightfall, Charlie Company, patrolling an area just west of Tay Ninh City, came across a spot where the jungle in front of them simply stopped. Stretching east to west, as far as they could see, was a very wide road—a really good road, capable of supporting heavy truck traffic as well as large bodies of troops. They had hit the jackpot, or, in this case, a tributary of the infamous Ho Chi Minh Trail.* The temptation to leap onto the road and see where it might lead was pretty powerful, but it could also be fatal. Was the route mined? Was it a trap? Was the NVA lying in wait?

When a B-40 rocket flew out of the woods and exploded in the middle of the column, Charlie Company had their answer. Several men went down; one machine gunner had his thumb blown off. Nicholson's squad was nearest the probable location of the enemy gunner who had targeted the company. He and several of his men lobbed grenades into the grass ahead and sprayed the area with rifle and machine gun fire. Nothing more came in their direction so they assumed that either they had blown away the opposition or whoever had been there had fled.

Taking a position away from the roadbed, Charlie Company elected to halt for the night. It was rapidly growing dark, and trying to set up perimeters and ambushes after sunset was problematic at best. There were no fires or hot food that night, but Nicholson had several cans of warm Coke in his backpack, courtesy of his

---

* The actual Ho Chi Minh Trail ran parallel to North and South Vietnam along a series of trails, roads, and waterways that were in neighboring— and neutral—Laos and Cambodia.

latest care package from home. He distributed all he had to his men, keeping just one for himself. It would be another miserable night in the jungle, compounded by the certainty of the enemy's presence.

Fortunately, the dark hours passed without any further unpleasantness. By 0700 on March 8, the company was rousted and ready for another day. The plan of action was to parallel the newly discovered highway and see where it went. Charlie Company took up a long, sinuous patrol position in the safety of the jungle and about 30 feet inside the tree line along the road. They humped along for hours, recrossing the road about noon, taking up another parallel position on the other side. More helicopters than usual shadowed the column from overhead. Obviously, something was up, and somebody knew something he wasn't sharing with the rest of the grunts down on the ground.

At approximately 1500, Nicholson and his squad were somewhere near the middle of the long, snaky line of Charlie's forward progress when they broke out into a clearing about 100 yards across. Nicholson could see the lead elements of the company plunging back into the jungle ahead. It was nice to be out in the open instead of sweating and pushing through endless miles of trees and vines, but not that nice; out in the open they were sitting ducks. That's when Nicholson saw him—one lone NVA soldier. It hadn't taken much: just a clump of gently swaying elephant grass (tall, tough, native grass), but on this hot, humid and stifling day, with no breeze at all, no grass should have been moving. The point man's instinct, carefully honed to a razor's edge after weeks of combat, had picked the enemy out of the monotonous background. Nicholson wordlessly signaled for the platoon's grenadier to move up to him. As soon as he did, Nicholson pointed to where he had seen the gook (slang for "local" or NVA). The grenadier whispered that he couldn't see anyone. Out of frustration Nicholson asked the grenadier to hand over the launcher. He shrugged and did. Nicholson dropped his pack and sank to one knee. He placed the grenade launcher on his shoulder, sighted carefully, and pulled the trigger. *Whump!*

The clump of grass disintegrated, dirt and green confetti flying everywhere. It was a perfect shot. But had he gotten the NVA? Was there an enemy there in the first place? No one could tell, but Nicholson decided he would count it as a kill anyway. *Had to be*, he mused. He handed the launcher back to the grenadier, reshouldered his heavy pack, and trudged ahead with the rest of the platoon. Then the shit hit the fan.

The lead elements of Charlie Company, the line ahead that had plunged back into the jungle, was suddenly under intense enemy fire. The crackle of rifle and light machine guns of all types shattered the oppressive heat of the lengthening afternoon. Birds squawked and flew into the air, desperate to escape the noise and flying lead. Nicholson's squad was told to push ahead and establish an eastern perimeter.

Nicholson's men quickly ran forward and angled off to the right. They broke through into yet another clearing, but this time they were handed a pleasant surprise: termite mounds, many of them. These nests were over four feet tall, almost as wide at the base, and hard as cement. They were perfect cover. The squad fanned out, two and three grunts behind each mound. The sounds of the battle in front of them grew even louder and Nicholson expected that swarms of screaming NVA would explode from the jungle in front of them at any second—but they did not materialize.

After roughly fifteen minutes, Nicholson decided to scramble back to the hastily established CP (command post). The platoon leader that day was Sgt. Rocky Hirokawa, twenty-five, from Gardena, California. He was calmly sitting on his haunches, waiting for orders. Near Hirokawa's elbow was one of Nicholson's best buddies, Solomon "Pineapple" Palikiko, a rifleman from Hawaii. Both men were a scant 35 feet from Nicholson. Half crawling, half running, Nicholson made his way back to Hirokawa.

"Rocky!" Nicholson shouted above the din. "Do you want us to do anything?"

"No" was Hirokawa's terse reply.

"So, what's going on?" Nicholson probed hopefully.

Hirokawa only shrugged. Pineapple gave Nicholson a nervous glance.

Frustrated and concerned, Nicholson decided to return to his termite bastion and do what grunts do best—wait. He began crawling and scuttling on all fours, trying to keep low. He had made about 20 feet of progress when something hot, solid, and powerful punched him in the upper right arm and slammed him to the ground. Nicholson knew he was hit, and any grunt's first instinct is to try to find out "How bad?" This usually means popping up to do a quick check of all extremities, and that was what Nicholson foolishly attempted. *Wham!* He was pounded again, this time from the back. He wisely decided to stay down.

Mortars! This was a new element in the enemy equation. Nicholson could feel the hot shards piercing his neck and back. Nausea rose up, and head-pounding pains enveloped him. He could taste something sweet and sticky in his mouth, and he could smell the overpowering coppery odor of blood and burning flesh everywhere— his own blood, his own seared skin.

The NVA were walking their mortars across the battlefield. They would fire two at a time, virtually on the same spot, then click the sighting piece up or down to zero in on a different location. Nicholson had been zinged by shrapnel from one mortar round, and then a second round, delivered on almost exactly the same coordinates, smacked him again. The actual ground zero for both blasts was almost squarely on top of Hirokawa and Palikiko.

As the mortar fire moved away, Nicholson was able to struggle to one knee. The entire right side of his body was soaked in bright red blood. His right hand had curled awkwardly up against his chest. It was not receiving any blood flow, and the muscles and tendons had involuntarily contracted, making the limb totally useless. He glanced back at the CP. Hirokawa was a gelatinous mess and obviously dead. Palikiko was lying on his back, his midsection ripped apart. His gray intestines, splayed all over his thighs, were steaming, even in the thick jungle air. Nicholson had to fight back the bile rising in his throat. Medics were already swarming over the victims.

He managed to crawl back to his termite mound. Another grunt from Charlie was there, calmly smoking a cigarette. Despite his best efforts at recollection, Nicholson, to this day, does not know who that man was. Out of pure frustration, Nicholson raised his shattered rifle and fired two magazines, left-handed, at the jungle. It was all he could do before collapsing at the base of the mound.

"Why don't you fire?" Nicholson yelled at his moundmate.

"Nothin' to fire at, Dave" was the nonchalant reply from the Smoking Man.

"Well, if that's the case, do you mind giving me a hand, then?"

"Sure, Dave. No problem."

Between them, the two men managed to remove Nicholson's blood-soaked shirt. They packed his worst wounds with a couple of the thick padded bandages that all grunts carried in their pockets. The blood stopped flowing freely, and some feeling even returned to Nicholson's right arm. He was able to uncurl his fingers and shake some life into the crippled appendage. Next on his list of priorities was water and a smoke. The canteen's contents were hot and tasted like warm plastic, but cold champagne would not have gone down any better. He inhaled the proffered blood-soaked cigarette. Life was suddenly looking better, and he felt as if he might actually survive.

The fight raged on, but amazingly, except for the mortars, it stayed ahead of Nicholson's position. Soon thereafter the call went out to have the wounded report back to the CP. Nicholson wanted to stay but realized that he was more of a liability than an effective rifleman, so he reluctantly trudged back to the CP. On his way to the medevac he passed Palikiko. Two medics were frantically working him over. Pineapple was awake, ashen and grim-faced. Their eyes met. Nicholson didn't see any way that his pal could survive. He reached out his left hand, which Palikiko eagerly grabbed, and firmly so.

Fighting back tears, Nicholson murmured, "Oh, Pineapple, you're gonna make it."

Palikiko said nothing. He just squeezed Nicholson's hand even harder.

[Author's Note: Sgt. Rocky Hirokawa has an honored place on the Vietnam Wall. Solomon Palikiko does not. Somehow, he survived.]

Nicholson made it back to the casualty marshaling area. There were dozens of men, some desperately wounded and obviously near death, others somewhat more mobile, like Nicholson. Then an F-4 Phantom rumbled overhead, flying incredibly low and impossibly slowly. The men below could hear the *click* of the release latches over the sounds of battle. Two enormous pods fell away from the Phantom, one from under each wing: napalm.

The explosions rocked both sides of the lines, and the ground trembled underfoot. Then, as if a vision from Dante's *Inferno* had suddenly sprung to life, a solid sheet of boiling flame rose 50 feet into the air. Each upturned GI face could feel the heat. The NVA who were under the wall of fire felt nothing: They were incinerated in a heartbeat. As the flames died down, the jungle grew eerily quiet, but the shock and awe didn't last long. Radios started crackling commands again, the sound of helicopter blades split the air once more, and the roar of battle recommenced.

For SP4 Dave Nicholson, the war, at least for a while, was over. He would be flown out that afternoon to receive treatment for his wounds. So would forty-one other men from Charlie Company—plus three dead. "Lucky Charlie" had, indeed, been turned into "Hard Luck Charlie," and the worst was yet to come.

4

"HUMPING JUNGLE"

MARCH 21, 1970, FSB ILLINGWORTH

Charlie Company was then under the command of Capt. George Hobson, who had taken over only nine days earlier. Charlie's previous CO, Capt. Joe Gesker, had been wounded in the fighting on March 8 and had been flown to the hospital in Tay Ninh City. On the morning of March 21, the company set out from the recently established and newly christened FSB Illingworth, heading north. Their orders were to recon the immediate vicinity and uncover any evidence of an enemy presence. The "immediate vicinity" was a heavily forested piece of War Zone C between FSB Illingworth and the Cambodian border, about five miles away.

Former PFC John Banicki, who served with Bravo 2/8 in 1971–72, maintains a Bravo 2/8 veterans Web site and provides an excellent contemporary description of what life was like on a fire support base:

Fire Support Base (FSB) or Landing Zone (LZ) as they were called earlier in the Vietnam War were where we would rest between patrols. Most patrols lasted from 12 to 15 days out in the jungle looking for the enemy or his activities. We would then spend 3 or 4 days on an FSB. The larger FSBs would have 105 or 155 mm howitzers, a mortar platoon, command & control bunker, mess hall, medical aid station, and other supporting resources. The FSBs were set up to support the maneuvering companies out in the jungle, other FSBs, and fire on suspected enemy locations. It was truly amazing how fast and accurate those guys were with their howitzers and mortars.

Our rest period would include pulling guard duty 24 hrs a day. Each infantry man would pull a 1- or 2-hour stint in one of the guard bunkers rotating among all of our enlisted men in the company. The 1st Cavalry FSBs were built in the form of a triangle with a combination sleeping and guard bunker on each corner. There was an M-60 machine gun, claymore mines, starlight night vision spotting scope, and a radio in each of the guard bunkers. There also was a shooting range where we would shoot up our old ammunition and make sure our weapons were in good working order.

Then there was latrine duty. When the cut-off 55 gallon barrel became full of human waste we would add fuel oil and a little gas to burn the waste up. THIS DID NOT SMELL GOOD. There also was garbage detail. We would pick up the trash barrels on a mule (small motorized cart) and transport it outside the fire base perimeter and dump it into a large pit where it was later burned.

While on the FSB we would receive mail and any packages from back home. A good cold pop or beer was had by spinning it on a block of ice when we could get our hands on one. We could also take a well deserved shower. This consisted of a tripod with a canvas bucket that had a shower head attached to it. You would stand on a wooden pallet to keep out of the mud. No privacy but it sure felt good. A trip to the barber and medical aid station were usually a necessity. The jungle was not kind to our bodies as in BIG BUGS, man-eating ants, leeches, and plants that had an attitude. Our feet also took a real beating during the rainy season.

[Used with permission of John Banicki.]

MARCH 24, 1970, SOMEWHERE NEAR THE CAMBODIAN BORDER

During the day on March 24, Charlie Company had discovered a "trotter": a trail through the jungle wide enough for two men to march along side by side. This was probably an offshoot of the larger and better-known Ho Chi Minh Trail. It was interesting to Captain Hobson in that the trotter was suspiciously close to FSB Illingworth, just to the south. Were the NVA planning some sort of mission against the FSB?

Hobson had a Kit Carson Scout with his company (also known as "KC," these were former enemy soldiers who had defected, then agreed to serve with the Americans or the ARVN). The KC discovered a thick blue communications wire that had been strung along the trotter. Only battalion-sized units or larger carried or operated this type of equipment. Hobson wanted to tap into the line to try to hear what the NVA might be discussing but the KC argued against it vehemently: Tapping in would surely give notice to the NVA that their comm line was compromised, and it would obviously alert them to the presence of the Americans.

As Charlie hunkered down for the evening, establishing their defensive perimeter and assigning watches, they set up several claymore antipersonnel mines, with trip wires, along their immediate section of the trotter. Anyone using that trail during the night would be in for a nasty surprise.

As darkness settled over the region, and very near the vicinity of Charlie Company, another group of soldiers was shutting down their activities for the day. These men were the skilled, experienced, tough, tenacious, and motivated soldiers of the 272nd Regiment, 9th Division, North Vietnamese Army. They were entrenched in superbly camouflaged bunkers, some with interconnecting tunnels. The complex was stocked with sufficient rations and enough small arms, machine guns, recoilless rifles, and rocket-propelled grenades to inflict serious damage on any opposing force. The 272nd was in charge of defending a supply base within the complex and protecting the trail that Company C had run across. These were the enemy soldiers with whom both Charlie Company and Team Alpha would soon tangle; these were also the men who would attack and try to destroy FSB Illingworth on April 1.

The 272nd Regiment was one of the enemy's toughest and most experienced fighting commands. They had clashed with the ARVN and the Americans on numerous occasions. They did not have the array of weapons and firepower their opponents could field, but they had something perhaps even more powerful to back them: their iron will and seemingly infinite patience. At this point in the conflict, the NVA knew that the Americans were losing heart for participating in the war and were actively trying to turn over the waging of the conflict to their ARVN allies. The NVA were firmly convinced that once the Americans left, the house of cards that was the South Vietnamese government would fall, and when that happened, they would win. It was just a matter of time, and the clock seemed to be moving in their favor.

Also working to the NVA's advantage was the disposition of their typical trooper versus the mind-set of his American counterpart. Every NVA soldier had been raised inside a Communist propaganda system that stressed devotion to the state. Although their average ages were remarkably similar, nineteen to twenty-one, their training and expectations were not. An American draftee could start counting his days in uniform (730) almost immediately upon reporting to boot camp; the NVA draftee faced an indeterminate period of service. American GIs didn't start training together as a unit until after they were assigned to their terminal commands. In Vietnam, final assignments weren't determined until after the replacements stepped off the transport planes and reported to the various replacement companies. NVA soldiers started training as three-man cells as soon as they were inducted or enlisted; three cells formed a nine-man squad, and each squad was led by a combat veteran. The NVA grunt was fighting for his homeland, on his own turf. American grunts, for the most part, were simply fighting to stay alive, do what was required of them as best they could, and make it back to "the World."

0200, MARCH 25, 1970, CHARLIE COMPANY, NEAR THE CAMBODIAN BORDER

At 0200 the next morning, one of the claymores that Hobson's men had rigged along the trotter went off with a loud *whump!* An enemy hand grenade sailed back toward Charlie's lines. It exploded in the brush nearby. It did no damage except to some bits of the endless vegetation and the vestiges of the men's frayed nerves. Charlie went on high alert, expecting the worst, but nothing further happened during the inky and seemingly endless night.

0600, MARCH 25, 1970, CHARLIE COMPANY

As daylight broke, a patrol from Charlie discovered that the exploded claymore had produced bloody results: An NVA warrant officer had stumbled over one of the trip wires. Documents on what was left of the body proved both valuable and disturbing. He was carrying detailed maps and sketches of Illingworth, just as Captain Hobson had surmised. This could not be good. It signaled that the NVA had reliable intelligence on this nearby American compound; worse, it probably meant that they were preparing to do something about it. It also indicated, de facto, that if the NVA were willing to take on a major fire support base, they had sufficient resources in the immediate area to do so.

Captain Hobson got on the radio and called up his battalion commander, Colonel Conrad. It wouldn't take a rocket scientist to conclude that all the evidence Hobson had gathered was a strong suggestion that the patrol ought to turn around and head back, but Colonel Conrad wanted more info. Were there any signs of how large the enemy force might be? Had Hobson and his men seen any evidence of what types of weapons the NVA might have? Conrad directed Hobson to push on—to make contact, if need be, then radio back.

It was not what Hobson necessarily wanted to hear, but orders were orders. He hid his reluctance and his concerns and told his company to pack up. They would move on and try to find out more. They dragged the bloody remnants of the unfortunate NVA officer off the trail and covered him with fronds and branches.

It was going to be another blistering day. The men stripped down to the bare essentials of clothing necessary to push through the unforgiving jungle. Packs were adjusted so that the straps would dig into a minimum of flesh and the 90 pounds of gear per man would ride as comfortably as possible. Weapons were wiped down and rounds were chambered, but the safeties stayed on. Anyone who had dry socks put them on, even if they were filthy. No sense tempting immersion foot. Laces were bound tight. Plastic bottles of insect repellent were kept handy: not for the bugs, for the stuff was pretty much useless against the gargantuan mosquitoes of Vietnam, but for the leeches that would inevitably sneak onto shins, calves, and any exposed flesh. Cigarette packs were ripped from the C-rats cartons and stuffed in handy pockets. Quick gulps of canned peaches or beef stew were downed along with sips of warm water from brackish canteens. A few lucky grunts had packets of powdered Kool-Aid to mix with the tepid water.

Even though the trotter was right next to them, Charlie would not take the easy route. Too dangerous. If the NVA were nearby, the trail would be patrolled and defended, and Hobson was certain they would have interlocking fields of machine guns set up along it. It was what he would do. No, they would shove through the brush parallel to the trail instead and try to do so as silently as possible.

There was one change to the usual pattern, however, and it wasn't popular with the men. The usual method of jungle patrol involved snaking along, single file. A point man or point element led the way, of course, but the NVA had long ago gotten wise to that gambit and unless opposing forces literally stumbled into each other blindly, being on point was probably no more dangerous than being anywhere else in the line. The NVA had gotten very good at ambush, and their favorite tactic would be to allow the van of the column to go past the initial kill zone. Once about a third of the patrol had passed, the NVA would jump in and, as if dissecting a snake, cut the column into three or more pieces, surround each segment, then wipe out each group, in detail.

Hobson knew this, which was why, on this day, he set up his route of march in two parallel columns about 20 yards apart. He also exchanged the point with regularity. This would allow those in front frequent relief from the heat and the exhausting work of pushing through the jungle, but it meant more turns on point, which the men did not like. The parallel columns had another potential benefit, however, and it was one that Hobson had tried to drill into his men during his short tenure as their commander: "If we get hit, fan out, make a circle, set a perimeter."

Two files marching abreast made it easier to immediately anchor both ends of the lines, then push out from the center of each line to form a defensive perimeter. It was the jungle equivalent of the blowfish's defense: If someone or something pokes you, stop, puff up the middle, and point all your weapons outward.

Stealth would still be the order of the day, nonetheless. Despite all the war movies to the contrary, nobody on point was flailing away at the jungle with a machete. That was a Hollywood artifice

long ago abandoned by the troops in the field. Making noise got
you killed.

1500, MARCH 25, 1970, CHARLIE COMPANY, ON PATROL

Toward the middle of the afternoon, the point elements of Charlie
came across more clear signs of enemy activity. The patrol halted.
Hobson, the KC, and several of the veteran NCOs went forward.
Freshly hewn tree stumps poked up from the jungle floor. Some of
the trees that had been harvested were more than half a foot in
diameter—just the right size to provide beams and posts for bunkers. The trees that had been felled were carefully chosen: the remaining neighbors still maintained the overarching canopy above,
thereby keeping the area from the prying eyes of the Loaches and
observation aircraft that constantly crisscrossed the skies.

Hobson and the KC also spotted a strange-looking stand of
sticks pounded into the floor of the makeshift clearing. Having
served a previous tour as a military adviser to the ARVN, Hobson
thought he recognized what this meant, and the KC confirmed his
suspicions. It was an animal trap, used to snare small game that
would supplement the daily rice ration. This was more bad news:
It indicated that a more permanent installation, such as a bunker
complex, might be nearby. Small groups of enemy troops, especially
those on the move, would not take the time to set such elaborate
snares.

It was very clear by then that Charlie Company was getting
closer and closer to a potential confrontation. How far away could
the NVA be? Not far, based on these unmistakable signs of entrench-
ment. Hobson gathered his officers and NCOs and told them to
cinch it up yet another notch. They would continue north, since
that direction had brought them to this state of affairs and in obvious proximity to their targets. Hobson changed the point arrange-
ments yet again, this time deploying a three-man element. If there

was, indeed, a major enemy installation or bunker complex out ahead, more than one set of eyes would be needed on point.

The progress of the entire company slowed to a crawl. Each suspicious movement, no matter how insignificant, was thoroughly investigated. If a clump of grass moved without benefit of a breeze, the point element signaled a halt. A patrol of five to ten men would then move ahead, cautiously probing and pushing until the suspicious activity was thoroughly checked out. When the all clear was signaled, the point element would move up and take over again. So it went, each exhausting, backbreaking, sweating yard, until darkness halted their northward progress for yet another miserable night of hunkering down to cold food, bugs, fitful catnaps, and eternal watchfulness.

1700, MARCH 25, 1970, TEAM ALPHA

Late in the same afternoon, Team Alpha was completing another day of "cloverleafs," fanning out from the previous night's NDP in looping patterns through the nearby jungle. Their mission was the same as Charlie's, only using different equipment. They, too, were trying to locate enemy forces in the area and their encampments, if any. They had not turned up very much that day, just a few old signs of movement; nothing active or threatening. That was OK with the men. They were another day, another twenty-four hours closer, to DEROS (date estimated return overseas—"going home"), whatever amount of time that might be for any individual trooper or grunt. They began to settle in for another evening of frayed nerves and potential ambush, but, as was Captain Poindexter's daily habit, they would never camp twice in the same spot. To stay in one position for more than one night invited discovery by the NVA and increased the odds of an attack or a pounding by mortars manyfold. As the combined troop finished its preparations, the maps placed them just west of the abandoned town of Katum.

1800, MARCH 25, 1970, TEAM ALPHA

As the day ended, about three hundred American soldiers, slightly fewer than two hundred infantry, slightly more than one hundred cavalry, are far out in no-man's-land, way in advance of any other friendly forces, except for one small, stationary fire support base. They are beyond reach, except possibly by helicopter, and even at that, only the men encamped with Team Alpha are in a position to accept helicopter traffic. Their only orders are to recon the enemy, find them if you can, destroy them if you do. That is all they know, accept, and understand about their orders. It seems sufficient to them; along, of course, with their own imperative, which is soldiering on with minimal damage in order to protect their futures beyond "the 'Nam."

They are pretty remarkable men even though they are, in truth, fairly unremarkable in terms of the entire hierarchy of the American fighting machine. They are not Green Berets or (in a later decade) elite Delta Force operatives. They are not Navy SEALs, Air Force Special Forces, or Recon Marines. They are regular grunts. Their average age, including the officers and senior noncoms, is about twenty-two. Other than having attended armor or infantry basic training, they had no idea where they would end up until they got to the units to which they were ultimately assigned. They have been thrown together by circumstance from every corner of America and all walks of life. Outside the commissioned officers, the vast majority of them have only high school degrees and little or no college experience. Should they be fortunate enough to survive, the great majority of them will go back and marry hometown girls and become part of the vast backbone of America that produces the clerks, mechanics, postal workers, plumbers, construction guys, electricians, and transit drivers that this country could not do without.

These "average Joes," who were way out in the boonies, with absolutely no idea what would happen next, would be called upon, in the next twenty-four hours, to exert incredible courage in the face of frightening odds. They would be called upon to "do the right thing." This is the heart of this story: what ordinary soldiers ended up doing under extraordinary circumstances.

How these particular men responded to the situation they were thrust into would determine many things. For that moment, though, with the inky blackness of equatorial night upon them, the opposing forces were not yet aware of one another. That would change in the blink of an eye, and for all these men the world would never be the same again.

5

ONE BAD ROUND CAN RUIN YOUR WHOLE DAY . . .

Crickets. That's what Sgt. Ronald Vaughan, twenty, from Pensacola, Florida, was listening to—the crickets, and a few lizards. Just like back home, sonorous chirps from nocturnal dating games drifted over Alpha Troop's NDP on the stifling but relatively peaceful evening of March 25, 1970. Another exhausting day of cat-and-mouse between Team Alpha and the NVA was finally over. Cloverleaf after cloverleaf had been run. The Sheridans and the ACAVs had busted three to four klicks of dense, sweltering jungle. The infantrymen of Company A had been right there with them, sometimes riding along, sometimes hopping off and poking through thickets of bamboo and sawgrass looking for enemy bunkers. It was a day of negative contact, however, which was both a blessing and a curse. Any day without a gun battle was a good day, but it also meant they didn't know where the enemy was, and that could always produce an unwanted surprise.

Sergeant Vaughan was the TC in charge of A-33. Somewhere around 2300, things were finally settling down to the point where small groups of men who were still awake could engage in quiet conversation, sip a last cup of coffee, or, if not on duty, try to get some sleep. Vaughan, like everyone else, was thoroughly exhausted. As he sat in the TC's seat behind the .50 cal, he was fighting off the fatigue, but he still had an hour to go before he could wake up his relief.

Each section and each track commander were responsible for their own watches. It was fairly common for every trooper to get at least one two-hour stint of guard duty each night. Nobody ever got six straight hours of sleep under field conditions, never mind seven or eight. Before the first watch was set, each track was supposed to erect a section of chain-link fence across the front of the vehicle. The fence was normally kept rolled up on the track during the day, then unrolled each night and affixed to vertical posts in front of the track. The cumbersome wire was a bitch to put up, especially after a long, fatiguing day. If, however, an enemy-launched RPG snaked into the laager during the still of the night the chain-link barrier was intended to entangle the rocket before it could hit the track. Pain in the ass or not, the men dutifully deployed the screens. Likewise, each TC made sure that a claymore was set up in front of the fence. The antipersonnel device was placed to face the menacing jungle ahead, and a detonator wire was strung from the mine directly to the TC's cupola in the track. Should the NVA elect to try to crawl up into the lines, they would have to get by the claymores first. Not a pleasant prospect—if the man on watch was awake, that is. Ronald Vaughan was awake—mostly—and listening to the crickets.

Capt. John Poindexter was very much awake although, like the rest of his men, exhausted. At 2300, he was just finishing his rounds. His twenty-odd Sheridan tanks and ACAVs were carefully circled, each about 10 meters from the next, all guns pointing outward toward the menacing black of the jungle surrounding their clearing. As a choice for an NDP, this dry lake bed had been a pretty good one. It was flat, spacious, and relatively insect free. Poindexter was convinced that one advantage of never sleeping in the same encampment two nights in a row was that the insects didn't have time to catch up with the men. The other obvious advantage, of course, was far more beneficial: The NVA were constantly kept guessing as to where the troop might be.

Between each vehicle, dug into shallow depressions, were Capt. Ray Armer's infantrymen. Poindexter had to step over or go around some of them as he checked on each track. One of the last tracks in line was from 2nd Platoon. Gentle snoring indicated to Poindexter that the trooper on watch was more than likely not awake. He rapped on the man's gun shield.

"Huh? What the . . . Oh, it's you, Captain, what's up?" came the yawning reply from within.

"Not you, it seems" was Poindexter's accusatory reply. "Are you going to be able to keep your eyes open or do we get the next man up?"

"No, sir, I'm cool. Don't need to wake nobody else." A brilliant smile shone in the moonlight.

"OK. Stay alert."

"Yes, sir."

Poindexter moved on. Sleeping on watch was a very serious breach of the UCMJ (Uniform Code of Military Justice). Punishments could be draconian. Poindexter had every right to relieve the trooper from duty on the spot and send him under guard to the rear to await trial and punishment. If he hadn't been running on adrenaline and trying to bear up under the overwhelming fatigue, he might have given it serious consideration, but he wasn't any less tired than the kid himself. Besides, the solution could be worse than the problem. Putting one trooper on report meant two fewer men: one under arrest and one to guard him. There was no "rear" to go to anyway. The troop was way out in the boonies and thoroughly isolated from the rest of the battalion. Then there was this: tossing a trooper into LBJ (Long Binh Jail) would probably represent a vast improvement in the man's lifestyle, given the conditions under which they were operating. No, Poindexter would take the man at his word—this time.

Satisfied at last that he had done all he could to settle the men and their positions for at least the next few hours, Poindexter wearily headed for his M-577 command track. The M-577 was a vertically extended version of the regular M-113 ACAV that allowed a couple of men to stand inside. It housed the operational radios and a cramped desk space that served as the administrative and communication center for the troop. The command track's operating space could also be extended by deploying a large tentlike attachment at the back of the vehicle. Such was the case this night. Poindexter pushed aside the entrance flap and stepped into the stifling heat of the interior. The radio operator on duty, Sgt. Greg Steege, twenty-two, from Denver, Iowa, handed the captain the radio traffic that they had received from headquarters: pretty routine stuff, nothing urgent.

"You got the times for the mad minutes?" Poindexter wanted to know.

"Yes, sir, right here," Steege said.

"Good. That's all for me for a few hours—hopefully."

Twice, sometimes three times a night, the entire troop engaged in "mad minutes." At specified intervals during the night, times that were changed every day, the radio operator would get on the command net and order every TC on duty to commence firing, blindly, at the jungle in front of his vehicle. These random evolutions were meant to surprise and obliterate any NVA sappers (enemy infiltrators) trying to sneak up on the laager. It hardly ever nailed any enemy troops, and it was certainly not sleep-inducing for the Americans, but it kept everyone on both sides on their toes and had the beneficial side effect of awakening any troops who were supposed to be on watch who were not. In addition to the mad minutes, the mortar crew would have specific assignments for each evening, and they, too, would lob rounds into the jungle at selected coordinates where enemy activity had been detected or was suspected. An NDP was actually a noisy place at night, punctuated only by the crickets' soulful pleas and the lizards' high-pitched chirps.

John Poindexter stepped outside the M-577, stripped off his dusty, begrimed fatigue jacket, and flopped down on his cot. Sleep was nearly instantaneous, but before he drifted off, he tried to unwind his mind just a little. This night, he reflected on the duties that had been thrust upon him. He had saluted smartly and said "Yes, sir" when he was offered command of Alpha, but he had had no idea how crushing the responsibilities would be. He was not afraid; in fact, fear was hardly ever a factor for him, except for those rare times when he was truly in the heat of battle with the bullets whizzing all around. No, it was more the fatigue combined with holding the lives of so many in his hands that weighed so heavily upon him. *Man,* he thought, *I'm only a couple years older than most of them myself. A fine situation we've gotten ourselves into.*

Then you had to add the general discomfort to the mix. Dust and dirt were ever present. They filled your eyes, your ears, your nostrils, and your lungs, even at night. Showers were a luxury and infrequent. The best most of the men could do was strip naked near a 5-gallon jerry can perched atop an ACAV and take off the cap, letting gravity provide an impromptu and incomplete cleansing.

The air, always filled with fine particles of dirt, was constantly soaked with the stench of diesel. The petroleum fumes permeated everything, even the food, which, though usually plentiful, wasn't very tasty and was frequently eaten cold. The peaches tasted like diesel; so did the ham and eggs, the canned spaghetti, even the Kool-Aid and the cigarettes. When you weren't being shot at, you were always in danger of falling branches, slashing grass, toppling trees, heavy pieces of metal flying through the air, sprains, broken bones, sharp objects, deep cuts, scorpions, snakes, mines, and insects of gargantuan sizes, the likes of which were never seen back in "the World." It was a miserable, backbreaking, bone-aching, debilitating environment—and then you might just get blown away or have one or more appendages hacked off.

Well, Poindexter sighed as he fell back on the cot, *at least we could bury the trash today, and the latrines are downwind.* He was asleep in seconds.

A little farther down the line Sgt. Donnie Colwell was also looking forward to getting a little rest. Colwell, TC of the medic track, hauled a stretcher outside and plunked it down next to his vehicle. He'd be off duty at midnight, which was moments away, and he was ready to sack out.

Thirty-three of thirty-nine, he mused. *We've been on the line and engaged in combat operations for thirty-three of the thirty-nine days we've been out here so far. Shit, I'm tired.*

The three mortar tracks were about 50 feet away from him. He could hear the crew on duty, Sgt. Joe Wakefield and SP4 Floyd Coates, chatting while they opened 81 mm mortar cases and stacked the rounds carefully on the back ramp of their mortar track.

Looks like they'll be firing the 81 mm tonight instead of the four-deuce. Good. That one's a bit quieter, Colwell thought absently. *Not that you can get much sleep with all these fireworks going off anyway,* he grumbled to himself.

Under these conditions the men had to learn to sleep differently. It was never quiet in an NDP, at least not for very long. If the mortars weren't going off, there were the mad minutes. With a little practice, you could screen all that out. Pretty soon you grew used to the familiar chatter of your own guns and the outbound *whoomp* of the mortars. Colwell knew he could sleep through all of those distractions: He'd done it many times. He also knew he'd be fully awake and on his feet in a heartbeat if the sounds changed, to the high-pitched whistle of an incoming round, for example. Or the *clack-clack-clack* of the AK-47. These were sounds you definitely did not want to sleep through.

Alpha Troop's mortar section chief was Sgt. Francis "Bud" Smolich— "Sergeant Smo" to just about everyone. Six to eight years older than most of the enlisted men in his troop, Smolich had taken a long time to get to where he was. Bud had actually volunteered for the army at seventeen but was initially classified 4-F. He tried again at twenty-one. This time he was classified 1-Y: also not medically qualified, but inching closer to the top of the pile and someone who could be qualified in times of national emergency. By the time he was twenty-seven, Smolich was married, but the Selective Service System was reaching way down the list and definitely experiencing a national crisis: Vietnam. He finally got his "Greetings from your Uncle Sam" letter and after basic training was shipped off to Fort Ord, California, for mortar school. More advanced mortar indoctrination at Fort Polk, Louisiana, followed. Two days before he could have slipped through the army's tightening cordon of those without enough time left on their enlistments to get orders to Vietnam, Smolich received his instructions: back to Ft. Ord, then off to Southeast Asia. On landing at Tan Son Nhut, he received his final posting notice: Alpha Troop, 11th ACR, "somewhere in the jungle, War Zone C."

Smolich's section consisted of three special-purpose M-113s, each configured for the storage, handling, and deployment of the mortars assigned to Alpha Troop. Two of the ACAVs were equipped with the heavy 4.2" or "four-deuce" mortar, which weighed over 300 pounds and could toss 3.5 kilograms of high explosive over 4,000 meters.

The third track carried the lighter 81 mm mortar, which weighed a little over 120 pounds and fired an HE (high-explosive) round that could range out to over 5,000 meters. Tonight, they would be using the 81 "mike-mike" (mm) and tossing rounds out to three or four predetermined sets of coordinates: all trail intersections where enemy activity was suspected. They were going to be firing every hour and dropping up to eight rounds on each target.

Each of the mortars was hard-mounted to a swiveling base plate inside the rear section of the mortar tracks. The ACAV's rear ramp was lowered during firing operations and jacked up on blocks to level it. This would provide a handy platform on which to prep and stow the rounds that would be fired. The senior man of each mortar's two-man crew would work out the firing solutions on a portable plotting board and set the elevation and traversing mechanisms on the mortar to match the map coordinates. The second man would handle the ammo. His job was to carefully set the proper propellant charge for each round to be fired, pull the safety pin, then drop the round into the firing tube. With a good mortar crew, and Sergeant Smolich had very good crews, the well-rehearsed operation would proceed like clockwork.

The next senior man in the mortar section was Sgt. Joe Wakefield, twenty-four, from Cincinnati. He was on his second tour in Vietnam.

"Which watch do you want tonight, Joe?" Smolich inquired of Wakefield.

"I'd better take first watch, Smo. If I go to sleep now you'll never get me awake again tonight."

"OK, you got it." Both men, like everyone else in the troop, were tired beyond ordinary comprehension.

Smolich walked away, leaving Wakefield with his junior mortarman, twenty-one-year-old SP4 Floyd Coates from Culpepper, Virginia. He found a reasonably comfortable spot on the ground on the far side of one of the four-deuce tracks, threw down a blanket, flopped to the ground, and was asleep instantly.

2400, MARCH 25, 1970, TEAM ALPHA NDP

The explosion shattered the night shortly after midnight. Flames shot skyward from the middle of the NDP. The entire compound was illuminated as brightly as if a parachute flare had been dropped squarely in its midst. The ground trembled, and the echoes of the blast ricocheted off the sides of every vehicle with fearful metallic *twangs*. More explosions. Screams. It was all wrong. These were not the familiar sounds of ordnance moving outward, toward the enemy, but neither were they the warning signals of incoming fire. There were no high-pitched whistles preceding the *crumps* of inbound artillery. There was no snaking, twisting *hisssss* of an RPG wending its way into their inner circles. No green tracers from the NVA's AK-47s split the air. Something terrible had happened, that was certain, but no one knew quite what—not in those first few moments anyway.

Fatigue and the need for sleep were instantly obliterated. Sergeant Smolich was close to the epicenter of the blast. He was instantly awake and on his feet, the initial ball of expanding heat washed over him even though he was still standing behind the protective wall of a track, and thankfully so; otherwise he could have been badly singed. Barefoot, he sprinted around the end of his ACAV to find Joe Wakefield's mortar track completely engulfed in flames.

Oh my God, they must've taken an RPG was Smolich's first reaction. Staggering in the light and heat of the burning track, he raised his arm to cover his face and tried to get closer. He couldn't get near enough to do anything for the two men he could see. One was on the ground, not moving. The other was sitting upright, in the back of the track, framed by the glowing conflagration. He was not moving either.

They've got to be dead was Smolich's sober evaluation. Then other mortar rounds scattered about the ramp, and the back of the burning track started cooking off (exploding spontaneously due to the nearby heat).

Shit! I've gotta get these other tracks outta the way! was Smolich's next panicked thought. *If we don't, there's gonna be a lot more dead guys soon.*

Smolich turned from the grisly scene before him and began shouting for assistance. He needed help, fast, to get the other mortar tracks started and out of the immediate area. Several men rallied to him, and among them all they got the other two mortar tracks started and lurching away from the fires and flying shrapnel.

Ronald Vaughan was jolted from his heavy-lidded peering into the jungle walls. He was about 50 yards away from the explosion when it occurred. Instantly, he fired up his track's cold and coughing engine. He shouted for everyone else to get off the ACAV. All he could think to do was race to the scene and try to help—but he didn't want to endanger any of his own men to do so. His thought was to place his ACAV between the exploding ammunition and the rest of the troop. The track lumbered over to the raging fires, and then he stopped it. Someone, Vaughan does not know to this day who it was, raced over and leaped onto his ACAV. The two men spotted another trooper writhing on the ground. Vaughan dropped the ramp. He and the unknown soldier jumped out, hauled the wounded man up onto the deck of the track, leaped back in, and drove away from the flames. Vaughan had as yet no idea what had happened, but he knew the crickets would be silent for a while.

Donnie Colwell was less than 50 feet away. His medic track was in the center of the NDP—not out on the circular perimeter. He was up and sprinting toward the disaster seconds after the initial blast. The flames were already so intense that it was difficult to get close to the scene. Acrid smoke stung his eyes and crawled down his throat, nearly choking him. Colwell was not a medic, but as the TC of the medic track he had seen more than a few fatalities and woundings. It was not hard to assess the damage here. Sergeant Wakefield had been blown off the track by the explosion. He was alive, but barely. Colwell knew, however, that he could not survive: Only his torso remained. Both arms were gone at the elbows, and he was missing everything else from the top of his groin down. Another trooper appeared at Colwell's side. In the heat and the smoke he couldn't make out who it was. Colwell pointed to the second man involved in the blast, Floyd Coates. He was still inside the back of the mortar track. Might the two of them be able to grab Coates and pull him out if he was still alive? Colwell peered at Coates, hard.

No way, he finally decided. In the growing light from the flames he could see Coates's throat had been ripped away by the blast. He had been killed instantly, and the flames were starting to reach him.

Another man was sitting upright just a few yards away, screaming in agony. This turned out to be twenty-year-old SP4 Walter "Chip" Andrews from Garnerville, New York. Andrews was a substitute mortarman. He had not been part of this evening's crew, but he had been nearby when the initial detonation occurred. He raced to the scene to help. Bud Smolich had seen him running toward the fires and had shouted for him to stop—to get away. Smolich knew there was nothing that could be done for Coates and Wakefield, and he was afraid Andrews might be caught in a secondary explosion. Andrews ignored Smolich, and that was exactly what happened. As Andrews approached the shattered track, a mortar round cooked off right in front of him.

Colwell and the other trooper (it turned out to be medic Craig Wright) ran over to the agonized Andrews. Shrapnel had blown a large hole completely through Andrews's left forearm, but that was not the worst of his injuries. His midsection had been sheared away by slicing metal fragments, and his intestines were lying in a grotesque heap, covering his right thigh and leg. The two would-be rescuers nonetheless grabbed Andrews, one man under each armpit, and started to drag him away. At that moment, however, more rounds starting blowing off, the heat became too intense to stand, and more deadly shards hissed and zinged everywhere. Colwell stared down at Andrews. He had stopped breathing, and his eyes had rolled back in his head.

"He's dead. Let's get the fuck outta here."

Colwell and Wright abandoned the effort to pull Andrews away. They ducked and ran for their own lives.

Captain Poindexter was off his cot like a shot. His first reaction, like almost everyone else's, had been *We're under fire!* He figured that one of the mortar tracks had been hit by an enemy RPG or something like it. His second reaction was *We're lit up like a Christmas tree. Every NVA gunner for miles around has a perfect target!*

Sprinting toward the flames, Poindexter shouted over his shoulder to his radioman, Sergeant Steege, "Call Stone Mountain Control now! Get an emergency dust-off headed this way!" He knew there were going to be casualties. *Might as well get 'em moving*, he grimly assessed.

Then Poindexter's tactical mind clicked into gear: *No muzzle flashes from the jungle . . . no incoming rounds . . . no RPGs . . . we're not taking enemy fire! What's going on? Did we do this to ourselves? How?*

Poindexter didn't have to issue any orders. He could see that his men were reacting to the emergency as their instincts and training dictated. They were cranking up their vehicles and moving them outward, expanding the circle, getting men and machines out of harm's way and the reach of the greedy flames and exploding rounds. Others were focusing on rescue or standing by alertly, armed and ready to repel enemy invaders, if necessary.

Sergeant Smolich ran by, shouting orders to a couple of his men. One mortar track lurched forward, away from the disaster. Another mortarman literally dove into the back of the second, as yet unaffected mortar track. Seconds later, the engine coughed to life and this track, too, ground forward, so hot that it was smoking. That the track and the driver escaped immolation and the cooking off of its fuel or rounds was, indeed, a minor miracle.

Poindexter and a few of the men got as close to the fire as they could. They crouched down and kneeled at its periphery, worshippers at a fiery rite that had taken a turn toward insanity. Poindexter stared as hard as he could into the maw of the rapidly distorting

ACAV. The aluminum frame was yielding to the demands of the intense fires and beginning to re-form. It was then that the cause of the tragedy became all too apparent. The tube of the 81 mm mortar was clearly visible, backlit by the flames. It was splayed open like some perverted, peeled, metal banana.

Son of a bitch! A round exploded in the tube was the captain's instant and accurate analysis.

The conflagration seemed to stall, if only a little. It was then that Poindexter saw the shape of one of his men lying in the dirt, maybe 15 yards ahead. With a supreme effort to ignore the intense heat and stifling smoke, he crept forward. He reached the man—he recognized the face of one of his sergeants, Joe Wakefield, staring up at him.

My God, he's alive!

Poindexter's eyes teared up with the intensity of the smoke and heat. He could feel the hot breath of the inferno searing his skin and heating his fatigue trousers to the point of ignition. Blindly, he reached down, grabbed the body under the armpits, and tugged.

He's lighter than I thought, Poindexter abstractedly judged. *Maybe it's the adrenaline.*

Poindexter could only "see" through his own glowing eyelids, but he backpedaled as best he could with Wakefield's body beneath him. Once the intense heat abated, Poindexter stopped. He dropped Wakefield's form and sank to his knees. He opened his eyes. Wakefield was staring up at him, imploring.

"Why did this have to happen to me? Why me? Why?" he begged.

Poindexter flashed back to a moment a few days before this. Wakefield had come to him requesting a transfer. He had had enough of life in the field, and since he was on a second Vietnam tour, a dispensation might have been granted. Poindexter had said no. Sergeant Wakefield's departure would leave a big hole in Smolich's mortar section, both in terms of manpower and experience. Request denied. Fate sealed.

The gallant captain looked down into Wakefield's face once more. He was inches away. The light in Sergeant Wakefield's eyes had gone out. He was dead. It was then that Poindexter focused on what remained of his former sergeant and realized why he was such an easy burden . . . and why death would be a blessing.

S. Sgt. Dennis Cedarquist was completely incredulous. He couldn't believe that his friend and fellow noncom Joe Wakefield was dead. It wasn't five hours ago, just before dark, that the two of them had been kicking back, relaxing, listening to their favorite music— Motown. Wakefield had just gotten a brand-new reel-to-reel tape player, and he was so proud of it. He took it with him everywhere. Cedarquist could still see Wakefield's smile in the flickering shadows.

Eventually, all the fuel and ammunition the hungry fire could reach was consumed. A tenuous quiet once again enveloped the expanded NDP. Had the NVA chosen to attack at that juncture, it might have been a propitious time for them to do so, but for whatever reasons, they did not. One by one, the men absorbed yet another unexpected but arbitrary act of random violence and moved ahead. Perimeters were reset. New watches were posted. What passed for sleep overcame those who wanted just another day to be done. Slicks arrived to haul off the wounded, which were few, fortunately. The dead could wait for morning.

Donnie Colwell remembers what he heard that night as clearly and as distinctly as if it were yesterday, despite the chasm of over forty years. As he lay there, seeking the sleep that for whatever reason would not come, he could hear Floyd Coates, just a few yards away, say to Joe Wakefield, "Hey, there's a piece of tape on this warhead."

Wakefield's response was, "That's OK, drop it anyway."

Moments later, the world came apart.

The 81 mm mortar shell in common usage during Vietnam had a safety pin at the top that needed to be pulled in order to activate the round.

An experienced mortar crew, like Wakefield and Coates, would prep their rounds for the evening's mission by taking the ammo out of the case, stacking it on the back of the mortar ACAV's ramp, and setting each propellant charge for the required distance for each target. Only at the actual time when the round was about to be dropped down the throat of the mortar tube would the gunner pull the pin. In this regard, the shell was like a hand grenade. If the pin was not pulled, the round would not fire. Sometimes, even if the pin was pulled, the round would not fire. If this happened, the crew had the challenging and nerve-wracking task of physically picking up the mortar tube and trying to dump the faulty round out of its mouth. These "duds" would be removed from the mortar track, set aside, and usually destroyed the next day.

What if a mortarman picked up a round from a fresh box of ammunition and saw that the safety pin was missing? Suppose the hole from which the pin had been removed was taped over with a simple, innocuous piece of masking tape. Suppose you are tired, fatigued beyond belief, and you just want to get the night's exercises over with. The safety pin needs to be removed in order for the round to fire anyway; so, someone's done that for you, why not just drop the round?

Dropping a round into the mortar tube fires the shotgun shell inside the bottom of the projectile as soon as the base of the round hits the firing pin embedded in the base of the mortar. The shotgun shell blasts the round upward and ignites the propellant at the base of the shell. The shell will fly as far as there is burning propellant to push it skyward. Once it dives back to earth, the fuse in the nose of the round takes over: It can be set to detonate on impact or at any time from zero to twenty-five seconds after the round is fired. Somehow, the fuse in this round detonated the instant the shotgun shell was fired.

Was it, plain and simple, a faulty round? Was it manufactured in error at the U.S. Army munitions factory in Watervliet, New York? Was it a dud round that somehow accidentally got recycled into a case of fresh ammunition? Did the absent safety pin affect the timing of the fuse, no matter how the crew might have set it? Was it a tragic mistake brought on by crushing fatigue and the desire to simply get on with the mission and then get some sleep? We can never know: Those who could testify to the immediate facts of the situation are long since dead.

SP4 Ray Tarr, twenty, from Kittanning, Pennsylvania, was trying to sort out his vivid memories of the mortar incident and its unsettling aftermath. As he and several others sat on the ground, watching the ill-fated 81 mm track burn and start to become a distorted mass, he heard another trooper say that when he got back "to the real world" he was "never going to talk about this again—ever!"

SFC Robert Foreman nearly jumped down that man's throat. Foreman looked the bitter and frightened trooper straight in the eyes and said, "Oh yes, you will. We all will. We'll need to, and people will need to know what happened here."

6

FIRESTORM

0600–1100, MARCH 26, 1970,
CHARLIE COMPANY LINE OF MARCH

The anticipation was more than palpable. For two days, Charlie Company had been on tenterhooks. There were incontrovertible signs all around them that the NVA were nearby—and probably in numbers no one wanted to contemplate. Every movement, every sudden snap of a twig, every frightened bird that went screaming off into the jungle caused the men of Charlie to reflexively duck and tuck into a crouch. They were not afraid. They were beyond fear, just doing a job and desperately hoping to get a call on the PRC-25 (portable field radio) that would tell them, "You've done enough. Come on back." Getting whacked, after all, was just a roll of the dice.

The call did not come. In fact, the radio traffic yielded just the opposite. Colonel Conrad was growing impatient with Charlie's progress, or what he perceived as a lack thereof. As careful as Captain Hobson was trying to be, the boss was anxious for him to make contact, to bring on a confrontation that would, at least, confirm the multiple and absolute indications that there was an NVA force lurking somewhere nearby. The maps and notes found on the unfortunate warrant officer Charlie had bagged were driving all the division intelligence types into paroxysms of concern. FSB Illingworth and all the forces that were roaming about in War Zone C were essentially hanging out to dry, ready to be snatched off the clothesline unless the enemy could be located first.

"Goddammit, find them!" was the order of the day.

Scanning the local terrain and making some observations from the vantage point of his Huey, Colonel Conrad had determined that there was an open zone not far from where Charlie was cautiously probing. From the air it looked like a better path for Hobson's men than the thick and punishing jungle they were trying to navigate. In fact, it was a section of jungle that had been devastated by an old B-52 strike. Using the carpet-bombing tactics that the air force was growing famous for, some mission in the not-too-distant past had blasted a wide swath of lunarlike craters and shredded jungle waste across the nearby landscape.

From above, it looked like a quicker way to drive northward and let Charlie make some progress. Conrad ordered Hobson to get his men over there ASAP. To the airborne battalion commander, hovering some 500 feet above the jungle, the strike zone looked like a highway. To the men on the ground, the craters were depressions big enough to swallow a tank. They would have to walk around them. What looked liked flattened jungle from the air was, in reality, a nearly impassable jumble of broken tree trunks, busted limbs, and sprouting regrowth. In truth, for the men of Charlie with their heavy weapons and 90-pound packs, it was more difficult than pushing through the jungle; plus, they were out in the open, exposed, with the tropical sun beating down on them like a blowtorch from hell.

Nevertheless, Charlie Company would do as they were told. They changed direction and angled across the moonscape carved by the bombers. It didn't take long for Conrad to recognize his mistake. Mercifully, he radioed Hobson to get the men back into the jungle—quickly.

With a collective sigh of relief, the column plunged back into the greenery on the other side of the bomb-damaged track. Visibility was immediately reduced to a few feet in either direction, but at least there was shade. With the trailing elements of the company once again under the canopy of trees, Hobson called a standing halt. The men reached for their canteens. Hobson and his platoon leaders took a break to reorient their line of march. A new point element was set, and the company headed off again.

It was shortly before noon when the wall of green that Charlie was trying to shove aside suddenly pushed back. Muzzle flashes erupted all around them, and men started to fall. SP4 David Solis, twenty, from Winslow, Arizona, was the first to die. An enemy bullet tore into his forehead, and he was dead before the thick jungle matting could break his fall. PFC John Paul Didier Jr., twenty-one, from Rockford, Illinois, was leveled in the same initial fusillade, his right femoral artery ripped open. AK-47 and enemy machine-gun fire seemed to come from every angle.

It was not yet clear what had happened, but Hobson quickly discerned that the company was taking fire from at least two sides, if not three. His conclusion was obvious: They had finally found the NVA; worse, they were entrenched in what appeared to be a bunker complex—and Charlie Company had inadvertently walked right into the middle of it.

Hobson knew they had to get a perimeter established, and pronto. Seasoned troops with fire discipline would fan out and form a circle. Getting green troops to do so in the face of countless muzzle flashes was an exercise in leadership. Men like S. Sgt. Preston Dawson knew what to do.

Dawson, due to a lack of officers, was leader of Lonely Platoon. He was new to Charlie, but not to combat. He began grabbing men and shoving them into position. Some of his troopers had never been in a firefight, and they were frozen in place. Dawson began whacking men on their helmets and backs or kicking their asses, literally, to start returning fire. They began to settle down and respond.

1130, MARCH 26, 1970, NVA BUNKER COMPLEX

Captain Hobson had been in a number of engagements before, but nothing like this. He figured that his forward element had walked straight into a well-planned fire zone of two, maybe three bunkers. It looked like there were more bunkers ahead, so pushing forward was probably not a good option.

As soon as the firing started, enemy soldiers began boiling out of their well-hidden spaces. Dawson shot three of them dead before they could raise their rifles, but many more scurried off into the surrounding jungle. It was like kicking over an anthill.

Hobson considered turning the whole column off to one side or the other, but that presented additional challenges: If they were already well into the complex, a turn could take them deeper into a probable killing ground. The whole company could end up in a maze from which there was no escape.

Retreat to the B-52 strike area they had just navigated was equally distasteful. It would completely expose his men while they tried to maneuver through the tangled limbs that covered the ground or skirt around the gaping craters. The jungle, as bad as their position was, at least offered some concealment.

There wasn't much choice for the moment, so Hobson and his officers and NCOs concentrated on firming up the perimeter, setting up a casualty collection point in the center of their lines, and trying to get some help.

The NVA wasted no time in cutting off all of Charlie's avenues of retreat. An undetermined number of enemy grenadiers were immediately detected behind Charlie, blocking access to the B-52 strike zone. RPGs from that direction would soon be winging their way toward Charlie's lines.

Every bunker within range was dialed in on Charlie Company. Later events would prove Hobson's initial assessment to have been correct; that is, the company had walked straight into the open end of a horseshoe lined with enemy fortifications. When the NVA commander ordered additional troops to peel off into the jungle and slip behind Charlie, he had them boxed in on all sides.

The intensity of the fire from both the Americans and the NVA ratcheted up. Dense brush, thick bamboo, fields of stout grass, and the interminable greenery helped conceal one foe from the other, but it was, after all, not armor or masonry. It was only chlorophyll in one form or another and, ultimately, very poor shelter from hot, flying lead. Men might not be able to see one another, but it didn't prevent them from killing each other. The uncaring bullets and lethal grenades would see to that. Casualties began to mount, and, at least for Charlie Company, the available ammunition began to decline precipitously. By the end of the first hour of combat, half of Charlie's arsenal was gone.

1230, MARCH 26, 1970, NVA BUNKER COMPLEX

A lull occured in the fighting, reason unknown, but welcome nonetheless. Sweating and winded from his last inspection of the perimeter, Hobson crouched down at the base of a large acacia. His RTO (radio telephone operator) and KC came over and dropped down beside him. Hobson looked up. Tiny patches of blue sky were visible through the canopy of trees above, but they were certainly not big enough to afford any sort of window for vertical extraction. The umbrella of foliage also made it difficult, if not impossible, for anyone circling overhead to see the grunts of Charlie and drop them any supplies.

Hobson hurriedly considered his options. With the state of his ammunition and the extent of his casualties, there was no longer any chance for a retreat—nor would he have attempted one, since doing so would mean leaving behind wounded men too incapacitated to move. He would never surrender. That just wasn't in his schema. Neither could he attack. His company was no longer strong enough to punch a hole in the enemy's encirclement. In his own mind, he was already committed. They would fight on as long as they could, even though the only choices right then seemed to be death, wounding, or capture. If any other possibilities were in the cards, they would be limited by whatever hours of daylight were left. That was out of his control. If there was to be any relief, and it didn't look good at the moment, he would have to leave that up to someone else. Right then, he was busy keeping himself and his men alive as long as he could. He did have another fleeting and unpleasant thought: If things did not work out well, he was worried that he would be remembered not as George Hobson, the battling company commander from the 2nd of the 8th, but as Vietnam's George Armstrong Custer.

1245, MARCH 26, 1970, NVA BUNKER COMPLEX

During the brief hiatus, the boom and crash of the artillery from FSB Illingworth was more obvious, but it was not much help. Charlie's current position was still very much in range of the big artillery pieces at Illingworth, and the American gunners had been trying to reach the NVA since the action had begun, but the opposing forces were intermingled. The long-range shells could reach their targets, but there was an equal chance of blasting Charlie's lines as there was of hitting the enemy's bunkers.

Slicks couldn't make much of a difference either. Not that they hadn't tried. Colonel Conrad had been calling for resupply and medevacs for over an hour. Several brave pilots had made the attempt but had encountered such intense ground fire from the NVA that they had had to turn back.

There was the additional problem of not having a viable landing zone. Charlie had certainly had no time or opportunity to carve one out. The B-52 strike area would be impossible to land in due to the gigantic bomb craters and entangling brush, to say nothing of the machine gunners and RPG grenadiers who lay in wait, itching for a big, fat target like a Huey. The overhead canopy was too tall and too thick to accommodate a jungle penetrator (an anchor-shaped hoisting device that a hovering helo could drop through thick foliage). Parachuting in some rangers or infantry reinforcements was also out of the question—they'd get tangled in the trees and could be picked off before they got to the ground.

The AH-1 Cobra attack helicopters took a turn at it, along with Air Force F-4 Phantoms, but here again, the opposing forces were too mixed up for these otherwise superior weapons to have any effect other than delaying what seemed like the inevitable.

The bottom line was that Charlie was in a great big nutcracker and there wasn't a hell of a lot anyone could do to help them. It was entirely likely that those members of the company who were still alive by nightfall would be quickly overrun and dragged off into the dark. By the next morning any survivors would be across the Cambodian border and on their way to whatever hellish POW camp the NVA would provide.

7

BIG BROTHER IS WATCHING

1200–1330, MARCH 26, 1970, LT. COL. MIKE CONRAD'S
COMMAND HELICOPTER

Lt. Col. Mike Conrad was growing more and more desperate. He had a good company of grunts totally enveloped by a determined enemy and facing probable death or capture. He—and they—were running out of options, time, and bullets faster than a Saigon hooker could make a twenty-dollar bill. This was definitely not what he had had in mind for Charlie Company's plan-of-the-day, but he wasn't shocked. Well, maybe a little. He certainly had pressed George Hobson to get on with the mission, which was locating an enemy force they knew had to be lurking somewhere nearby. Still, Conrad was surprised by the size of it, and the fact that the NVA were clearly dug into a formidable position and weren't about to give it up without a serious fight. Charlie Company was surrounded by—what?—hundreds of well-armed, experienced troops. Hobson had less than ninety men, many of them in their first serious action and, no doubt, scared shitless. Who could blame them? Conrad certainly wouldn't.

Conrad's Huey circled warily just behind Hobson's position. As the rotors noisily chattered above his head and the pilots did a dance with death and the NVA gunners below, Conrad's razor-sharp mind tore through his mental index cards. He'd seen plenty of action on his current tour, and the one before this, but here was a new set of challenges. He called upon everything he had been taught at West Point (Class of '56) and all the career-enhancing stops he had made in between, and there had been many: the 11th Airborne, a tour in Lebanon, the 82nd Airborne, an adviser's tour in Vietnam in 1963–64, Rensselaer Polytechnic Institute for a year of grad school, three years on instructor duty back at "the Point," the prestigious Command and General Staff College at Fort Leavenworth, and then this, his first truly important field command, as CO of the 2nd of the 8th. He was definitely on the army's fast track, but that was far from his mind right then. He had a bunch of his men gripped in an iron vise, and he had tried everything he could think of to pry the jaws of that vise open. Nothing was working.

For a brief moment he flashed back to the recent briefings he and the other battalion commanders had gotten from General Casey, the 1st Cav's new second in command. Casey was smart, aggressive, and determined. He, like Conrad, had been in Vietnam before and this time was determined not to repeat what he saw as some of the leadership mistakes of the past. The worst of those mistakes, in Casey's mind, was complacency. Unlike some others, Casey appreciated that the NVA was a skilled, determined, and wily foe, not an enemy that would be cowed by the brute, overarching force of superior American arms. Casey, with his boss's blessing, would try some different tactics in the 1st Cav's area of operations, which, of course, included War Zone C.

Casey's idea was a simple but effective one: keep the enemy off balance and keep them guessing about the 1st Cav's intentions. Casey knew it would be impossible to blanket the whole operations area and force the NVA to surface. Instead, the 1st Cav would hopscotch across the region, moving ever closer to the Cambodian sanctuaries that the enemy would want to protect with ferocity. Casey's men—artillery, armor, and infantry, finally coordinated as one—would plant an FSB here, another there, fan out from each base, point and shoot, prowl and probe, then abandon each FSB in succession, establish another, and keep on moving. It was a far different strategy than the one that had been utilized before, which involved seeking out large set-piece confrontations, erecting substantial, semipermanent bases, and then pushing the ARVN out in front and making them fight for their country, with American backup.

Casey told his subordinate battalion commanders, like Conrad, "We're going to break a lot of brush, we're going to move fast, and we're going to hit hard."

The second and riskier part of Casey's strategy was to provide tempting targets for an increasingly agitated NVA. He wanted to smoke out as many hidden complexes as could be found and expose as many enemy regiments as the army could unearth. On this day, much to Charlie Company's discomfort, the aims of General Casey had proven wildly successful; consequently, Conrad had to figure out a way to pull Hobson's nuts out of the fire.

As soon as Conrad heard the first radio calls from Hobson, he dashed to the Huey assigned to him as battalion commander and told the pilots to "move it." The slick was over the scene of the action within minutes but started drawing ground fire as soon as it came in range. Conrad told the aircraft commander to back off. It wouldn't do him—or Hobson—any good if the NVA shot them down or if they had to crash-land in the middle of Hobson's perimeter.

Conrad had Hobson constantly marking his positions with smoke (special grenades that spewed only colored smoke) so that he could effectively identify the location of Hobson's lines. This would give Conrad a reference he could use to direct any artillery that might be able to reach and cover the grunts. Conrad also called for TACAIR (tactical air support). Cobras and Air Force F-4 Phantoms tried to oblige. The F-4s attempted to drop 250- and 500-pound bombs on the coordinates they were being given, which they hoped were the enemy's bunkers and not Charlie's perimeter. They were flying lower and slower than prudent aviation parameters and current operating guidelines dictated.

Medevacs were ordered up, but they couldn't get through the ground fire or find a spot to land. Any attempt to haul the wounded up through the treetops was out of the question, too.

Resupply slicks lumbered into the area, but all of them were chased away smoking or on fire and certainly full of holes. Three of the birds that tried were damaged so extensively that they were later placed in an indefinite "no-fly" status.

1330, MARCH 26, 1970, CHARLIE COMPANY'S COMMAND POST

"Stone Mountain Two-Nine, this is Racer Two-Nine."

"Go ahead, Racer Two-Nine," Conrad responded to Hobson.

"I'm getting down to the last of my smokes. Ammo's down to a few magazines per man. No more machine-gun ammo. About 20 percent casualties now. If we don't get some more ammo soon we're going to be SOL"—shit out of luck—"Over."

Conrad sighed heavily. He could hear the concern in Hobson's voice. Hobson wasn't ready to panic, and from all Conrad knew about the experienced and stoic company commander he doubted he would ever panic, but there was certainly desperation in that tone, and who could blame him? Conrad mustered up his calmest radio voice.

"This is Stone Mountain Two-Nine. Roger. We've got some more air on the way. Hope they can execute a kick-out for you, so get ready to mark your position again."

Conrad didn't know who or what was trying to fly into this maelstrom, but he had heard, on the net, the call sign of another one of the 1st Cav's Hueys seeking directions to Conrad's position. Apparently, there was going to be one more desperate attempt to get some ammunition to the stranded grunts of Charlie.

That's one brave goddamned pilot, Conrad mumbled to himself, *or a complete idiot.*

Suddenly another voice broke into Conrad's reverie and popped into his headset.

"Stone Mountain Two-Nine, this is Writer Two-Nine, over."

Poindexter! Conrad chided himself for not considering that option yet. Then he had a thought—a desperate one.

Maybe, just maybe. He knew he was grasping at one very thin straw.

8

"SADDLE UP"

The last thing on Sgt. Bud Smolich's mind on the morning of March 26 was the strategy that had thrust his unit deep into War Zone C, hard up against the Cambodian border, chasing the North Vietnamese. He was too busy cleaning up the disaster of the night before.

As Smolich surveyed the sickening damage, he could only wonder, *What the hell happened? Did somebody make a mistake? Nah, I trained these guys myself. They knew what they were doing. Had to be a defective round.*

The problem was that no one would ever know exactly what happened: the three men directly involved, or what was left of them, lay under ponchos awaiting dust-off to the division morgue.

All Smolich knew for sure was that he was staring at a mortar tube splayed open like a perverse metal flower and that one of his three precious mortar tracks was a smoldering, gutted hunk of twisted junk. Then there was the stench. Smolich and his men were still finding pieces of the bodies. Three of his best men were gone, one blown all to hell, one whose head had nearly been torn off, and one gutted as he tried to help the other two. Then all three had been roasted through-and-through by the intense fires. Others had been wounded; he was not sure exactly how many.

The disaster cooked off mortar rounds that had been stacked on the ramp of the ill-fated track as well as some rounds sitting in piles nearby. Shrapnel had flown everywhere. Smolich, a veteran of many months of combat, was still wearing the fatigue trousers that had caught fire as he tried to save his men. His eyebrows were singed, he had numerous first-degree burns, and his eyes were red rimmed and watering from the latent heat and smoke.

Sure as hell not what I signed up for was all his numbed brain could contemplate at that dispiriting moment. When he was finally done with his onerous tasks, Smolich decided he had better report to the CP.

"When I walked in, the first sergeant [Holloman] and Captain Poindexter looked like they'd seen a ghost. They both thought I had been one of the men blown up inside the mortar track. The captain bear-hugged me and Sergeant Holloman, thankfully, took me off the KIA (killed in action) list."

Even with all that had happened since midnight, Smolich's day would prove to be far from done. In just a few more hours his mettle would be tested yet again, under even more trying circumstances.

Captain Poindexter was contemplating the randomness of war and the myriad ways by which one could run afoul of even the most careful preparations. *Was it all just the luck of the draw*, he wondered, *and if so, could one ever know when one's luck was about to run out?*

Poindexter was poking around the ACAV that had become a death trap for three of his men. As he did so, his radio operator yelled at him from 100 yards away that the higher-ups were on their way. Judgment from on high, battalion level at least, if not division, would be swooping in soon to probe the disaster. They would ask all the logical questions, as they had the right and authority to do, but who could answer for the fickleness of war?

Poindexter would not have long to reflect upon his sadness or his concerns. He could hear the *whop-whop* of the incoming slicks. He glanced at his watch: 1100 hours. It was already another blistering, humid, uncomfortable day. At least it was the dry season. They wouldn't have to contend with mud plus the heat.

The official party helicoptered in to inspect the accident site. Lt. Col. Mike Conrad, CO of 2nd Battalion, was among them, as was the battalion sergeant major. While the officers met with Captain Poindexter, the sergeant major tracked down 1st Sgt. Jerry Holloman, the troop's senior NCO.

"Your men look a little crusty there, First Sergeant," the well-tailored sergeant major was heard to comment to Sergeant Holloman.

Holloman took his superior NCO aside, out of earshot of the men, and in no uncertain terms explained the facts of jungle life to the crisply attired, rear echelon sergeant major. Holloman related that his men had been in almost constant combat for weeks, had fought several serious engagements, had sustained many WIA (wounded in action) and several KIA, and had been operating for a very long time in an extremely adverse and isolated environment. In even earthier terms, Holloman told the sergeant major just where he could stick his opinions, and it would be somewhere in the nether folds of his neatly starched trousers.

The delegation stayed only a few minutes—just long enough to see that the tragedy wasn't caused by negligence. Expressing sympathy and rendering handshakes, the team disappeared almost as quickly as it had arrived. There were promises of replacements for the men lost as well as delivery of a new mortar track as soon as one could be located. A red-faced sergeant major's ears were still ringing as he jumped aboard the departing chopper, pressed pants on fire.

1200, MARCH 26, 1970, TEAM ALPHA NDP

"Writer Six, this is Writer Two-Six." It was 1st Lt. Mike Healey, commanding 2nd Platoon. Poindexter had sent him out two hours earlier with a platoon from Ray Armer's infantry company to conduct a cloverleaf to the north.

When he heard Healey's radio call, Poindexter jumped from his canvas chair again and stepped into the baking heat of the command vehicle. Radio Operator Steege passed the handset to Poindexter.

"This is Six," Poindexter responded.

Steege slipped past his boss in the cramped quarters of the ACAV to go outside and grab soft drinks. He returned in seconds with two lukewarm beverages.

"Six, this is Two-Six, what's going on? We can hear lots of heavy fire out ahead."

Healey was Poindexter's most seasoned lieutenant: a solid officer with a good head for the realities.

"Two-Six, this is Six. Some grunts are getting hit to the north—out by the dry streambed as far as I can tell. They've got lots of casualties. It looks bad."

"Roger that, Six. Has Stone Mountain Two-Nine said anything about us yet?" Healey inquired with more than a little self-interest. He was smart enough to understand that Team Alpha was the only friendly unit nearby that could possibly be called upon to lend any assistance.

"Nope. What are you doing?" Poindexter asked while signaling to Steege that he wanted his maps.

Healey reported his position, and it was clear to Poindexter that Healey and his men were the closest assets to the beleaguered grunts of Charlie. Healey also revealed that they were not uncovering any enemy activity in their sector and there were no fresh signs. This didn't surprise Poindexter: He knew exactly where the enemy was operating at that moment.

Of Poindexter's other two platoons, One-Six was temporarily

led by SFC Willie McNew. Three-Six was commanded by 1st Lt. Robin Henderson—the newbie lieutenant. They, too, checked in from their patrol positions. Both were farther out and in the opposite direction of Healey and the growing battle to the north. Poindexter carefully marked each position in grease pencil on his grubby plastic overlay and issued orders for all the patrols to halt and stay put until they heard back from him.

Inside the command track, it was over 100 humid, baking degrees. A tiny electric fan blew stale, pungent air with an erratic *whirr* punctuated by a *tic-tic-tic*. One of the fan's corroded blades was knocking against the wire cage surrounding the straining propeller. Poindexter stared at the charts looking for the answers he already had but didn't want to see. He'd almost rather be out with one of the patrols in the jungle. At least it was cooler there, in the shade of the greenery, and someone else would be here, making the tough decisions.

Poindexter took the soda can offered by Steege. It was warm to the touch and the contents barely drinkable. He drank it anyway. He turned and walked the few steps to the ramp leading out of the sweltering tin box. Poindexter plopped back in his canvas chair, long legs and arms seemingly unfolding everywhere. Several field mechanics and a couple of the mortar crewman were nearby pretending to be busy. They were not—they were there to catch the first wisps of the elusive "word," the definitive "dope," on what might happen next. When and if caught, the smoky tendrils of the conversation would be passed quickly to the rest of the men: It was a "jungle wireless" of great efficiency.

Inside the command track, the radio sprang to life once more.

"Stone Mountain Two-Nine, this is Racer Two-Nine." Captain Hobson was calling Colonel Conrad—again. There was some desperation in his voice as he reported, "I'm down to the last of my smokes. Only a few magazines per man. About thirty casualties now, over."

Conrad tried to sound reassuring, but outside of begging for supplies to keep coming and attempting to effectively direct artillery and air strikes, there was not much else he could do. Everyone within earshot of the radio knew that Charlie had only two options: a breakout or a miracle. There was also the clock to consider. There were about seven hours of daylight left. Even if Charlie's ammunition held out—and that seemed problematic—they had to be out of there by dark or it would be over. After nightfall, the NVA, who were experienced nighttime operators, would pick Charlie apart man by man until they were all dead or captured. By morning only the KIAs would be left for the Americans to recover. Any survivors would be across the border and on the way to Cambodian POW camps.

"Well, what are we going to do?" Ray Armer asked in the stifling shade of the command track. "It's a little over four klicks from us to George."

Armer's question hung in the air like a bad smell in a tight space: No one could do anything about it, but you couldn't ignore it.

Poindexter knew that his metal mounts and Armer's riflemen were the only forces close enough that could come to Charlie's aid. The two captains stared uncomfortably at each other. Poindexter, as the designated troop commander, was technically the senior officer in charge. Armer waited to see which way Poindexter's thought process was leaning. The choices were all bad: They could sit tight and wait for orders, but if they did so, more men would die as they sat on their butts. Armer could dash off into the jungle with his men, but without Poindexter's tracks he could never hump enough jungle to get there in time. They could all mount up and ride to the rescue, smashing through the jungle as they went, but if they got there before Charlie was overrun, would there still be enough time to extract before dark? Engaging the enemy on their turf at night was a guaranteed suicide play.

It was Jerry Holloman's turn to weigh in on the matter. As the senior enlisted man in the troop, it was his job to represent the grunts.

"Four hours for the whole trip, maybe more," Holloman finally offered. "The busting looks pretty bad, but at least there aren't any streambeds between us and Charlie." As difficult as the jungle itself could be for ACAVs and tanks, the unstable walls of dry stream- beds could pose insurmountable obstacles.

Holloman had expressed the possible and the positive. To complete his obligation to the men, he would also have to voice the probable and the negative.

"On the other hand, it probably means a night operation on the way out, and the men haven't had any sleep for two days."

Poindexter knew Holloman was right on all counts, especially the fatigue factor, given the tragedy of the night before.

SP4 Larry Roberts was like a man adrift. He was the TC of ACAV A-13, but "Lucky 13" wasn't: It had hit a land mine in a mi- nor skirmish the week before and was presently "inop" and being repaired. He had extra time on his hands, and as a result he was hang- ing around the command post trying to pick up on whatever might be going on. Roberts wasn't a soldier handcuffed by the niceties of the usual command structure. In other words, he was not afraid to ex- press his opinions on military matters despite his relatively low rank in the pecking order. He had overheard most of the conversation so far and felt compelled to offer his opinion on the possibilities that seemed to be ripening.

"There's a real good chance of an ambush on the way out there with all them dinks around. Do you really want to volunteer . . . sir?" He spat as he laid down the challenge. A small puff of red dust rose from where his spittle plowed into the dirt.

Ray Armer was quick to answer. "Hell, no!" The standard dic- tum for the war at this stage was "Never volunteer for anything." Everyone knew that. Any officer who was too quick to volunteer his men, especially on missions that were designed to get officers "me- daled up," was instantly suspect.

Then Armer tossed the challenge right back. "But if I was with those guys I'd sure want *somebody* to try to get me out."

There it was in the air, again.

Poindexter knew all eyes were on him. He also knew that what he did next would determine the course of some—possibly many— lives: some of his men's, some of Ray Armer's, some of George Hobson's. Maybe all of them.

Poindexter had a solid troop. They were well trained and motivated. They had performed admirably to date. There were the usual complainers, but there weren't many shirkers. In a war with a thousand reasons not to take risks and a hundred opportunities to get off the front lines, his men had stood tall. Hard drugs and pot were everywhere; feigned psychoses were common; racial quarrels could lead to reassignment; malaria was purposefully contracted by some to avoid combat; equipment could easily be sabotaged; and so forth. Not in Alpha Troop. For whatever reasons, and Poindexter could only hope it was through luck and decent leadership, his men had decided to do their best and soldier on. If they took this on, though, it would be a real gut check.

Poindexter was also thinking that Colonel Conrad and the rest of the infantry-oriented officers in the battalion had no clear idea of what Team Alpha might be able to do in this situation. Alpha Troop had only recently been assigned to them. *That's probably why we haven't gotten the call*, he mused.

On the other hand, maybe Colonel Conrad was holding them back as a last resort. *If that's the case, it's going to be a real disaster by the time he tells us to get moving.* Poindexter knew that even with the tanks leading the way, he could only plow through so much jungle per hour. There might not be enough time to get there and back—if they could even get there at all. The chances for a happy outcome if they got tangled up in a night operation were too slim to even contemplate.

There was also another pucker factor that made the hair on the back of Poindexter's neck stand at attention as he sat there sweating: *Maybe we're the real target. Maybe the NVA picked on Hobson knowing we'd leap to the rescue. We've been a pain in their asses for weeks. Maybe they're really after us!*

More Cobra gunships streaked overhead, racing to the north, and the sounds of the battle could be heard more clearly than before. Within the tight circle of Alpha Troop's command tent, however, the silence was deafening.

SP4 Don Dush, twenty, an M-60 gunner assigned to Poindexter's command track, was part of the small group at the heart of the NDP that day. He was new and had yet to go out on his first mounted mission. Like most low-ranking enlisted men, he was not comfortable around the senior officers. He just wanted to keep a low profile and not get in the way, but even a raw replacement like Dush knew that momentous decisions were about to be made. He recalls hearing the radio traffic and watching the intensity of the expressions around him.

"I didn't understand the operational end of things, but it wasn't too difficult, looking at those faces, to know what was going to happen before anyone said anything," Dush remembers.

Doing nothing, with American lives at stake, was the least acceptable option. Both Poindexter and Armer knew they could never live with that. Poindexter sighed, yet resolutely dictated, "Saddle up."

Ray Armer had been sitting quietly, sweating in more ways than one. Once Poindexter made his decision—their decision—he, too, knew it was the right thing to do. He looked up. Poindexter and Armer locked eyes. Armer smiled grimly. They nodded to each other in a way that meant their fates were sealed, but that it was still OK. Wordlessly, each captain stood and busied himself with his preparations.

Armer picked up his rifle and went off to gather his platoon and squad leaders. He would maintain his command post on Poindexter's track, but he wanted to be sure that all his men understood what was about to take place. A company of grunts from their own battalion was in serious trouble. He was convinced that his men would want to go to their aid.

Poindexter raised his voice to his radio operator, who was inside the command track. "Steege, call Stone Mountain Control and tell them we're preparing to react. Don't say to what. Conrad will know, and I don't want the wrong guys to know."

"Yes, sir. Anything else?" Steege acknowledged from inside the M-577.

"Yes. Tell One-Six [1st Platoon] and Three-Six [3rd Platoon] to get back here right away. Then call Two-Six [2nd Platoon] and tell Healey to keep busting jungle north—no, wait, don't say 'north.' Just tell him to keep moving in his current direction as rapidly as possible, and that we'll be joining up with him as soon as we can."

"Yes, sir, got it."

Poindexter's directive to Healey had been purposefully vague. *He'll figure it out. He's a good man,* Poindexter said to himself. Poindexter knew that Healey could hear what was happening just ahead of his position, and the cavalry always rode to the sound of the guns. Plus, everyone knew that the NVA were monitoring the American radio nets, so rather than say "move north," thereby telegraphing their intentions, Poindexter had not specified a direction.

Next, Poindexter motioned for Holloman. The troop's top sergeant jogged over to join his commander.

"Top, I want you to take charge here while we're gone."

"Yes, sir."

"Make up two squads from what men we have here and the two platoons coming back. Have Smolich get one of the two mortar tracks we have left ready to go—keep the other one here. Steady men only—don't need any still freaked out by last night going out with us. Dig in on a small perimeter with what you have left. I know we haven't moved the NDP for two days, but I think the NVA are preoccupied right now and not looking this way. Keep in touch with me by radio every hour."

"You got it, sir." The capable and experienced Holloman saluted, then moved off to carry out his orders.

Poindexter glanced around the NDP. Men were hustling everywhere. No further orders needed to be given. There were no gripes, no swearing, no complaints. It was just another mission. It was why they were there. Might as well get it done.

S. Sgt. Gus Gutierrez casually leaned on the .50 caliber machine gun atop his Sheridan. His twenty tons of aluminum and steel, A-27, was nicknamed *American Woman*. Below Gutierrez's feet, inside the turret and lower in the tank itself, was the remainder of his crew: a loader, a gunner, and a driver. The big 300 hp diesel was running smoothly, idling in place. They were fully stocked with canister, grenades, and machine-gun rounds, but Gutierrez had taken the precaution of jamming as many extra ammo cans and spare machine gun barrels as he could in the confined spaces—just in case.

He watched as the other Sheridans and ACAVs in 2nd Platoon busied themselves with their own preparations. The platoon was already out in the jungle, somewhere ahead of the NDP, conducting a routine patrol. Lieutenant Healey would know exactly where they were: He had the maps. Captain Poindexter had called them on the radio moments ago and given them new instructions. Gutierrez closely scanned the faces of the other men—and Lieutenant Healey. Healey looked very serious, the other men anxious. The rumor was that some 1st Cav guys had gotten themselves into trouble and needed rescuing, and they were the only unit nearby who could help.

Well, Gutierrez mused, *if we're going to do something about this situation, Poindexter's the guy to do it.*

Many of the troopers, after Poindexter had taken command of Alpha Troop, had joked about the new captain's cockiness and swagger. He looked like a tall, skinny bantam rooster just looking for a fight. Today he was going to get one. It made many of them more than a little nervous: How far would Poindexter push them to prove who ruled the henhouse in War Zone C?

No doubt the Sheridans would be busting jungle momentarily, and Gutierrez and his crew would be in the lead. *American*

Woman was one of the troop's newer tanks, and one of the most reliable.

She's primed for this one, Gutierrez was thinking. *Ah, well, we'll go clean up this mess and be back by mail call. As soon as those dinks catch wind of us coming, they'll pack up and disappear into the jungle—just like they always do.* Gutierrez had no idea how wrong that projection would be.

PFC August Whitlock, twenty-one, was a field cook. His main duty was to bring hot chow to the troops in the field from the mess halls behind the lines whenever combat operations permitted. This would happen when a slick was available to bring the food, plus the mail, ammunition, spare parts, and whatever other small supplies the troop might need. He had flown to the NDP the night before, and the plan was for him to fly back the next morning. The shit had, of course, hit the fan the previous evening with the mortar accident, and today there wouldn't be any time to send a slick back to get him before the troop moved out. However, he was not just a cook: He was also a trained rifleman, and with the shortages the troop was experiencing he found himself detailed to go on the day's mission.

As soon as Poindexter had made up his mind to try to rescue Charlie Company, Whitlock and the rest of the troopers started packing up. Whitlock noticed something he had not seen before, however—a bit of a ritual as it turned out. Many of the troopers going out into the jungle, one by one, started seeking out the men who were being left behind at the NDP. Silently, with little fanfare, each trooper handed off something—a letter, a picture, a small package, whatever seemed too precious to carry off to the fight—just in case he didn't make it back. It was only then that Whitlock began to appreciate the magnitude of what was about to happen. As he said much later, "This was going to be something bigger than any of us realized."

SP4 George Burks, twenty, from Huntsville, Alabama, was a gunner on Sheridan A-19. From the time the *Star Trek* series had first captured the attention of sci-fi fans everywhere, Burks had been hooked. He was, indeed, a "Trekkie." As the word filtered down to the troops, who were tagged with the task of busting enough jungle to attempt this risky and harrowing rescue, all Burks could think about was the classic *Star Trek* conundrum centered on the "Kobayashi Maru Test." The *Kobayashi Maru* scenario was given to all command-designated cadets at the fictional Starfleet Academy. It was meant to be a challenge to their powers of reasoning, deduction, morality, judgment, and fitness for command. In truth, however, it was a diabolical problem for which there was no classic right-or-wrong answer, and it also placed every cadet in a "no-win" situation.

The nub of the puzzle was a setting in which the *Kobayashi Maru*, a civilian fuel carrier, accidentally stumbles into the dreaded Neutral Zone and collides with a "gravity mine." Without help from a friendly rescuer, the ship, its crew, and all three hundred of its passengers will perish. The primary challenge is that any penetration of the Neutral Zone by any Federation warship will automatically generate a combat response from the Klingon Empire and trigger a certain resumption of the devastating war that the Neutral Zone was established as a barrier against.

Each "captain" cadet must decide what to do when, as part of the simulation, a distress call is received from the *Kobayashi Maru*. Do you dash in and rescue the stranded civilians and thereby risk resumption of a horrible war; or, to keep the Federation safe, do you stand by and leave the *Kobayashi Maru* to its fate? It struck Burks that Team Alpha was facing its own *Kobayashi Maru* scenario, and the odds of making the right decision seemed equally grim.

The only cadet who had ever beaten the problem and scored a "win," naturally, was the universally famous Capt. James T. Kirk—and in order to win, he had snuck into the computer room the night before the test and secretly reprogrammed the computer. Some might call that cheating, but in the world of the future Starfleet it was dubbed "original thinking" and Kirk received a commendation.

Alpha Troop's brave captain had made his decision: *The "Klingons" be damned. We're going to rescue the* "Charlie Maru." Burks could only hope their captain had some "original thinking" up his fatigue-jacket sleeve somewhere as they plunged into their own version of the "Neutral Zone."

9

TOUGH CHOICES

When the firefight erupted, enveloping Charlie so quickly and furiously, PFC Paul Evans, eighteen, two weeks in Vietnam, and only then experiencing his first serious action, dove face-first behind an anthill. He tried to press himself as flat as he could into the jungle floor. Vietnamese anthills were huge and hard as concrete. They actually provided decent cover, at least on one side, but in this situation, the bullets were ripping the air over Evans's head from all directions.

S. Sgt. Preston Dawson, bellowing loudly, somehow avoiding getting torn to shreds, rumbled over to Evans's position. He grabbed Evans by a shoulder and shouted at him, "Look up!" Amid the roar of the battle and all the chaos, Dawson got Evans focused and told him to get behind some logs a few feet away where several other men were setting up a firing position. With AK-47 rounds smacking into the dirt all around him, Evans managed to hump the few yards from the anthill to the log barricade without getting nailed. He dove over the log pile smacking into both one of the RTOs and one of Charlie's medics. "Doc" was trying to patch up the KC, who'd taken some shrapnel in the shoulder. The KC was wincing in pain and spouting some Vietnamese that was gibberish to Evans.

Evans uncurled himself and managed to get into a decent firing position behind the downed tree trunks. The firing ramped up another notch. Several enemy rounds slammed into the wooden wall in front of Evans, ripping out large chunks of wood. Instinctively, Evans pulled the trigger on his M-16. He was on full automatic. The recoil from his own rifle knocked him off balance. His bullets flew in all directions, and not just at the NVA. He came within inches of blowing off Doc's foot. Everyone nearby yelled at him at once.

"Jesus, Evans!"

"Fuck, Evans! What the fuck are you doing?"

"Evans!" Dawson roared. "Cease fire!"

Evans blinked behind his thick glasses and relaxed his trigger finger. They all glared at him.

Dawson crawled over to Evans and stared intently into his face. "Evans! Look at me! You OK?"

Evans took a deep breath.

"Your first firefight?"

"Yes, Sergeant."

"Here." Dawson reached behind his back for the canteen on his web belt. He brought it around, unscrewed the top, and handed it to Evans. "Take a swig."

Evans gratefully downed a huge swallow. His throat had been choked with dust, dirt, smoke, and fear. The water, though warm, somehow tasted sweet. Strawberry Kool-Aid.

"Thank you, Sergeant."

Dawson cracked a small smile and put a big hand on Evans's shoulder. "You gonna be OK now?"

"Yes, sergeant. I was just . . . just . . ."

"I know, son. We all are."

"We gonna get outta this, Sergeant?"

"Don't know, son, but we're gonna need every grunt to be cool. You gonna be cool now?"

"Yes, sergeant. I'm cool."

"OK then, get back up behind that damn barrier—and set your rifle on manual. We need to save some ammo. Pick your targets."

With that Dawson was gone, off to another position down the line. Evans hunkered lower and tried to find targets. He couldn't see any, so he just took shots at any brush or foliage that moved. He began to realize they probably weren't going to get out of this alive, but somehow, knowing he wasn't alone seemed to make it a little more OK. He was part of the team finally and under the influence of the calming effects of strawberry Kool-Aid.

Nineteen-year-old Pvt. Ken "Mississippi" Woodward, from—you guessed it—a little town in Mississippi called Quitman, had convinced himself that he, too, might die that day. After three hours of relentless combat, two KIAs he was pretty sure of, and probably another thirty to forty woundings, the company was down to about fifty to sixty effectives. They were out of water and nearly all of their ammunition, and no help was on the way. His platoon, Scotch, was out on Charlie's perimeter roughly in the 180- to 270-degree sector of the 360-degree combat circle. Scotch had seen the least amount of action at the outset of the battle, but that had soon changed, and was changing still.

It was rare, in these deep-jungle confrontations, to actually see the enemy unless they were about to overrun you, but as Woodward sat there clutching his rifle and staring into the thickest brush he had ever seen, several NVA soldiers ran across the front of his position. Everyone opened up on them, but it was unclear if they hit anyone. What was very clear was that the NVA were tightening the noose around the company. Woodward's sector was the only part of the line where there had been any hope of fashioning an avenue of retreat—up until then, that was. Woodward was RTO for 2nd Squad of Scotch. He shifted his M-16 to his left hand, stamped the butt of the rifle into the ground, picked up the handset with his right, and started to shout into the radio. He was anxious to tell Captain Hobson what they had seen, and what he thought it meant.

As Woodward reported the new developments to the beleaguered Hobson, a tremendous blast of small arms and RPGs, a wall of steel, came flying his way. Everyone nearby hit the jungle floor once more, but not before three or four more grunts, Woodward couldn't tell who exactly, were cut down. Shouts of "Medic! Medic!" went up. Considering the direction from which this intense shooting had originated, the men of Scotch knew, for certain, the NVA they had just seen running past them were responsible for it. It also meant the enemy was blocking the last possible avenue of escape: They were completely encircled—and probably doomed. Even so, no one panicked, at least none had yet. Rather, to Woodward's amazement, they all still seemed determined to go down giving a proper account of themselves.

As bullets whizzed overhead, Woodward crawled all over the immediate area, scrounging for extra magazines from the men who could no longer fight.

We're screwed . . . Damn, we're screwed was all Woodward could repeat to himself, over and over.

Rather than making him scared, it was making him angry, and he became even more intent on taking as many of the dink bastards with him as he could.

It is supremely difficult to describe what thoughts flow through the minds of men who are under the kind of duress imposed by intense ground combat operations. In the case of the men of Company C, on this particular day, the task was even more challenging considering they were not only trying to stay alive but also fighting an enemy they could rarely—if ever—see. Added to this stress were the extra burdens of running out of the means to carry on the fight and knowing that they were surrounded with very little hope of survival (other than miracles). The mental challenges for these men were, to say the least, extreme.

Under these kinds of combat conditions, some men will simply give up, physically and emotionally, and enter into a nearly catatonic state of fear that is beyond the ability of others to reach. These men will shut down, pull within themselves, and become useless ciphers. Nothing can force them to move. No amount of bullying, shame, shouting, or physical pressure will get them to recommence firing their weapons or otherwise contribute to the outcome of the battle in which they have become entrapped. Men like this often lose control over their most basic bodily functions and end up pissing or shitting themselves and quivering uncontrollably. There is no way to effectively train soldiers for this condition, or arm them for its potentiality. Predicting its occurrence is beyond the scope of any psychological test that has yet been devised. The only way you find out if you are part of this unfortunate subset of mental misfits is to become one. There were plenty of frightened men in Charlie Company on March 26, 1970, but all available contemporary evidence indicates that every one of them—even the newest replacements—passed this basic test of courage. Some went way beyond the basics of what others might call "cutting it" and performed extreme acts of heroism, not all of which were ultimately recognized.

Some men will enter into a state where their training takes over completely and almost all of their actions become instinctual and in accordance with what they have been taught or learned, perhaps in previous combat. These men somehow force those parts of their brains that are in control of fear and panic to shut down or at least shut up. It is the same thing, on a much lesser scale, of course, as the swimmer standing on the shore, ready to plunge into a freezing surf. This participant in the annual "polar bear plunge" knows he shouldn't be on this beach in January, shouldn't be risking the shock to his system, is going to feel instant numbing cold and intense surface pain; he pushes all of that aside and jumps into the freezing water anyway. Soldiers like these allow their best and most dominant survival instincts to take complete control. They shove everything else aside to carry on with the job at hand. It was evident that such men were in the ranks of Charlie that day.

There are even some men who can function on a totally conscious level, supremely aware of every facet of all the dangers surrounding them. They see everything and analyze it all. They are frightened and anxious, but they can push those concerns aside and take the actions they need to take to survive or help their comrades make it through the day. There were men like that in Charlie as well.

Lastly, there are those who haven't got a clue what to do except to do as they are told. The fear is there but secondary to the dynamic of the group. Incapable of independent thought or action in regard to the survival of the men with whom they fight, and, of course, themselves, they depend on those who demonstrate no fear to tell them what to do. Many times the uninitiated, the youngest, the "newbies" fall into this category, as might well be expected. If they survive they might, at some future date, graduate to the ranks of the instinctual automatons or the high-functioning thinkers. For the moment, they need guidance, reassurance, and sometimes a kick in the ass. Charlie Company had many of these men in their ranks that day.

The X factor in all of this, of course, is what happens when all the possibilities for survival are exhausted. What do you do when the last rounds of ammunition are expended? When it's clear that the enemy is about to walk into your lines unimpeded and either shoot you down where you stand or bind your hands and march you off to a tiger cage in a filthy POW camp, what then?

It's fairly obvious what the catatonics would do—nothing. What about the rest? Do you surrender, make them kill you by going down swinging, or save the last bullet for yourself? By 1400 on March 26, the men of Charlie who were still conscious and not so severely wounded as to have lost the capacity for lucid thought were trying to figure out which option fit best. They were, indeed, that desperate.

10

"BUSTING JUNGLE"

1st and 3rd Platoons made it back to the NDP in less than half an hour. The command elements of Alpha Troop—consisting of Poindexter's ACAV, A-66; A-81, the medic track; A-86, one of the remaining mortar tracks; and the FO's (artillery forward observer's) ACAV, formed up with the returning platoons and headed off into the jungle to catch up with 2nd Platoon. Poindexter radioed his intentions to Colonel Conrad, who acknowledged and approved the captain's initiative.

Within another half hour, the entire troop was back together and diligently trying to shove aside the roughly 4 kilometers of jungle growth that separated them from the beleaguered grunts of Charlie. As the formation pushed ahead it was aligned as a giant *E* (if you were looking down on it from above). The open side of the *E* faced in the direction of the intended "busting." The top and bottom tines of the *E* each consisted of one platoon with a Sheridan in the lead. The third platoon was the spine of the *E* and covered the back of the formation. This platoon could act as a maneuver element if need be, quickly breaking to one side or the other to provide support where needed if the troop was suddenly attacked—which all of them expected would be the case. The middle and shortest tine of the giant *E* was the command element, with Poindexter's track immediately behind a Sheridan borrowed from 1st Platoon, followed by the mortar, FO, and medic tracks.

The jungle in this part of War Zone C was particularly dense and forbidding. It had not yet been touched, for whatever reason, by any of the lethal defoliants that the American forces had grown too fond of using. In addition to the thick grasses, choking vines, and nearly solid thickets of brush, there were groves of native hardwood trees, especially giant acacias. Most of the trees were far too large for the Sheridans to topple, so they snaked around them. From the air it looked like the giant *E* was constantly wiggling, changing shape and undulating like a nest of metallic snakes slithering over the forest floor.

Meter by meter the formation slogged ahead, making good progress at first, almost 100 meters every five minutes or so. Then the flora seemed to take sides, this time in favor of the enemy. It appeared to get denser, thicker, more resistant. It was some of the worst busting any of the troopers had experienced. The Sheridans quickly overheated, forcing the platoon leaders to rotate the lead tank every thirty minutes or so. An exhausted Sheridan would pull over and let the next tank take the lead. As soon as the replacement passed, the worn-out crew of the tank being replaced would swing the main gun off center, just enough to gain access to the coolant reservoir cap. The cap was carefully loosened, releasing giant geysers of scalding-hot steam. It was as if some extremely strange species of land-whale were suddenly breeching amid the forest, gasping for air—and more water.

One Sheridan, A-18, the balkiest and oldest of the troop's complement, overheated so badly that it nearly caught fire; even the insulation started smoking. The tank's enterprising crew simply opened the hatch and began pouring 5-gallon cans of water directly into the engine compartment. Under most conditions, this desperate act of extreme maintenance would likely cause the engine to seize or simply quit. This one did not, however, and the tank simmered down and lurched ahead once again.

Every track in each line carefully followed the vehicle ahead of it. This minimized the need for additional busting and also helped ensure that the trailing tracks would not roll over hidden mines, booby traps, or natural obstacles that could twist a track right off.

The troop had to maneuver around old bomb craters and tree stumps, too, and despite the fact that they were traversing crunched-up vegetation, the ride was far from smooth. In fact, it was constantly jarring and bone rattling—especially for the infantrymen of Company A, who were unaccustomed to riding to a fight at all. Sitting atop the ACAVs or on the rear decks of the Sheridans, some of Ray Armer's men were bounced off when one of the tracks smacked into a large depression or irregularity. Others were rudely swept off the vehicles by trees or branches that took one last swipe at their tormentors before crashing to the jungle floor. Bamboo rattled the sides of the tracks and smacked some of the riders. Razor-sharp grasses slashed by, whipping against exposed skin. Then there were the insects.

Captain Armer and his RTO were sitting on the back of A-66. The tank leading the column at that time was commanded by SFC Robert Foreman. Foreman's Sheridan hammered down a tree that apparently had been home to a rather substantial wasp's nest. By the time A-66, dutifully following the tank ahead, rolled over the downed nest the wasps were alert, angry, and swarming. This species of wasp was bright jungle green, overly large, and particularly nasty. They went after Captain Armer and his RTO with profound virulence. The radio operator was particularly victimized. In his furious attempts to get the stinging insects off his back, he accidentally allowed his radio to tumble from his shoulders. It fell directly onto the downed nest itself.

Captain Armer quickly realized that no one was going to retrieve the radio, which was crawling with angry wasps. Neither did he want to leave an operational PRC-25 where it might be picked up later by an enemy soldier: So he pulled out his .45 and put a bullet into the set. He then went back to swatting wasps.

The radio operator was stung so badly that a medic had to dose him up with painkillers. Armer refused medication, wanting to have a clear head for the battle he knew lay ahead. (He still bears the painful scars of the wasp stings forty years later.)

The ride into the jungle was also nightmarish for PFC August Whitlock, and it was a time of terribly conflicting emotion.

I'm a damn field cook, for crissakes, he kept saying to himself over and over; yet there he was, M-16 at the ready, bouncing on the back of an ACAV, headed to what would probably be a nasty firefight. Why? It was not that he was unprepared. He was, after all, a trained rifleman first, a field cook second. It was not that he was reluctant to fight. Scared, sure, maybe a little, perhaps even a lot, but not unwilling to go along with his fellow troopers, if they needed his help. He just didn't know what was really going on.

"What's the captain up to?" That was all he kept asking, to anyone who'd listen. Naturally, at the lowest levels of the rigid hierarchy, where Whitlock and all the other E-4s and below dwelled, the whys and wherefores were not always obvious, nor were they often explained. All Whitlock really knew was two things: One, he wasn't having any fun. The dust and bugs were everywhere, and the ride he was experiencing was hard and painful. Two, life was a jumble of feelings just then. More than a few men were still grieving over the losses of the night before. Whitlock was among the most affected. When he wasn't boiling up a pot of coffee or serving hot chow to the men, he was usually detailed to assist the mortar crews. He had become close to those guys, particularly Sergeant Smolich. Smolich had lost three good men, including one of Whitlock's best buddies in the troop, Chip Andrews.

Yet amid all his doubt and churning uncertainty another deeply felt emotion lay smoldering: a nascent fire of revenge. As Whitlock tried to hold on to his perch on the back of the grinding, bouncing ACAV all he could think was *Lousy, shitty war . . . I just wanna kill somebody.*

Back on Sheridan A-19, Specialist 4 Burks, the gunner, had to be ready to pull the trigger on the main gun when the TC yelled, "Fire!" His primary job, deep inside the tank, with a limited field of vision, was to shoot at whatever target he was directed to cover and do so with the correct ammunition. It was usually a process of eyeballing the target through the gun sight, zeroing in on it, watching for the green light that meant "OK to shoot," and carefully squeezing the trigger. Except today. He had a canister round loaded in the main gun, anticipating a fight against enemy troops. The powerful projectile held a lethal spray of thousands of tiny darts and could obliterate a company of massed men at distances of 200-plus yards. It was like having your own enormous shotgun. All Burks could see, though, was a wall of green constantly moving at him and sliding off to either side of the tank. Brush, grass, and small trees kept slapping the end of his big gun tube before being chewed up by the treads beneath him. He had no range, no bearing, no targets.

As Burks later said, it was "triple canopy jungle, very dense, dark, dreary, spooky, tense, scary. Very bad woods."

There was klick after klick of it to plow through. No one knew how long it would take, they didn't really know where they were headed, and they couldn't see what was coming at them—and all the time they waited for sudden blasts of gunfire or RPGs to roar out of the jungle on all sides.

Burks was stuck in an aluminum box with a diminished view of the outside world and every confidence that at any moment "incoming" would start hammering his thin-skinned box to scrap metal.

SP4 Don Dush's perspective was not much better than Burks's. Standing behind the right M-60 mount inside A-66, his view of the world from behind his gun shield was near zero. As the ACAV rolled over the crumpled vegetation, a wall of unending, monotonous green slid by, inches from Dush's face, left to right.

Dush later wrote, "The move through the jungle was a scary and most uncomfortable time. I really didn't know what to expect. I had not had a shot fired at me yet. I do remember listening to the air strikes and small-arms fire, seemingly for hours while we were enroute, and thinking how crazy it was that we were simply driving into that."

SP4 Raymond Tarr was serving as a loader on Sheridan A-38. The tank was nicknamed *Abilene.* The reasons for the name were unknown and probably lost to the history of a long-forgotten tank crew. Perhaps the previous TC was from Kansas—but no one knew.

Tarr's perspective on things, during the course of an actual battle, was even more restricted than that of a gunner like George Burks. Loaders were literally in "the belly of the beast" handling the dangerous caseless ammunition and sweating things out at the very bottom of the Sheridan. At other times, as when busting jungle, loaders usually rode atop the turrets and had the arduous but necessary task of making sure that downed tree limbs and miscellaneous jungle junk didn't clog the air intakes or accumulate on top of the vehicles.

As the troop drew closer and closer to the suspected positions of both Charlie Company and the NVA, the sounds of the fight grew louder and more ominous. Occasionally, Tarr would look up as he heard the artillery rounds roar overhead. He couldn't see them, of course, but the noise they made caused him to instinctively try. He could, however, catch glimpses of the helicopter gunships and even the Phantoms zooming by. Two planes, in tandem, flew so close to Alpha Troop that Tarr could actually see the flames trailing from their exhaust pipes as they crossed a short break in the tangled canopy overhead. When they released their bombs, somewhere out to the front, the ground quivered as if in a minor earthquake. That surely meant they were getting close.

Poindexter got on the radio and told the three columns to pop purple smoke grenades. Each platoon complied, and purple smoke wafted up through the treetops. Poindexter hoped—as did Ray Tarr and his buddies—that the smoke would effectively mark their positions and prevent them from becoming the unfortunate victims of off-target drops of airborne ordnance.

Other than the din of the battle ahead, the crashing and crunching of falling vegetation was the dominant sound in the ranks of Alpha Troop. A green mist of chlorophyll wafted through the gun slits of each vehicle and mingled with the dust and sweat-laden humidity. Teeth rattled as each track slammed into stumps, potholes, or solid objects hidden in the jungle debris, but, miraculously, not a single track lost a tread during the entire busting evolution.

Inside each baking aluminum shell, the strong smell of gun oil mixed with the pungent odor of unwashed human flesh. Men nervously fingered their weapons, constantly shifting and adjusting cans of ammo or the bandoliers of extra bullets. The popping sounds of gunfire, the smash of rockets, and the thud of the artillery drew them inexorably to the hungry touch of personal combat.

11

ANGEL OF MERCY

In the fall of 1941 a handsome kid from an Irish family hailing from Allston, Massachusetts, decided to go to college right across the river from where he had grown up. Since he was also a very smart kid, that college across the river was happy to welcome him into the Class of '45. Then, later that same year, the Japanese bombed Pearl Harbor. Somehow, continuing to study behind the ivy-covered walls of Harvard College no longer seemed the right thing to do, so after a year in Cambridge, George William Casey Sr. applied for a transfer and was accepted into the West Point Class of '45.

World War II ended before newly minted 2nd Lieutenant Casey could get into the fight, but he was ready for Korea, where he led an infantry company into combat on the infamous Heartbreak Ridge. He earned a Silver Star and a battlefield promotion for his bravery. He then served on the personal staff of a future Joint Chiefs of Staff chairman, Gen. Lyman Lemnitzer; earned a master's degree in international relations from Georgetown in 1958 and a second master's from George Washington University in 1965, this time in business administration; and, returning to his academic roots, was a military fellow at Harvard's Center for International Affairs in 1966.

With all of his intellect, the connections he was making, the educational background he was amassing, and his growing array of personal decorations and awards, Casey was definitely on the army's fast track for promotion and advancement. There were a few murmurs that Casey would become army chief of staff himself one day, perhaps even chairman of the Joint Chiefs. He was fashioning a solid career with extraordinary potential for future command—and general's stars—but there was even more to the man than that. Casey was known throughout the army as a "soldier's soldier." Not since the days of the famed five-star General of the Army Omar Bradley had the U.S. Army had a senior officer with such a reputation for care and concern for every man he commanded.

By March of 1970, Brigadier General Casey was on his second tour in Vietnam, this time as assistant division commander of the famed 1st Cavalry. He would succeed Maj. Gen. E. B. Roberts in the top job in the 1st Cav in May and be promoted to major general. Casey was a superb organizer and had a near-photographic memory. It was said he could name every single officer in the entire division and recognize each of them on sight, and was held in awe by his troopers.

When an aide came to the general early in the afternoon of March 26, 1970, with the news that one of his companies, Company C, 2nd of the 8th, was pinned down and fighting for its very existence, it was no wonder that he wanted to know instantly what could be done to help them.

1330, MARCH 26, 1970, LT. COL. MIKE CONRAD'S COMMAND HELICOPTER

Colonel Conrad was getting to be about as desperate and exasperated as Captain Hobson, but he tried very hard not to let it show in the radio exchanges he and Hobson were having. Conrad tried to be reassuring, helpful, and informative, but he knew Hobson was already out of machine-gun bullets, nearly out of rifle rounds, and running very low on smoke grenades. When the smokes ran out, which could be in minutes, Conrad would no longer have a way to effectively mark Hobson's position for the artillery and the TACAIR assets that were trying to help. Without smoke, observations would be guesswork, and that could be as lethal to the men of Charlie as the NVA. Conrad would have to call off the long guns and send the aviators back to base. It would be another nail in Hobson's rapidly closing coffin.

Hobson's men were scrounging ammo from the dead and wounded. They were squeezing off shots one at a time—no more rifles on automatic. The machine gunners were ready to throw sticks; they had nothing else to use. When Hobson's men finally ran out of bullets it would be over in a matter of moments. When that happened, Conrad would be looking for a shipment of body bags instead of pilots brave enough to try to penetrate the ring of steel around Charlie.

Then, literally out of the blue, came a radio call. Conrad could scarcely believe what he heard in his headset. General Casey himself, the assistant division commander, was inbound, piloting a Huey, loaded to the gills with machine-gun bullets, rifle ammo, and water. Casey would no longer ask his pilots to do what he wouldn't be willing to do himself, so he had called for his own personal helicopter to be fueled and loaded. It was unusual for a senior officer to take such a risky gamble, but on top of this, Casey was barely qualified to fly the mission. He was not a veteran helicopter pilot. He had only taken aviation training after he had been assigned to the 1st Cavalry. He reasoned that if he was going to command an airmobile division he ought to be able to do all the jobs that his subordinate officers were capable of doing—and that included flying helicopters. He had taken a short, six-week "crash course" in the basics at Fort Rucker, Alabama, earned his pilot's wings, then joined the division.

Casey always flew with a more experienced pilot, however. It was usually a junior warrant officer, lieutenant, or captain, and such was the case that day. Still, Casey was at the controls as the nimble slick bounced and jinked its way across the jungle canopy below, heading for a possibly lifesaving resupply of Charlie Company.

Conrad excitedly got back on the radio and told Hobson to get out a few of his last smoke grenades—help was on the way. Ammunition would be dropped on them shortly. He decided not to tell Hobson who was delivering it.

Despite his previous efforts to hold the line, Hobson's perimeter had shrunk. He had finally been forced to draw his circle tighter based on the dwindling number of grunts that were still standing and the pitifully small supply of ammunition available to them. To give the pilot the best indicator of his location, he decided to pop the smoke, which was purple, from the very center of his position. As soon as he could hear the sound of the rotor blades above the din of the battle he let the smoke swirl upward. Unfortunately, due to the thickness of the jungle canopy, the smoke became too diffused to clearly mark the right spot. What little smoke the trees managed to let through, the rotor wash from the slick blew away.

Pvt. Mississippi Woodward, out on the southeast corner of the perimeter, and carefully monitoring all the chatter between Hobson and the slick pilot, watched the purple smoke curl skyward. He and every other man lifted their eyes to the heavens, looking for the Bird of Deliverance. All of a sudden, a lull in the firing was evident. The Huey's shadow could be seen maneuvering somewhere above, the rotors slashing the humid air and whipping the treetops wildly.

Then, out of the corner of his eye, Woodward saw another plume of purple smoke swirl upward, but something was not right about it. It took him a couple of seconds . . .

Wait . . . wait . . . that smoke is . . . Holy shit! It's outside our lines! Woodward scrambled frantically for his radio. Somehow, the NVA had purple smokes! Maybe they'd captured some in a previous firefight. They were using them to try to fool the Huey pilots into dropping on their signal and not on Hobson's.

Woodward started screaming into his radio, "Ignore that smoke! Ignore that second purple smoke! The gooks have got purple smoke, too, how copy, over?"

If the slick pilots saw the second smoke or heard Woodward's frantic warning they never gave any indication. As soon as the ruse was detected, the NVA opened up again. This time the volume of fire seemed even greater, if that was possible, and it was all aimed upward. They were no longer concentrating on the men of Charlie. They wanted to bring down the slick. It wouldn't take much. One well-aimed machine-gun burst in the tail rotor or a lucky RPG hit and it would be all over.

The men of Charlie could see the Huey's skids rolling over and intermingling with the treetops. They could also hear the sickening sound of the enemy's bullets smacking into the metal of the aircraft hovering above them. The typical Huey had armor plating affixed to the bottom of the fuselage for just this purpose, but a determined pounding wouldn't hold off major damage for long.

Hobson gazed upward. The slick was almost directly above him. The pilot shouted into the radio that he still couldn't see any smoke and told Hobson to use the sound of the rotors to "walk" the bird to where he wanted the drop—and hurry. Hobson did that as calmly and as accurately as he could, and as he talked to the slick he realized the voice he was hearing was familiar.

Oh my God! It's General Casey himself!

There was no time for pleasantries, though. The Huey was getting slammed, and if it didn't get out of there soon, it and its crew were going to join Charlie Company on the jungle floor.

Casey made adjustments as best he could but finally had to commit. He instructed the crew to kick the boxes out—all of them— and do it ASAP.

Heavy boxes of machine-gun ammo, M-16 bullets, and cans of water began to rain down from above. Some split open on impact, scattering thousands of rounds of precious ammo across a wide arc. Some fell outside of Charlie's lines. Men ran out and retrieved them anyway, exposing themselves to incredible crossfires. Amazingly, not one man was hit. Several boxes fell right on target. The grunts of Charlie Company began ripping them open and passing the bullets around.

When the last of the crates was out of the Huey's side hatch, Casey jerked the stick over and headed east, back to base, his slick trailing smoke. The Huey had plenty of bullet holes in its skin, and General Casey's personal aide was seriously wounded. Even so, the mission had been a success, and in more ways than one. The desperate men of Charlie finally had additional means to carry on the fight. Beyond the invaluable cargo, they also had the knowledge that one of their own generals had cared enough to risk his life on their behalf. Both factors were immense morale boosters.

[Author's Note: George Hobson, for one, believes that General Casey was the first of three principal officers to save his men that day. The other two, of course, are Captains Poindexter and Armer. Hobson and others think that General Casey has not been properly recognized for his heroics on March 26.]

12

ENCOURAGING WORDS

Once the men of Charlie had a few more bullets and at least some hope, other critical items they needed became more obvious. Chief among these necessities was water. General Casey's slick had managed to drop a few containers of the precious fluid, but there was still not enough. Medical supplies were dwindling, too, and a few of the wounded men were hit so badly that they were hovering near shock from loss of blood. Plasma, painkillers, and bandages were disappearing rapidly.

Unexpectedly, Colonel Conrad raised the bar of hope even higher: He informed Hobson that more help was on the way. Just what kind of help was not specified. Certain that the NVA were on the same radio net and listening, Conrad would not disclose what type of force it would be, nor would he give any ETA or direction of approach.

It wouldn't be any sort of airborne force, Hobson reasoned. He knew what even the craziest of helicopter pilots would face if they tried to insert any additional troops into this cyclone of steel. They would be slaughtered either before or shortly after they tried to land.

It had to be a ground-based relief column, but the closest troops were over five miles away, back at FSB Illingworth, and as good as the 2nd Battalion's grunts were, they weren't superhuman. Hobson knew there was no way any appreciable number of infantrymen could hump that distance, in this jungle, in time to make any difference.

Could they come by truck—or jeep? No, not in this impassable terrain, a choking landscape without any decent mud tracks, never mind roads.

Maybe Conrad was just shining him on—hoping to keep his spirits up, encouraging him to hold on, to fight harder even if their promised relief was based on false hope?

Well, whatever it was, Hobson didn't have time to worry about it. He had a determined enemy to fight, and that was all he could process at the moment. He and Conrad also knew that any potential assistance needed to get there before dark, which was about five hours away. If no relief column had shown up by nightfall, it was going to be "game over." Hobson shoved the possibilities from his mind and went back to work.

1500, MARCH 26, 1970, TEAM ALPHA'S RELIEF COLUMN

Poindexter was lurching along atop A-66, sweating profusely and trying to get his bearings from the plastic maps he carried. The heat inside the ACAV was so intense it was melting the grease pencils he used to track his progress on the charts.

The goal, of course, was to navigate to Charlie Company's position as quickly as possible. With all the noise generated by five tanks and fourteen ACAVs crunching through the bush, there was no sense in trying to feign any sort of stealth approach. A beeline directly to the confrontation ought to be the best tactic, as long as there were no unknown dry riverbeds or steep obstacles along the route of march, but with the all-enveloping jungle canopy it was hard to get accurate bearings. Asking for help from TACAIR or Colonel Conrad, constantly circling above, wasn't a good option either, since it would certainly alert the enemy to Team Alpha's avenue of approach.

The jungle yielded only grudgingly, but the tracks ground ahead, carving the klicks from the stubborn greenery. The sun, unrestricted in its heavenly arc, had no problem racing for the horizon, however, and Poindexter could only wish for some way to halt its progress as he tried to speed up his own.

1530, MARCH 26, 1970, CHARLIE COMPANY'S INTERIOR LINES

SP4 Rick Hokenson, twenty-two, from Detroit Lakes, Minnesota, rested his hopped-up M-14 with its tactical scope atop the giant log he was hunkered down behind. Hokenson was a designated sniper, a job he had wanted since being drafted in '68. He had been around guns all his young life and had spent his happiest days hunting in and around Cotton Lake, right off Route 34, way up in northern Minnesota. Cotton Lake was, in fact, where he went in his head in times of great stress and anxiety, like right then. The images helped calm him.

After basic and advanced sniper training at Fort Lewis in Washington, Hokenson was offered two opportunities: Korea or Vietnam. Remembering clearly what the winters in Minnesota were like, he decided he did not want anything to do with frozen Korean foxholes. He wanted to go someplace warm. Vietnam was warm; besides, the 1st Cavalry had the coolest uniform shoulder patches. Thus it was that Hokenson found his way to Charlie Company. He had been there for almost a year, and his DEROS was rapidly approaching. He had fought with Charlie through some of its toughest battles: Valentine's Day 1970; March 1 through 8; the Great Rice Caper; and then this dust-up.

This was the worst one so far. Hokenson and the rest of Charlie Company were certainly in dire straits, that he knew. He had seen men going down all around him for over three hours, and things were only going from bad to worse. From his nearly invisible vantage point behind the downed trunk, he peered carefully into his Leupold 10×40 scope and felt his right index finger gently caressing the specially weighted 1-pound trigger pull. He idly mused that it would be a shame to lose or damage this beautiful rifle amid all the destruction going on around him. He knew that the special $900 M-14 and the $2,600 scope that the army had simply handed to him cost more than the Pontiac GTO he was secretly coveting.

The scope was amazing. The other grunts with their standard M-16s were having trouble identifying targets to shoot at. Hokenson simply aimed the scope in the direction of the nearest enemy bunker and could line up NVA faces clearly. He started shooting them one at a time, each anonymous face erupting in a cloud of red mist as soon as the M-14's big 7.62 cartridge (the same one used in the M-60 machine guns) plowed squarely into each of them.

With the terrible toll Hokenson and his rifle were exacting, it didn't take the enemy long to figure out where he was, and what he was—and that they wanted him dead. The first AK-47 round sent his way landed with a sickening *whump!* It was the exact same sound these rounds made when they plowed into human flesh. Hokenson put down his rifle and excitedly began to pat himself down. He knew he had been hit; he just couldn't figure out where, and it hadn't started to hurt yet. Then came three more body blows: *whump! whump! whump!*

Oh my God! I'm dead! was all Hokenson could think.

Again he felt around, looking for pools of blood, spilling guts, chunks of exploded flesh. Nothing.

Whump! again, but this time splinters of spongy wood flew everywhere. It was then that Hokenson realized he wasn't hit at all. The NVA rounds were simply sinking into the big log he was hiding behind—and the trunk was rotten, soft and full of moisture. The AK rounds were making the all-too-familiar sounds because the tree was not solid and had nearly the same density as a human body. Hokenson didn't have much time to ponder the physics of the situation, though. The next sound snaking its way toward him was much more ominous, and it didn't end in a *whump* but rather a very substantial *WHOOMPH!*

A well-aimed RPG slammed into Hokenson's barrier. The log was obliterated in a huge shower of pulpy wood. Fortunately, the trunk and not Hokenson absorbed the blast. It was time to find another shelter. Hokenson grabbed his M-14 and scurried back toward the next group of grunts along the perimeter.

It was then that Hokenson heard the latest rumor: that a group of cavalry guys were trying to bust through to help them. He hoped it was true, of course, but desperate situations always breed desperate stories. He still had a grenade in his pocket, the one that he was keeping for himself. As a sniper he knew that if he were captured he'd be one of the first to be tortured. The enemy hated snipers the most. He had already made up his mind he would not be taken alive.

1600, MARCH 26, 1970, TEAM ALPHA RELIEF COLUMN

Poindexter halted the column briefly. He knew they were getting near. The sounds of the battle they had been hearing all afternoon were very close. They found themselves on the edge of what appeared to be an old B-52 strike zone. Bomb craters were strewn in their path, and the swath of destruction, rotting vegetation, and dead branches stretched for a half mile in either direction.

Poindexter was simply amazed that they had come this far and had somehow avoided an ambush. The NVA commander was either very absorbed in the battle or supremely confident that he was not in a position to have to worry about the oncoming Americans. Still, it had been a minor miracle they had not been jumped somewhere along the way.

Poindexter felt they were finally close enough to the action that they no longer had to worry about radio communications; plus, surely, the NVA had scouted them out, or at least heard their throbbing diesels crashing through the forest.

He called Conrad. "Stone Mountain Two-Nine, this is Writer Two-Nine. I'm putting out smoke on my point. Can you give me a spot relative to Racer, over?"

"This is Stone Mountain Two-Nine, roger, wait. I'll come around and take a look." Conrad directed the Huey pilots to swing around and try to pinpoint Team Alpha.

Poindexter gave an order for the lead track in the column to pop smoke—a yellow one.

Moments later, Conrad came back on the radio. "This is Stone Mountain Two-Nine. Identify yellow. Make a half-turn to your left, Writer, and come around to a heading of three-three-zero. You've got about two hundred meters to go."

"Thanks, Two-Nine. Writer out."

Before issuing the order to turn and move toward Charlie's position, Poindexter gave each platoon leader specific instructions to elevate all guns until they made actual contact with Charlie and heard from him again. No firing until they had direct orders from him to do so. He made each platoon leader acknowledge the order.

Poindexter knew from previous experience that a clever enemy commander would not hesitate to insert a group of his own men squarely between Alpha Troop and Charlie's lines with the specific intention of sacrificing those men to draw the cavalry's fire. If they were suckered into this ploy they might wipe out a token group of the NVA, but they'd be firing right into Hobson's men, too. It was likely they would kill more of those they hoped to rescue than any NVA.

"Writer Two-Nine, this is Racer Two-Nine. I've actually got a few smokes left. I'll pop one when we have you in sight."

It was Hobson, and he seemed to have a note of hope in his voice that Poindexter had not heard during the hours of their approach.

1615, MARCH 26, 1970, SCOTCH PLATOON POSITIONS, CHARLIE COMPANY

There was no mistaking the sounds: the throaty roar of ACAV diesel engines and the higher-pitched whine of the Sheridan turbines. Hobson began to hear first one, then two, then many of them. He ran to the southeast perimeter of his lines and stared across the expanse of the B-52 strike zone.

There they are, by God. What a sight! They made it!

13

BREAKTHROUGH

It was Captain Poindexter's turn to contemplate crossing the lunarlike landscape of the B-52 strike zone that sprawled between his troop and the men of Charlie Company. Going straight across was surely the quickest route to the stranded grunts, but it could also be a path right into an ambush. Then there were the bomb craters themselves. Any one of them could swallow an ACAV whole. The sloping sides of the partially eroded depressions could trap a track's treads and twist them off if a driver was not vigilant. The piles of vegetation would make it difficult for his accompanying infantry to walk across the blast zone. They would have to hop aboard the tracks and ride—which would make them perfect targets for any NVA snipers, skilled riflemen, or machine gunners.

Going around the strike zone would mean another long delay in relieving the stranded men—and there was no guarantee there was a way around. They couldn't even see an end of the strike zone from their position.

Poindexter decided to risk moving straight across the zone. As he made up his mind to push ahead, a yellow smoke sputtered to life across the open gulf of sand and broken trees.

Poindexter picked up the radio handset. "Racer Two-Nine, this is Writer. Identify yellow."

"This is Racer Two-Nine, affirmative! Affirmative!" Hobson shouted, elated.

The drifting yellow smoke identified the spot where Alpha Troop should try to penetrate Charlie Company's perimeter—and it had the secondary effect of assuring that this wasn't a ruse and an attempt to suck the cavalry into the maw of the NVA's bunker complex.

The cavalrymen cinched everything down a little tighter. It was going to be a bumpy ride and one where a firefight could erupt at any second. Flak jackets were donned, helmets put on. A shower of empty soda cans spouted from the ranks of the vehicles as last-second lukewarm beverages were poured down dry and nervous throats. Towels that had been protecting oiled machine-gun barrels from the humidity and moisture were pulled away and tossed aside. Nervous trigger fingers itchily took weapons off safe.

The infantrymen of Alpha Company tried to flatten themselves on the decks of the Sheridans or the backs of the ACAVs as much as possible, even hide behind their bulky packs (which they had shed as soon as they had clambered aboard). Captain Armer knew that with the first incoming rounds all his men would ditch their rides in a heartbeat and dive for the bomb craters—an infantryman's natural instinct. He'd be right there along with them. He didn't like riding all that much himself.

In three parallel columns, the tracks carefully picked their paths across the bomb zone. Everyone skirted the craters, cautiously moving forward at what seemed a snail's pace. This was it. If this was a trap, it would be sprung right then. The whole troop was out in the open, vulnerable, and enclosed in a free-fire zone, naked as jaybirds.

Strangely, nothing happened. In fact, less than nothing happened: The small-arms fire across the way slackened, almost coming to a complete halt. Was it possible that the NVA were, indeed, completely surprised? Were they, as incredible as it seemed, seeing and hearing the cavalry for the first time that afternoon? Were they staring in awe at this sudden cavalcade of firepower and muttering the Vietnamese equivalent of "Oh, shit!" whatever that might sound like?

Poindexter was taken aback, not truly believing their luck. Had the NVA radio operator in charge of intercepting the American radio traffic been distracted? Wounded or killed? Had his radio been damaged? Had the NVA commander set a trap for them but in the wrong spot? Had the artillery and TACAIR really masked the approach of all these noisy, snorting diesels?

Whatever the circumstances, Poindexter was totally absorbed in the maneuvering by then and only gave it one passing thought: *What a relief!*

First Lt. Mike Healey's 2nd Platoon was the first to make it across the gap. His lead tracks plunged back into the sheltering vegetation. The NVA, who had insinuated themselves in Charlie's rear earlier and could have blocked the way, had mysteriously disappeared. Had they been eliminated? Had they been cowed by the approach of Alpha Troop's charging beasts and fled?

"Six, looks like we've got some of our guys out front here. They look pretty beat up," Healey radioed back to Poindexter.

Indeed, they were: almost too exhausted to get out of the way of the cavalry vehicles that carefully picked their way into Charlie's lines.

One of Healey's lead vehicles, *American Woman*, with Sergeant Gutierrez and his crew, pulled into Charlie's outer perimeter. Gutierrez, who had predicted they'd all be back by mail call (that wasn't going to happen), was flabbergasted.

"Upon entering the area of contact, my first sense that something terribly bad had happened was the sight of ponchos with jungle boots hanging out of one end. I felt my heart stick in my throat."

Poindexter's vehicles were next to plow across the gap and back into the jungle. As his command track, A-66, came to a halt inside Charlie's defensive circle, his right-hand M-60 gunner, SP4 Don Dush, gawked wide-eyed at the men they were rescuing.

Dush saw men who were spent. Only slowly, and with great deliberation, did they stand or otherwise come out from behind whatever firing shelters they had been using. Like springs that had been wound too tight, they seemed reluctant to uncoil. They stared at the men of Alpha Troop and their heaving, snarling machines almost as if they were apparitions, too unbelievable to be real.

On Sheridan A-38, SP4 Ray Tarr stuck his head out of the loader's hatch. His tank had halted inside Charlie's lines very near the casualty collection point. Wounded men were lying everywhere. Slowly, they began to rise, or if they could not get up they at least propped themselves on elbows or held on to the outstretched arms of other men. There were no cheers, but Tarr knew that he would never forget those upturned, filthy, mud-and-blood-streaked faces. There were some smiles, a few hands raised with big thumbs-up, but, as usual, the eyes told the story: Some were filled with tears of joy, but all radiated relief and thanks.

A little farther down the line on ACAV A-21, another young M-60 gunner, SP4 Larry King, was in the midst of the men who were still actively carrying on the fight. As soon as the tanks and ACAVs broke through this part of the encirclement, the survivors began leaping onto the tracks, hugging and backslapping their deliverers.

Captains Poindexter and Armer jumped down from A-66, touching terra firma for the first time in many hours. Captain Hobson spied his fellow officers and strode over to them immediately. The fatigue on Hobson's face was obvious, but the gratitude for the timely arrival of his rescuers was evident as well. The men shook hands.

"Sure glad to see you guys," Hobson exhaled wearily. "The NVA are very strong, at least a battalion, my guess. The main part of their complex is just north of my position, over there." Hobson pointed to an area off to his right. "About thirty wounded, 3 KIA. More than a third of the company in casualties." *[Author's Note: Captain Hobson believed he had three dead at that moment, but, in fact, it was only two. The actual number of dead and wounded from Charlie, based on the best after-action reports available, was more akin to half the company.]*

Poindexter and Armer simply nodded. They both stared at Hobson, incredulous that he was still standing. His empty bandoliers hung loosely across his shoulders, his web belt devoid of any grenades. It was clear that he was nearly done in physically, but it was also evident that he had not quit, nor had his men, despite the long odds, the horrific day, and the strength of their opponents. It was quite a display of mental and physical fortitude.

1645, MARCH 26, 1970, CHARLIE COMPANY CASUALTY COLLECTION POINT

Sgt. Donnie Colwell, TC of the lone medic track, gingerly maneuvered his vehicle among the bodies sprawled in all directions around the casualty collection point. Once he found an area large enough to park the ACAV, he pointed the blunt nose of the track in the direction of the enemy and dropped the rear ramp. The large slab of aluminum crashed heavily into the bloodstained grass. It seemed as if someone had taken a large paintbrush and slathered red in large patches, all around.

Colwell and his medic sidekick, SP4 Gary Felthager, dashed out of the ACAV. Colwell carried his M-16, Felthager his medical kit. Sporadic gunfire was still occurring all around them. One grunt from Charlie popped up from his concealed position in the brush and pointed to an area toward the left front of Charlie's perimeter. He shouted that there were still two men out there, wounded. Just as the man finished his report he himself was spun around, hit by an enemy round. Fortunately, the wound was relatively minor, but it certainly gave grim testimony to the fact that all of them were still in a hot zone.

Colwell and Felthager, with the assistance of a couple of grunts from Charlie, managed to crouch, half-sprint, and crawl to the two men who were still out on the periphery. The first man they reached was SP4 David Solis, gunned down in the first seconds of the ambush. He had been shot squarely between the eyes and died instantly.

PFC John Didier was lying in the thick brush a few yards away. He, too, had been shot down at the beginning of the battle. Colwell and Felthager had to crawl on their bellies to reach his position. Amazingly, he was still alive, but only barely. He had been shot in the middle of his right thigh. The wound was massive and had prevented him from moving more than a few feet from where he had fallen. Blood was everywhere—too much blood. He had been out there bleeding, trying to pinch shut his severed femoral artery, for almost six hours. Felthager went to work on him, but the look in his eyes led Colwell to believe it was probably too late.

The small group of rescuers attracted intense fire. Colwell decided to crawl a few yards ahead of Felthager to give him some room to work as well as provide some fire support. Unfortunately, the NVA spotted Colwell and began to lay down a withering fusillade on his position. Colwell tried to press himself into the earth as deeply as he could. The bullets flew closely above him and clipped enough leaves and branches to shroud him in foliage. He could not raise his head, never mind his weapon. He decided to slither back to where he had started.

When he got back to Felthager's spot he discovered that Didier had, indeed, expired. The untreated blood loss had been too great. The two men each grabbed a shoulder of the dead soldier and dragged him back to the casualty collection area. Under the unwavering dictum of "no one left behind," the two Alpha troopers did the same for Solis, risking their lives a second time to retrieve his body, too.

1700, MARCH 26, 1970, NEW TEAM ALPHA COMMAND POST, INSIDE CHARLIE COMPANY'S LINES

Now what? That was the nagging thought on the minds of all three captains as they stood together inside the revised perimeter encompassing the men of both Charlie and Team Alpha. Poindexter carefully assessed the condition of the men from Charlie Company. As he looked around, he saw wounded soldiers who probably wouldn't make it without the kind of medical attention they could only receive in the rear area. Of the remaining effectives, probably fewer than fifty of the original company, all of them had been through hell and looked it.

Maybe the best thing to do, he reasoned, *is to load everybody up and get out of here—back the way we came.*

Almost as soon as he considered that course of action, he rejected it. *No, the NVA commander, whoever he is, is far from beaten. He's got a powerful force in place, and until a few minutes ago, he had a good portion of us trapped. We're still in a tough spot, and if we leave now these guys will no doubt dog us every step of the way back. That won't work.*

In a perfect world, he'd send one of his platoons, Jeb Stuart style, racing around the entire enemy complex from the outside, probing for a weak spot in their defenses. Once found, he'd direct all the rest of his force to that point and pour through it.

Poindexter glanced at the sky, then his watch. *No time for that,* he ruefully determined.

Two parallel lines of reasoning suddenly codified in his brain. First, he thought, *How many chances are we going to get to take a real shot at an entire NVA battalion? We've been chasing them for months. They never stand and fight. Maybe this is it.*

Next, he rationalized, *One hard shot—right up the middle. We'll give them everything we've got. Maybe we get lucky and blow them away or at least scare them badly enough they'll leave us alone on the way back.*

As if reading Poindexter's mind, Hobson broke into his reverie.

"Whatever you're going to do, don't waste too much time. My guys need help."

Over on A-38, SP4 Raymond Tarr was thinking, *We'll pack these guys up now and get the heck outta here.*

Then something strange began to happen. Captain Poindexter began acting like a traffic cop, directing each of his fighting vehicles into positions along a great arc. *What the hell is he doing?*

Tarr then heard Poindexter shout over his headset, "Come on line and get ready for an assault!"

Oh, shoot.

Nothing else made any sense to Poindexter at this point. One quick, brutal battering, straight ahead, right into the heart of the NVA bunker complex. Superior firepower would undoubtedly carry the day. Once the troop had overcome the main resistance, he would break off one platoon, maybe 3rd, his least experienced, and have them clear an LZ nearby. Then he could call in the medevacs and get the worst of the wounded out of there and back to a decent field hospital.

The NVA will undoubtedly fold in the face of all this firepower. They always flee to fight another day. Once they move off, we'll pack up the rest of the men and get back to the NDP—maybe even before dark. At worst, if we can't break it off before dark, we'll laager up here for the night and take 'em out tomorrow.

14

"COMMENCE FIRE!"

1700, MARCH 26, 1970, TEAM ALPHA CP,
FRONTING NVA BUNKER COMPLEX

Alpha Troop had brought nineteen vehicles into the jungle, but before Poindexter could give the signal to push ahead, he was already down one main battle tank. A-18 had finally given up the ghost. The fires that had started in the insulation some klicks back would no longer yield to the constant application of the crew's cusswords and full jerry cans of water. Black smoke continued to billow from the engine compartment, and the crew was forced to abandon the tank. Twenty percent of Poindexter's big guns were rendered silent—a significant loss.

Of the remaining tracks, 1st Platoon, with Sergeant McNew in command, was out on the left of the line, closest to the suspected concentration of enemy bunkers. They would catch the initial brunt of any blowback from the complex.

Poindexter was close to the casualty collection point that sheltered the wounded men of Charlie too debilitated to carry on, plus the medics from Alpha Troop and their medic track. Also with Poindexter was 3rd Platoon, anchoring the center of the line. This was 1st Lt. Robin Henderson's command. Due to his lack of combat experience, and only that, Poindexter wanted to have him and his men close at hand.

Out to the right of the long arc of tracks was 2nd Platoon and 1st Lt. Mike Healey. These men and their tracks would have the farthest to go. The far right flank was anchored, in fact, in the B-52 strike zone, and they would have to swing rapidly to the left as if they were playing a grown-up version of the old schoolyard game Crack the Whip.

Captain Armer's infantrymen had split up, by platoon, then squads, then rifle teams, each element picking a track to fall behind. Each man dropped his pack where he stood. No sense carrying 90 pounds of extra baggage into battle. They stripped the packs of all ammunition and grenades and any lucky charms or favorite talismans that might be needed. They would come back later and retrieve the packs—if they came back, that is.

When the line of tracks went forward, the ground-pounders of Alpha Company would trail behind or stick close to the sides of the tracks, using them as shields, adding their firepower as targets presented themselves.

The men of Charlie Company who could still be called effectives would hold the casualty collection point and anchor the rear.

Up above, Colonel Conrad, still circling but dangerously close to being out of fuel, called back to Illingworth and said he'd be flying back to the FSB momentarily. He wanted them to get fuel and ammo ready. As his command helicopter peeled away, he called in TACAIR for one last raking of the enemy's lines. The Cobra gunships swooped in low and fast, firing a final barrage of rockets directly into the tree line and bunkers just ahead of Team Alpha. The F-4s followed, low and slow, almost wobbling as they approached. They were at stall speed as they wavered above the treetops. The pilots were sacrificing speed for accuracy even though by doing so they significantly increased their chances of being brought down by ground fire or pancaking into the jungle due to loss of lift. The fighter-bombers unleashed one last thundering load, hit the throttles, and pulled up and away.

The airborne ordnance was right on target but very close to friend as well as foe. In fact, SP4 Irwin Rutchik, an M-60 gunner on ACAV A-10, looked up to see a large bomb languidly drop from the sky not very far away. It exploded with a thunderous roar. The aircraft and its ordnance were so close to the ground that dirt, smoke, and fire shot upward, directly behind the tail of the very plane that dropped the bomb. Worse, debris and shrapnel spattered all over Rutchik's track as well as a couple of other tracks nearby. The gravity of the situation and being in the middle of this battle was not lost on Rutchik: March 26 was his nineteenth birthday, and he was sure it would be his last. Fortunately for him, it wasn't, but he swears that his ears are still ringing from that bomb forty years later.

SFC Robert Foreman stood resolutely in the turret of A-37 and surveyed the scene. He and the Sheridan tank he commanded were squarely in the middle of the slightly arced line of tanks and ACAVs facing the enemy's emplacements. Viewed from above, the long row of metallic steeds resembled an archer's bow, drawn tight and ready to let arrows fly. As the horsehide-and-muscle throwbacks of a hundred years ago might have done, these cavalry mounts impatiently pawed the earth, ready to spring forward. Diesel engines snorted, belching gouts of black fury, waiting for their drivers to unleash them. Up and down the line, machine gunners racked back their weapons, clearing their breeches, the modern equivalent of rattling sabers. Foreman waited for his CO, who was next to him in A-66, to give the word.

Poindexter surveyed left, then to his right. He glanced at his watch. It was 1700 hours straight up. The day was racing toward darkness. It was then or never. "Commence fire!" he shouted into the boom mike attached to his CVC (combat vehicle crewman) helmet.

Sergeant Foreman obeyed instantly. He was followed in seconds by the combined roar of the main tank guns throwing canister, the heavy machine guns spewing sheets of lead, and over two dozen light machine guns adding their staccato to the fray. It was as if a giant scythe had been taken to the foliage. Vegetation exploded, and a mist of green enveloped the battlefield. The canister rounds blew large, ragged holes in the jungle and instantly exposed any bunkers hidden behind the greenery. The machine guns functioned as modern-day weed-whackers: Their gunners worked them from a few feet in front of their tracks outward until they achieved an almost horizontal deflection. Nothing exposed within Alpha Troop's initial arc of awesome firepower could have been left untouched.

The barrage was so overwhelming that nearly all the NVA gunners fell silent. Were they stunned? Hunkered down in the bottoms of their bunkers until the initial assault blew by? Cautiously, the formation began to roll forward, firing at will. The drivers had to struggle within their limited ranges of vision to keep the line reasonably straight. Otherwise, it was possible for overzealous gunners, who were blasting away at everything, to track rounds into neighboring vehicles.

Dennis Cedarquist, a twenty-two-year-old staff-sergeant, TC of A-14, an ACAV emblazoned *Assassin*, was just to the left of Foreman. As the earsplitting roar commenced, all he could recall was the piece of advice he had gotten when he had first arrived in Vietnam the previous July: "If anyone orders you to start shooting, don't stop—ever—until they tell you to. You'll live a lot longer that way." Cedarquist had managed to survive unscathed for nine of his required twelve months in country, so he held down the handles of his .50 cal. Bark and limbs flew off the nearby trees, showering him and his crew with splinters and wood chips. He kept firing until he was forced to change belts. He wasn't sure he was hitting anything more than jungle, and they weren't encountering any return fire, at least so far.

Hey, whatever works! he thought. As soon as he could reload, he started firing again.

Nearby, on ACAV A-26, eighteen-year-old SP4 Fred Pimental was formulating similar thoughts about firing strategy. He was frightened out of his mind but became absolutely convinced that as long as he was emitting a continuous stream of bullets from his M-60 no one would be able to fire back at him through his wall of lead. This worked well until the barrel of his machine gun became so hot it malfunctioned. At that moment, all he could smell was the hot oil used to wipe down the guns. He dove down into the belly of the track to retrieve a new barrel.

A little farther down the line on the left, SP4 Larry Toole, on Sheridan A-17, squinted through his gunner's sight. The damage the troop had done to the surrounding jungle revealed a couple of formerly concealed bunkers, dead ahead. The front slots on each bunker started spitting heavy machine-gun fire. Just above Toole's head, he could hear the chatter of his tank's .50 cal as it opened a vigorous return fire. Without hesitation, he pulled his trigger, sending a 152 mm canister round straight into the bunker. He hollered for his loader to chamber another. He fired again, another point-blank volley into the second bunker. With grim satisfaction, he noted that the enemy's firing ceased. He had drawn blood. However, he also knew that his side was taking casualties, too. His headset came alive with frantic calls for medics, all up and down the line.

SP4 Fred Harrison, an M-60 machine gunner from Alpha Company, and temporary squad leader, couldn't believe his luck. Just as Company A and Alpha Troop were linking up for the first time, back at FSB Illingworth in early March, he heard someone shouting his name. He looked up and, in amazement, met the grinning face of his boyhood chum PFC Tommy Hudspeth, staring at him from the top of his ACAV. The two had grown up together in Riverside, California. Harrison knew his draft notice was coming, so he had gone down to the local recruiting station to enlist, hoping to get a choice assignment anywhere but Vietnam. That hadn't worked out very well. After basic training, while awaiting his fate at Fort Ord, California, guess who shows up to start basic? His friend Hudspeth, who had also decided to join up and get the inevitable over with. They weren't together long before Harrison got shipped out to Vietnam and assigned to Company A.

Six months later, thousands of miles from where they started out and with several hundred thousand men scattered over Vietnam, the two close pals found themselves a few feet apart in the middle of a hastily constructed fire support base in the middle of nowhere. What were the odds of that happening, and yet "there it was."

Harrison, at 6'6" and 200-plus pounds, even after half a year in the boonies, was known to all as "Big Fred." On the morning of March 26, 1970, as Team Alpha prepared to head out and intercept Company C, Hudspeth invited Big Fred to hop aboard his ACAV and ride to the fight.

A few hours later, there they were, staring into the maw of an angry battalion of the enemy. Harrison was amazed by what he saw: The initial barrages of the cavalry vehicles had stripped away part of the jungle as neatly and as cleanly as if a giant sword had been swept across the panorama before them.

"I clearly remember the lead tank busting through the jungle right down the middle of that huge bunker complex," Harrison recalled. "There were at least fifteen bunkers spread out in the first of the jungle we stripped away, immediately in front of us. Then, after that, you could see layer after layer of other bunkers spread out from there, row after row. We started taking incoming from every direction imaginable."

For a few moments, at the start of the battle, the NVA had been flattened by Alpha's tsunami of steel. Their initial response was weak and ineffectual. Were they not as strong as they looked? Had the initial charge overwhelmed their capacity to respond? Were they getting ready to bail out and sneak away, as they often did? Poindexter contemplated all this while simultaneously realizing that his troop was increasing its rate of fire alarmingly. If they kept this up they'd be low on ammunition in no time—and they had only moved forward about 10 meters.

Poindexter got on the radio again, this time bellowing, "Cease fire! Cease fire! Let's see what's happening. Acknowledge!"

Grudgingly, it seemed, the troop began to comply and the fire rate fell off.

"One-Six, Two-Six, Three-Six, casualty reports, over!" Poindexter barked into the radio. He was concerned not only about the alarming rate of ammunition expenditure but also the condition of his troopers and their ability to carry on the assault.

Sergeant McNew, of 1st Platoon, was the first to respond. "I've got two hit. They're on the way over to the medics. The grunts are carrying them."

Not too bad, Poindexter contemplated, *and Armer's men are pitching in to help get them to the medics. Good on them.*

"This is Two-Six. Only one man slightly hurt," 2nd Platoon leader Mike Healey reported, but seconds after making the report Healey himself was painfully wounded in the left hand by a chunk of flying shrapnel. He sank down in agony. After composing himself for a few minutes, he stood back up. He refused to leave his men and get treatment in the rear. This selfless act was not lost on his troops—or Poindexter when he heard about it later.

"Three-Six [Lieutenant Henderson]. Seems to be one hurt for sure, maybe one more."

Poindexter was relieved. No KIAs, that was certainly good, and very few wounded, at least so far. They could press ahead for a while longer.

There was no report from Captain Armer, though, and that concerned him. Armer was right behind him, and they could see each other, but Armer had no radio and thus no direct contact with his platoon leaders. Armer didn't know what his casualties were.

Almost immediately after Captain Poindexter had given the initial order to commence shooting, S. Sgt. Gus Gutierrez, riding atop A-27, had started directing his fire toward the jungle in front of his Sheridan. Unlike some others, however, he did get an immediate response—a puff of smoke and a raggedy trail from an RPG coming his way. It hit low and to the right.

Gutierrez and his crew responded with a volley, walking their rounds right back up the line of smoke that still hung in the air. The sergeant poured fire from his .50 cal into the spot where his vision had locked onto the initial burst of rocket exhaust. His gunner pounded the site with cannon fire. Gutierrez shouted to his men to clear away the jungle from the same area. Canister shredded left, center, right, then swung back and forth randomly to do it again and again. Gutierrez used his .50 cal like a fire hose washing away flames. Strangely, at that very moment, images of his parents, brothers, and baby sisters flooded his brain right alongside the vista of exploding jungle. Between the deafening roar and the perplexing visions, Gutierrez did not recognize right away that a voice was blaring in his headset, "Cease fire!"

The jungle fell silent except for the sound of the choppers above and the radios squawking with the lieutenants asking for damage reports.

Gutierrez stared ahead, and his mind returned to the moment. He could hardly believe what he saw: The tremendous fire of the troop had cleared away enough jungle to expose bunker after bunker. They were everywhere. This was a major complex, and it seemed each bunker was angled to create perfectly situated interlocking fields of fire. This was the mother lode of bunkers. There wasn't much time to admire its complexity or its potential to do great harm. Another RPG suddenly sizzled its way out of the complex.

Enemy gunfire began walking up the front of Gutierrez's tank. Rounds ricocheted off of the gun shield surrounding the .50 cal. Gutierrez turned and stared directly at Captain Poindexter, who was just off to his left. The sergeant shot him his best, "OK, sir, now what?" look. Poindexter gave Gutierrez a nod of approval, and the sergeant opened up again.

Gutierrez thought, *Shit, this is gonna get ugly.*

So it did. The NVA redoubled their efforts to stop the cavalry advance. The American troopers eagerly bore down even harder.

On A-38, SP4 Ray Tarr was busier than a one-legged butt-kicker. Part of his loader's job was to resupply the .50 cal ammo as needed, and his TC, S. Sgt. Curt Sorenson, seemed to be going through bullets like shit through a goose. Every time Tarr had to haul cans of ammo from the bottom of the tank he'd have to protrude from the unshielded hatch, thereby exposing himself to the gunfire. It was not fun, but he did, from time to time, get a peek at the battle raging outside his aluminum shell.

Back inside, his main job, of course, was to load the big gun. As luck would have it, right after they fired their very first canister round, the gun recoiled but then stuck in that position. It would not return to what is called "in battery," the position to receive another round and be readied to fire. Tarr's eyes got as big as softballs.

Oh, God, now what!

SP4 Don Grayson, Tarr's gunner, began screaming, "Pump it up! Pump it up!"

The frantic exhortation jarred Tarr back to reality. *The hand pump!*

Tarr dove down under the gun, found the backup hand pump for the hydraulic system, and began cranking as if his life depended on it—and it probably did. After three or four mighty shoves, Tarr could feel hydraulic pressure begin to build in the line again. Moments later, the main gun groaned, then slid forward, back into the proper position.

Tarr loaded another round, and Grayson fired, then another, and another. The hydraulic system continued to hold. The caseless rounds seemed to fly through Tarr's hands. Hot spent brass cascaded all over the inside of the tank from Sorenson's .50 cal, which was above him to the right. The sounds of the battle intensified. Bullets pinged off the outside of the tank's hull. Tarr nervously waited for the RPG that he knew could punch a hole in the tank's all-too-thin skin and obliterate him. Through his headset he could hear the screams of other men, some shouting orders, some shrieking in agony. The brass began to pile up at his feet. Soon, he felt, he'd be buried in shell casings. He had the uncomfortable feeling that maybe this day wasn't going to turn out so well. He became very frightened.

Then he glanced down. In the building mound of cartridge casings he saw, squarely in the middle of that ocean of glittering brass, a simple plastic container. It was the kind of big jar that Tarr remembered seeing so often back home in Pennsylvania—the huge jars that were used to pack those wonderful dill pickles. Except in this case, the jar had been cleaned out and reused to send a batch of homemade cookies to a soldier far away—Ray Tarr. The cookies had been baked and sent by a neighbor lady named Vera. Vera's son and Ray Tarr had been childhood friends and had grown up together. One boy went into the army; the other boy had joined the marines. Both had been sent off to Vietnam at about the same time. Then one was dead—of heatstroke—and the other was fighting for his life in a broiling tank in the middle of nowhere.

As Ray Tarr gazed down at the cookie jar, he realized that there were people out there who cared for him, who were thinking of him, praying for him. As that thought covered him with its balm, his courage returned. He would fight on. He would be OK.

Nothing about this assault seemed right to Capt. Ray Armer. As a dedicated, dyed-in-the-wool infantryman, it seemed strange to be standing or crouching out in the open, shooting at an entrenched enemy. That just wasn't how the infantry worked—normally. Taking on an enemy in a fortified series of works was fairly suicidal, something a trained infantry company would not do. Today they had the tracks, so, in one sense, they had some cover as they fought in the open. Armer cautioned his men that this could be deadly, too.

"Once we get into it, don't stand or work behind the tracks anymore," he told them. "Work between them. If these guys have to back up, they won't take time to see if you're standing back there. I don't want any accidents because of that."

In a firefight, as the company commander, Armer would normally be directing his men from a CP via orders to the platoon leaders and their sergeants, but today he didn't have a CP of his own. The overall CP was with Poindexter, and it was aboard A-66 and always on the move. Armer felt a little adrift with that, but to make the situation more manageable, he had turned over local control to his platoon leaders. He had trained them. He knew they were good. Two of them were West Pointers.

With not much else to do at that moment, Armer decided to become a rifleman. He started banging away at any target he could find.

Private Woodward had had just about enough for one day. A few hours before, he was convinced it was all over. With Team Alpha having shown up, he figured he actually might have a chance to make it. As he and his fellow grunts—those who weren't dead or severely wounded—sat down to catch a breather in the casualty collection area to the rear, Woodward assumed the rescuers would scoop everyone up and head back. That made the most sense, in his view. Then the world erupted in another spectacular outpouring of sound and fury. Woodward could scarcely believe it.

They're attacking! They're going after the NVA! What the . . . !

He watched in some disbelief as the long armored line let loose and slowly lurched ahead. Captain Hobson started yelling at the men to form up again, to fortify the perimeter. They were going to act as the rear guard and cover the casualty collection point, apparently.

Here we go again, he thought. *Looks like I'm gonna die after all.*

Woodward got up to move to the perimeter, and as he did so he flashed back to January, just three short months ago, and his first days in Vietnam. It seemed like eons ago. Then he absently went back to another year before that. He had just finished his first semester at Ole Miss, but he knew he was going to get drafted any minute. He decided to beat the draft and maybe get assigned to something he might actually want to do. So he enlisted in the regular army and was shipped off to basic at Fort Polk, Louisiana.

By January 1970, he was debarking an airlift at Bien Hoa. Like all newbies, he was shipped off to a replacement company (in this case, the 90th) to mill around until his name was called. They shouted "Woodward!" three days later, and off he went to the 1st Cav and their orientation camp, or "cherry school." On February 4, he was shipped out to Charlie Company.

Woodward was not reluctant, at first, to be where he was. As a "pretty normal" kid ("I was never in any real trouble") from conservative rural Mississippi, Woodward had been raised to say "Yes, sir" and "No, ma'am" and recite the Pledge of Allegiance with feeling. He believed in God and Country, and when it finally came his turn, he signed up, determined to do his duty, to do what his family and community expected of him. He had no qualms about it whatsoever—until Valentine's Day 1970, that was.

On that Valentine's Day, Mississippi Woodward, Dave Nicholson, and many of their fellow grunts, as Woodward said later, "had their innocence stripped away." The battles in Tay Ninh were "scary beyond belief" (as related in chapter 4). It was Woodward's first experience in combat, and although he and Nicholson and many others earned their Combat Infantryman's Badges during these trying days, Charlie Company also lost eleven KIA and fifty to sixty wounded. They had been ripped apart. Three weeks later, on March 8, they were devastated again. After this, Woodward no longer harbored any illusions about his real mission in Vietnam. He had been fully converted and knew that his true goal was to make it out alive.

Just when he thought he had made it and had survived another day in hell, they were at it again. He began to wonder if March 26 would offer a narrow escape from death after all.

This probably won't end well, he sighed gloomily.

The metallic line pressed ahead, but they were not making appreciable gains. Progress was being made in 5- and 10-meter increments, not more. They were in the heart of the NVA bunker complex: This would be where the enemy was strongest, best situated, and most determined. Poindexter knew that the relatively light casualty reports would not last much longer.

15

SLUGFEST

1800, MARCH 26, 1970, INSIDE THE NVA BUNKER COMPLEX

By 1800 hours, about an hour after the battle had commenced, Poindexter and Armer knew they were in a slugfest. The rate of fire was not subsiding in the least—on either side. The NVA commander, whoever he might be, had obviously decided he was going to stay put and fight it out. This was a highly unusual reaction from the normally cautious and somewhat skittish NVA. They were experienced, tough, and very brave fighters, of that there was no doubt, but in the face of superior American firepower, they usually preferred to fade away to fight another day or at least fan out into the jungle to gain a different tactical advantage. Not so today. For whatever reason, the NVA officer in charge of this regiment, probably an experienced colonel, believed he had the upper hand in this situation, and he was content to play the cards he held.

Perhaps he was also considering the time of day and the Cobra gunships still lurking overhead. If he were to abandon his fixed and very stout bunkers and attempt to flee to Cambodia, the gunships would have a field day blasting away at his retreating lines. He might lose his entire force in short order. Besides, it was only ninety minutes until darkness—he, as well as the Americans, knew that the NVA owned the night.

Poindexter became very concerned about the lack of forward movement. He was beginning to get bogged down. They had made too little progress through the NVA complex for Poindexter to allow a platoon to break away from the fight and begin establishing an LZ for the medevacs and a possible NDP for the troop.

As he began to consider his options, Captain Armer trotted up to the back of the command track. He hauled himself up onto the rear deck. He was breathing hard, drenched in sweat, and caked with the grime of battle. Little rivulets of sweat had streaked down both sides of his darkened face, creating the appearance of a war-painted chieftain ready for an all-out battle. His eyes were pink from the choking smoke and the nauseating diesel exhaust, but they were also shining with the eagerness of the pro in his element.

Amid the roar of the guns he had to practically place his lips against Poindexter's helmet to be understood. "I've got a few men hurt now. I'm moving up tighter between the tracks," he shouted.

Wanting desperately to know Armer's opinion of what was going on, Poindexter cupped a hand and shouted back at Armer's helmet, "OK. How's it look to you?"

Poindexter may have been expecting some sort of in-depth technical analysis—something that would help him decide what to do next. Instead, what he got was "No sweat. Most of their stuff is high now. We're getting to 'em."

That was it. Armer jumped down off the track and plunged back into the fight, ammunition pouches, grenades, and bandoliers bouncing on his frame as he loped away.

"No sweat"? Their stuff is "high"? "We're getting to them"? Poindex-

ter was more than a little amazed at his battle partner's sangfroid, but from the abbreviated report he at least understood that his infantry element was not being cowed by the enemy. If the NVA were "shooting high," it meant the Americans were getting close in and under their guns and probably forcing the NVA to keep their heads down. If that was the case, their aim might be less accurate, and that could cut back on casualties.

He glanced at his watch again. He decided they could press ahead, at least for a little while longer. Maybe they could break the enemy after all.

As the resolute line of tracks lurched ahead, slashing at the jungle and blasting the enemy bunkers, one ACAV, A-86, remained behind, on purpose. This was Sergeant Smolich's lone mortar track. The devastating accident of the night before had reduced Smolich's normal capabilities from three tracks to two, and one of the two had been left behind as part of the blocking force holding the NDP. Now it was time for them to add whatever they could to the battle. The mortarmen were jittery as hell about dropping rounds: Were there any more "defectives?"

Smolich suggested to Poindexter that the skies above be cleared. He wanted to get the choppers and fixed-wing controllers still orbiting nearby out of the way. Smolich didn't want to compound one tragic accident with another by unintentionally shooting down one of their own air assets. The sergeant also told the other mortarmen to get out of the track and away from the vehicle. He would fire the first few rounds himself just to make sure that everything worked OK.

Holding his breath, Smolich dropped the first round into the tube. It went off perfectly, flew upward smartly, nosed over as it should, and landed with a satisfying *crump* right in the heart of the NVA bunker complex. Everyone exhaled. The other mortarmen ran back to assist Smolich and promptly forgot their concerns.

Second Platoon was on the extreme right, moving well, conducting a wide sweep. Lieutenant Healey's men were having good success in clearing their sector. One challenge they faced, however, was maneuvering around some of the crumbling B-52 craters. A wrong turn by a driver could turn an ACAV over. To consolidate his ground without more danger to his tracks, Healey ordered a partial dismount so some of his men could sweep the area on foot, clearing it of whatever NVA might have survived their initial onslaught.

SP4 Bryan Cupp was the last to jump down and join the sweep. He stared ahead at a football-field-sized area where there was little vegetation left unblasted. He was the last man down off the tracks because his TC had been busy stuffing Cupp's pockets with grenades. The rest of the sweep team had already moved out and ahead.

As Cupp started forward, his eye caught movement ahead and off to his left. Two NVA with AK-47s jumped up from a small bunker that had been hidden underneath a pile of palm fronds and discarded branches. They had either snuck into the sector unnoticed or perhaps had been hiding there all along. They were intending to fire into the backs of the unsuspecting sweep team. Unfortunately for them, they did not notice Cupp coming at them from behind their hiding spot. Without hesitation, Cupp raised his M-16 and hosed them down. Nonchalantly, the twenty-year-old Ohioan went over to the bunker, dragged the two dead bodies out of the entryway, stripped them of their weapons, and popped one of his grenades. He tossed it into the bunker to clear it of any more surprises. The baby-faced youngster had become a killer of men.

The battle became a contest of wills between Poindexter and the NVA commander. Neither was showing the other any sign of quitting the fight. Team Alpha continued to probe for a way to outflank the NVA or, at least, to break their spirit. The NVA kept giving back as good as they got. Poindexter and his subordinates knew they were inflicting heavy casualties. Time and again their canister rounds plowed into bunkers where NVA were simply obliterated. The .50 cals and the M-60s literally cut men in half. Two-man RPG teams would pop out of holes to fire their rockets, then be shot dead before they could load another round. Somehow, the NVA were replacing men as quickly as they were lost.

Aboard the command ACAV, Sgt. Dennis Jabbusch, the TC, was bellowing for another can of .50 cal ammo to be passed up. While he waited, he poured a pint of lubricating oil over the barrel of his glowing gun. He noticed that the M-60 gunners had nearly gone through the entire first layer of ammo cans. Only one more layer to go.

Outside the command ACAV the ground was littered with spent brass and empty olive-hued ammo cans. At this rate, they'd be out of rounds by dark. This was of less concern to Jabbusch, however, than his rotation date, which was only eight days away. *Ammo be damned*, he thought as he kept his trigger fully depressed.

1815, MARCH 26, 1970, CASUALTY COLLECTION AREA

Mississippi Woodward slumped to the ground. He and the other exhausted and thoroughly depleted men of Charlie watched with a combination of pride and sheer relief as Team Alpha pushed into the NVA bunker complex. Their battle was not yet over, however. Although they were no longer the primary focus of the NVA's attacks, they were still taking fire. This time it was from the rear of the combined battle formation, behind the main advance of the tanks and ACAVs. As Woodward and others tried to catch a breather, Captain Hobson tried to be everywhere, making sure that he had a complete cordon around the casualty collection point.

Woodward, like everyone else, was soaked in sweat and drenched in adrenaline. He finally found a canteen that still had water in it and drained what was left. It was as warm as bathwater, but it tasted like pure, sweet relief. He checked his ammunition. Three magazines left. He'd have to scrounge more, and he noted grimly that there were enough wounded soldiers lying nearby who would no longer need the bullets they possessed. Incredibly, the tempo of the firefight accelerated once again.

Jesus! Haven't they had enough? Woodward thought with amazement. *How are those little bastards keeping this up? They're taking a beating from the cavalry. How many more troops could they have?*

Apparently they had enough to attempt to overrun the American forces yet again. Woodward and many others witnessed numerous NVA scurrying through the nearby jungle in an effort to get behind Charlie's position one more time. Hobson and his NCOs hollered for everyone to "light 'em up!" The attackers were soon beaten down, but not without more wounds being inflicted on the men of Charlie. The medics were working furiously.

Woodward noticed one downed solder they had missed, so he grabbed him up and helped him to the medic track. Woodward laid him down and started to run back to his position. Just as he did so he heard a loud explosion and was slammed to the ground. Fearing the worst, he jumped back up to examine himself. Shrapnel had gashed his left knee and right ankle. He turned to hobble back to the medic track, then stopped. He looked at the critically wounded men nearby. It appeared to him that some were not going to make it. He glanced again at his wounds—his first marks of combat. *Nah, later,* he shrugged and humped back to take his place in the line.

Charlie Company's medical supplies were all but exhausted. The arrival of Alpha Troop and their medic track, with TC Sgt. Donnie Colwell and SP4 Medic Gary "Doc" Felthager, was a godsend. Felthager quickly began disbursing bandages, morphine "sticks," and plasma. Then the two men scoured the casualty collection area for soldiers who had not yet been tended. Colwell acted as Felthager's armed escort since the NVA didn't bother to distinguish between noncombat medics and regular infantrymen. Colwell watched in awe as the self-effacing Felthager saved a "significant number" with his daring and quick applications of lifesaving triage.

"Writer, this is Racer Two-Nine. We've got dinks behind us here. But don't stop. We can hold."

This was George Hobson radioing to John Poindexter that the NVA were in their rear area yet again. The NVA were going after the command's weakest point, the casualty collection area, and the decimated remnants of Charlie Company.

"Six, this is One-Six! I'm being flanked! I'm being flanked! I'm taking heavy fire from the left! What do you want me to do?"

This frantic radio call burst into Poindexter's headset from the normally unflappable Sergeant McNew, way out on the left with 1st Platoon. This meant, undoubtedly, that the NVA commander had sent an unknown number of his soldiers sneaking through the jungle to try to enfilade 1st Platoon as they moved ahead. The platoon was being hammered on two sides, and if they continued to advance it would soon be three as the NVA began to slip around to the rear of the entire formation.

Poindexter radioed back that McNew should turn his last ACAV 90 degrees to the left and face the danger, then keep turning his vehicles to the left every 25 yards or so until he ran out of vehicles. In essence, McNew was "refusing the line," a tactic that was first made famous in American military history by the legendary Civil War colonel Joshua Lawrence Chamberlain. As Chamberlain and his 20th Maine defended Little Round Top at Gettysburg, the former college professor, who was about to be outflanked by the 16th Alabama, refused his left by bending his line backward 90 degrees. By so doing, he probably saved the Army of the Potomac from certain defeat and perhaps even turned the tide of the war in the Union's favor.

This battle, this day, was certainly not a "Gettysburg" by any stretch, but to the men involved it was just as important, just as life-threatening. Poindexter's directions, coming from someone who, like Chamberlain, was very much a citizen soldier and not a West Point professional, proved equally auspicious and every bit as effective. It was a brilliant decision, made on the fly, and probably prevented the entire operation from being outflanked and overwhelmed.

The extent of the enemy's bunker complex was being exposed bit by bit as the fight wore on. This was good in the sense that the troopers up and down the long mechanical line could finally see most, if not all, of what they were up against. It was bad in that what they saw was a very formidable force that wasn't going to simply run away. On top of this reality was the fact that both sides were practically muzzle to muzzle: The heart of the compound was barely 25 meters ahead. This left little room for Alpha Troop to maneuver, whereas the NVA had the entire surrounding jungle within which to work.

Poindexter figured there were forty-five minutes of usable daylight remaining. It was a certainty there would not be enough time left to establish either a local NDP or clear a landing zone—even if he could afford to break off one platoon to do the work, and he couldn't. They were still under heavy fire, and he needed every gun up and on the line.

A-19 was out on the perilous left with Sergeant McNew. His gunner, SP4 George Burks, was firing as fast as his loader could clear new rounds—but Burks was also keeping one ear on the radios. The reports were sounding more and more bleak—too many vehicles bogged down, too many wounded, too many cries for help. His platoon was in echelon formation, facing the jungle on the left side. The men on the Sheridan with Burks could see the blurry, half-concealed movements of the NVA flowing down their flank. In a moment of pure whimsy, Burks imagined the actions of the enemy appearing like a bowl full of goldfish squirming through the woods.

The tankers and the ACAVs on the left started firing into those woods. The shadows dissipated or fled, but there was a shocking number of them. *Oh shit, we're fucked!* was Burks's next thought, and then he gloomily envisioned the need for a second rescue—this time of many dead cavalrymen.

1820, MARCH 26, 1970, TEAM ALPHA AND CHARLIE COMPANY, COMBINED BATTLE FORMATION

Lieutenant Henderson, commanding 3rd Platoon, was still deferring, as well he might, to his platoon sergeant, SFC Robert Foreman. Henderson had to "make his bones," and this firefight would ultimately qualify. In the meantime, he carefully absorbed everything his experienced platoon sergeant was doing. Foreman did not fail Henderson or his men.

The platoon was in the middle of the formation and on point. Whenever there was an opportunity, Foreman inched his Sheridan forward. If there was a crack in the enemy line, he skillfully exploited it. The powerful Sheridan main guns packed a wallop, that was certain, but the skins of the tanks themselves were very vulnerable. The aluminum hulls could be pierced by heavy machine-gun bullets, RPGs, and large ordnance. Experienced TCs like Foreman knew this, of course, so as they blasted away they tried to maneuver to advantage. It was desirable to keep as small a profile to the enemy as possible. Simply put, this meant trying not to expose the long, flat sides of the track to direct fire.

The TC, who commanded from the turret and fired the .50 cal, was terribly exposed. To alleviate this problem, a field modification for the TC's big machine gun had been made: An extra steel rim was welded to the circumference of the turret. Steel shields were attached to the rim on a ball-bearing array that could rotate. It was far from a perfect solution, but it measurably increased the survivability of the TC in combat.

As the opposing forces pushed and shoved against one another, Foreman slowly moved forward, the nearby ACAVs advancing with him. The NVA shoved back. Drivers, gunners, and loaders all sustained wounds, and as they quit their vehicles to get medical attention, substitutes endeavored to take their places. A number of stand-ins came from Alpha Company. Although these men had no experience whatsoever in operating the Sheridans or the ACAVs, some of the guns, like the M-60s, were familiar to them. In any case, they did not hesitate to step up and try to take over whenever a need presented itself.

Poindexter could clearly see that a stalemate was developing. Team Alpha still had sufficient ammunition left and the determination to use it, but darkness was approaching swiftly. The NVA were showing no signs of fleeing, and nightfall would shift the momentum to their side. It was time to consult his battalion commander. Conrad, who had gone off to refuel, was back, circling above and behind the battle once more.

From inside A-66, Poindexter reached for the radio communications control box and switched over to the battalion frequency. Just as he opened his mouth to call Conrad, a thunderous explosion enveloped him and tossed him, unconscious, to the ammo-strewn deck.

Sgt. Bill Daniels, the gunner on A-37, was firing round after round of canister into the bunker complex. He felt as if he and his loader were acting like a fine-tuned machine: spot-load-shoot, spot-load-shoot. They were working as smoothly and as swiftly as the physics of the gun and its reloading would allow. The noise was deafening, and blasts were emanating from every direction, but there was a symphonic cadence to it all, a combat-generated harmonic: war set to Ravel's *Bolero*.

Then, suddenly, one of the instruments dropped out of sync. It was right after a weird vibrato slammed and shook the tank. Daniels noticed the change right away: The .50 cal had stopped firing. Brass casings were no longer cascading into the belly of the Sheridan.

Daniels hollered into the intercom for his TC, Sergeant Foreman, "Shoot, Sarge, shoot!" No response. Daniels glanced over his shoulder and up into the turret. Foreman was standing there, but all Daniels could see of him, as usual, was the lower half of his body. Strangely, his arms seemed to be hanging limply at his sides. Daniels turned back around to look out his view slit—maybe he could see what was happening above.

At that moment Foreman fell on Daniels, a .50 cal ammo can fell on Foreman, and something that was on fire fell on them both.

The loader yelled, "We're on fire!" Out the loader's hatch he went.

Daniels yelled at SP5 Rod Lorenz, the driver, "Man, they got the sarge and this thing's on fire! Get out!"

Daniels struggled under the weight of Foreman's body, the tangle of equipment all around him, and the fire that was coming closer. His emergency egress was normally over or around the main gun, but that way was blocked, so he squeezed himself under the gun, an incredibly tight space of about a foot and a half, and somehow managed to get through.

Foreman didn't respond to Daniels's desperate shouts. Reluctantly, he bailed out of the tank. Unluckily, he landed in an anthill and was immediately covered with angry, biting insects.

SP4 Floyd Clark, twenty, from Mt. Solon, Virginia, was the right M-60 gunner on A-34. His track was to the left of the blast that hammered Foreman's tank. He clearly recalls seeing the NVA grenadier who fired the shot that killed Foreman. He popped up squarely in front of A-37. No aim was required—he was practically on top of the tank. A tremendous flash, a shattering explosion, and clouds of dust. Clark was safeguarded by the sides of his ACAV and his gun shield, but as soon as the air cleared he peered out from behind his gun to see what had happened. Sergeant Foreman was no longer standing in the turret of A-37, but Clark did see several long strips of bloody cloth hanging from the branches of a tree right behind the Sheridan.

16

THE HIGH-WATER MARK

John Poindexter regained consciousness facedown on top of the remaining ammo cans that constituted the temporary deck of A-66. Warm brass casings littered his immediate field of vision. The ringing in his ears was intense. His head was throbbing and hurt like hell. He dared not move a muscle until his blurry vision began to refocus. The smell of expended ammo, dirt, and blood filled his nostrils. *My blood*, he wondered?

The M-60 gunners in A-66, Topper Hart and Don Dush, had been thrown to the deck as well. They, too, were beginning to come around. Hart had blood flowing freely down his left arm. The arm was, in fact, a bloody mess. Dush appeared to be stunned but otherwise unhurt. Poindexter could see all this by simply rolling his eyes around as he lay there, still reluctant to move.

What happened? Poindexter's brain wanted to know. *Maybe Foreman tracked his gun too far to the right and accidentally blew us away. Nah. Not Foreman.*

Poindexter began to carefully test each extremity, first to make sure they were all there. Every appendage seemed to answer the initial call except for his left arm. Curiously, it was not working, or so it seemed. He struggled to stand. As he did so, he took a swipe at his brow and aching head. His right hand came away hot with blood. Some of it crossed his lips and he tasted it.

As he shakily regained his footing, the din of the battle returned in all its ferocity. Although still ringing, his ears were starting to function again. He observed Hart roll off the back of the ACAV, left arm dangling uselessly at his side. Hart fell into the brush but popped right back up and trotted off to the medical station nearby. Dennis Jabbusch, the driver of A-66, was nowhere in sight. Dush had recovered his senses enough to jump back on his gun, and he began firing again, but other than what Dush could contribute to the battle, Poindexter realized that A-66 was essentially out of action.

His left arm was still not responding. He glanced down at it. It was still there, but it wasn't in very good condition. The pain had not fully penetrated the shock of his wounding, but it would soon. His best guess was that he had been hit by some shrapnel and it had torn up the forearm pretty good. He was bleeding profusely from somewhere, but from exactly where he could not tell. The parts of the forearm that weren't crimson were already turning purplish with bruised flesh. At least one bone, it seemed to be from his index finger, was sticking out from the wound. All in all, it looked pretty grotesque—and pretty serious.

Where was Foreman? The other 3rd Platoon tracks?

Poindexter peered over the side of A-66 and in the direction of where he last remembered seeing Foreman's tank. Dark smoke was circulating around A-37's turret, and then he saw it: There was a nasty, ragged hole in the gun shield just in front of where Foreman would have been standing.

An RPG, no doubt, Poindexter concluded. *Went through that shield like a hot knife through butter. Ah, that's not good.*

The RPG that ripped into A-37 had been the proverbial thousand-in-one shot. The morbid Vietnam saying "There's no such thing as 'close enough' except in horseshoes, grenades, and napalm" could also be applied to RPGs. Notoriously inaccurate, they were still deadly, and they only had to get "close enough" to wreak havoc. On the scale of bullets to bombs, they packed a punch somewhere between a hand grenade and a four-deuce mortar round. This particular rocket had apparently hit A-37's gun shield full on, just in front of Foreman. It passed through, meeting little resistance, its warhead hitting Foreman squarely in the chest. The still-intact munition and attached rocket motor pranged off the back of the turret and flipped upward before finally exploding in a lethal shower of red-hot gas and shrapnel. It was this minicloud of razor-sharp destructive power and concussive force that leveled Poindexter, Hart, Dush, and the entire crew of A-14, the ACAV on the other side of A-37. Several of Ray Armer's infantrymen were dinged, too. In a split second of lucky marksmanship, the NVA had killed one very fine soldier, wounded at least a dozen other men, and taken three fighting vehicles out of action, at least temporarily.

It was the pivotal point of this sharp, intense engagement. Poindexter's most forward element, the heart of his line, was out of the fight. Lieutenant Henderson was the only officer in the vicinity who could take decisive action, but he was immobilized—not with fear but inexperience. His lead Sheridan was a smoking wreck, fate of the crew unknown. His captain was down and obviously wounded, and the command vehicle dead in its tracks. Henderson's ACAV had been peppered with shrapnel and two of his own crewmen wounded. Worse still, for Henderson, his mentoring first sergeant was dead, and he couldn't reach anyone on the radios.

Had the NVA commander seen this situation—perhaps he did, maybe he didn't, no one knows—and been prepared for it, it would have been the perfect moment to send his men streaming through the temporary gap in Poindexter's formation. It would have been the classic "breaking of the line," something General Robert E. Lee had attempted to do with Pickett's Charge at Gettysburg 107 years prior. The NVA could have split the American force into two nearly equal pieces and begun to roll up each half.

Pickett's men were mowed down before they could reach the stone wall in the center of the Union lines, but a few of them got there. History would forever label that gallant but futile charge the "high-water mark of the Confederacy."

In this battle, this day, in a subsequent century, in the far-off jungles of Vietnam, another high-water mark was reached. In this case, the result was nearly the mirror image. The NVA, inexplicably, stayed put. At the exact moment when a full-blown assault could have broken the American lines, the NVA elected to remain in their bunkers.

It didn't take long for Ray Armer to figure it out, however. From his spot on the battleground, trying to position his infantrymen where they could do the most good, he heard and saw the explosion that crippled A-37, A-66, and A-14.

Armer got to the smoking tank as quickly as he could, climbed up on the rear deck, and crawled into the turret. He peered into the murky interior. It was quite clear to him that nothing could be done for Sergeant Foreman. His body lay in a ragged heap on the deck below, nearly torn in two. The rest of the crew was nowhere in sight. Armer grabbed the bloody handles of the .50 cal and began to sweep it across the jungle in front of the disabled Sheridan. He could only fire a few shots before the gun jammed. He tried to clear the jam but couldn't. Maybe the RPG had damaged it somehow, but in any case, the gun was done. He whipped his M-16 off his shoulder and began firing, going through several magazines.

After a few moments, Armer jumped down off the tank again— *No sense making myself another target up there*, he thought—and began shouting to as many of his men as he could find, moving them up to take positions between the disabled tracks. Soldiers crept up into the gaps, commencing a suppressive fire.

Ray Armer's decisive actions at that point in the battle plugged the holes in the American line well enough to cause the NVA commander to hesitate—and not press his considerable advantage. It was a pivotal moment in a desperate exchange.

Aboard A-66, SP4 Don Dush had shaken off the impact of the rocket blast. He was amazed to still be unscathed and in one piece, although he had certainly had his bell rung. Captain Poindexter was standing there bleeding, yelling something Dush's deadened eardrums could not hear. He finally recognized Poindexter's lips to be mouthing the words "Fire! Fire!" Dush jumped back on his M-60 and stared at where Poindexter was pointing, which was an area just in front of their track. Had he seen something? Dush saw nothing—no enemy troops, anyway—but he did not want to disappoint his captain, so he pulled the trigger and promptly shot off one of the track's radio antennas and blew up the tool box.

Oops . . .

Dush corrected his aim and began ripping the jungle apart. Out of the corner of one eye he saw his partner, Topper Hart, roll off the ACAV and limp off to seek medical assistance. He noticed Poindexter drawing his .45 and jumping off the track, too. He quickly disappeared.

Where the hell is he going?

A-66's TC, Sgt. Dennis Jabbusch, suddenly popped back up from the bowels of his cupola. Blood was running freely from beneath his CVC helmet, but he seemed to be functioning normally nonetheless.

Jabbusch tried to get the .50 cal working again, but it was useless. It had been damaged too badly, so he gave up and retrieved his M-16 and a can of grenades and began wailing away.

Dush's gun barrel was overheating badly, so he decided to swap it out, but the replacement barrel was balky. Dush was having difficulty getting it to fire long bursts. He fiddled with it for a minute and thought he had it fixed. Satisfied, he went back to look for targets. Instead of enemy bunkers, filling his field of vision was a sight the likes of which he had only seen in the movies. It was similar to watching the cinematic action suddenly morph into slow motion, just as the hero ducks a punch or sees an arrow or a bullet coming directly at him. Everything slows down as the character, for effect, one frame at a time, bends his body to get out of the way. Except in Dush's case, he froze. He didn't get out of the way. Instead, he simply watched, fascinated, as a large piece of metal, a shrapnel fragment, came flying directly at him. It resembled a miniasteroid, tumbling and turning through the atmosphere, crashing into the earth's outer layers. Fortunately for Dush, the fragment had already expended much of its energy, but in one last endeavor to do some damage, it flew unerringly toward Dush's gun shield, bounced off of it, and then smacked Dush squarely in the lower lip. The impact knocked him backward forcefully. His entire visage instantly felt like it was on fire.

His first thought was *Oh my God! I've lost my face!*

Dush dove down to the belly of the track to find a medical kit— and a mirror. His lip was bloody, swollen, and purple, but he still had his face. Now he was mad. The fears that had previously gripped him evaporated. The fight had suddenly become personal.

Ray Armer scrambled over to A-66 to find Poindexter. He wasn't there, which he thought a little strange. *Where the hell could he have gone?*

He did find Don Dush, who was having trouble getting his M-60 working properly. The other M-60 was abandoned, but it was clear it had been damaged. The .50 cal was silent as well. One trooper, Armer, guessed it was the TC (and it was, Jabbusch), who was firing an M-16 and pitching grenades as furiously as he could. Dush had found a thump-gun (an M-79 grenade launcher). He handed it to Armer, who within seconds had it tossing grenades into the NVA bunkers.

Topper Hart was back, heavily bandaged but unwilling to abandon his post. He tried to get his M-60 back online, to no avail. With his one good arm he, too, began tossing grenades like a madman. Dush acted as a loader, passing magazines to Jabbusch, HE thump rounds to Armer, grenades to Hart, and M-16 rounds to the Company A guys who were coming to the back of the track looking for more ammo.

Slowly, the wounded elements of 3rd Platoon and the troop commander's ACAV began to reorient themselves and get back into the fight. Sgt. Jim Crew, TC of A-39, had the last working Sheridan in 3rd Platoon. Sergeant Foreman had been a very close friend of Crew's. When he heard on the radios that Foreman had been killed he was enraged. Without waiting for orders, he pushed his tank ahead, passing the still-abandoned A-37. He started blasting away again, this time a man on a mission of revenge.

Crew's main gunner, SP4 Lowell Walburn, had been lucky enough to spot the grenadier who had fired on and killed Foreman. He was hiding behind a large anthill 50 yards ahead. Walburn laid the crosshairs of his aiming scope on the anthill, ordered the loader to pop an HE round into the main gun, and carefully fingered the trigger. Walburn waited patiently. Moments later, the NVA grenadier cautiously came around the right side of the anthill, slowly bringing his rocket launcher to bear, lining up another shot. Walburn pulled the trigger. The powerful 152 mm shell ripped the anthill to shreds before plowing into a bunker and erupting in a roar of dirt, sand, splintered logs, and body parts. The offending rocket launcher went spinning off into the jungle. At least some retribution had been exacted for the death of Sergeant Foreman—but not nearly enough in the minds of those who had known him well.

One element of 2nd Platoon was close to the near disaster threatening 3rd Platoon. This was Sergeant Gutierrez and his crew. Gutierrez had driven his Sheridan forward into the fight by angling off to the left a bit. Unfortunately, as he discovered quickly, this had placed his right up against a previously unseen ravine. He was cut off from the rest of his platoon, all of them ending up slightly behind him, to the right, and across the ravine. This left him temporarily exposed on his right flank. The next tank to the left of Gutierrez was A-37, Foreman's Sheridan, which had become a smoking wreck. Gutierrez had, in fact, seen it all happen.

"A loud explosion came from my left, and I turned to see Sergeant Foreman whiplash backward behind his gun shield as he was hit. I saw the trail of destruction work its way along the side of the tank and Captain Poindexter grimace as he was hit."

Gutierrez was the lead element, totally in the open and in the foremost part of the battle. From his perch atop his tank he could actually peer into some of the bunkers and see the enemy moving back and forth within them. The bunkers were prime targets, but there was just one problem: A-27 was down to its last canister rounds and firing high-explosive rounds might cause a blowback that would affect their own troops—that's how close the opposing forces had become.

Gutierrez decided to press ahead with his .50 cal blazing and his gunner, SP4 John Biggs, firing his M-60 as rapidly as he could. The .50 cal got so hot that Gutierrez could actually depend on the last foot or so of any belt he loaded going off all by itself. While that happened, he'd reach around behind the turret cargo racks where the Sheridans carried their extra .50 cal ammo.

Gutierrez's loader, PFC Stanley Carter, with the main gun mostly silent, had little to do, so he busied himself with passing grenades up to Biggs and Gutierrez. Each man took turns pitching them into bunker after bunker. The idea was to keep the NVA's heads down until somebody—anybody—began to plug the holes to the left.

Sgt. Donnie Colwell was all over the battlefield. Rather than stay behind in the relative security of the casualty collection area, he drove his medic track right up to and just behind Poindexter's command track. *Better to treat the wounded from here,* he figured.

With chief medic Felthager, he roamed across the front line trying to pull wounded men back and get them treated. Sometimes he had to threaten to inflict additional injuries on men who were too stubborn to stop what they were doing and pay attention to their bleeding wounds, broken bones, or lacerations.

Colwell had witnessed A-37 take the RPG hit. He had seen Sergeant Foreman drop down and the crew bail out of the tank. To Colwell the Sheridan looked like it was doomed as it sat there smoking. Victims from A-37, A-66, and one or two more tracks started staggering and stumbling toward the medic track. Colwell saw Captain Armer jump up on A-37 and try to work the .50 cal, to little avail.

When Armer jumped back off the tank Colwell figured, *Hell, he's an infantry guy. He probably doesn't know how to work the .50 cal.* So Colwell decided to give it a try—besides, there was at least one man down inside the tank. Maybe he needed help. Colwell grabbed his M-16 and quick-marched to the stricken Sheridan, bullets whizzing all around him. He crawled aboard the rear deck and worked his way to the turret.

Just one quick look inside the belly of the tank and at Sergeant Foreman's mangled body told him there was nothing he could do to help Foreman. Then he assessed the .50 cal. It was a mess—*shot to shit.*

By then, Sgt. Jim Crew was pushing his tank forward to plug the hole caused by the disabling of A-37. Colwell reasoned correctly that the crippled Sheridan needed to be pulled off the line. A-38's gunner, Don Grayson, and A-37 gunner Bill Daniels had decided they could safely check on the status of Foreman's tank. Colwell convinced the two to attempt driving the track off the line. Fortunately, the engine restarted, but the radios were dead; so, with Grayson driving, Daniels on the ground to guide Grayson, and Colwell squatting atop the rear deck to give driving directions to Daniels, the three men were able to pull A-37 back and out of the direct line of fire.

While crouching on the rear deck giving directions, Colwell was keenly aware of dozens and dozens of telltale green tracers flying at the troops from all directions. They were, he ruefully realized, completely surrounded.

Well, ain't this just fuckin' grand? Colwell swore under his breath, desperately hoping he wouldn't see one of the green tracers whipping inexorably toward him.

17

PEREGRINATIONS

During the next few minutes, one of the most bizarre incidents of the entire battle unfolded. The actions were witnessed by a number of troopers who were there, but the principal character in this minidrama, John Poindexter, has no clear recollection of the events described. Nor would he, necessarily, given that he had just been knocked senseless and seriously wounded. From the accounts of at least six eyewitnesses, here is what occurred:

After the RPG hit on A-37 and the wounding of a number of men, including himself, John Poindexter was effectively out of touch with 3rd Platoon. He had lost Foreman, of course, but also all contact with Henderson. His command track was, at least temporarily, immobilized. He desperately needed to know what was going on, so he hopped off the crippled command track and set out on foot to try to figure out what was happening.

The pain level in his wounded forearm was rising, and he was losing blood at a fairly alarming rate. He curled his shattered limb up against the left side of his chest. This eased the agony somewhat and helped stem the flow of blood, or at least hid it from view. In his right hand, he carried his trusty .45. Almost as soon as he stepped off his command track, he raised the pistol and fired it directly into the nearby jungle. Was he aiming at someone? Did he hit anyone? Was this a puny signal to the enemy that they had not completely obliterated the critical center of the line? Was he simply lending his meager firepower to the fray? He does not know.

As he walked among the wreckage of the battle he came across a dead NVA officer. He apparently recognized the man's status by his silver belt buckle and the web belt with pouches that NVA officers typically wore. He stripped the corpse of its belt, walked back to A-66, and threw it on the deck of the track. Perhaps there was some intelligence to be had in those pouches, but there was no time to search them. Poindexter also realized his .45 magazine was empty, although he was not exactly sure how, where, and when he had fired all those rounds. He nudged Dush and motioned to him that he needed help reloading his handgun. Dush reloaded Poindexter's .45, and off the captain went, yet again, to tromp the killing grounds.

A few moments after setting out again he bent down to examine another dead enemy body. *Yup. Another officer.* He had just removed this mangled corpse's web belt, holster, and pouches when two AK-47 rounds slammed into the ground at his feet. He whirled around, stood, and fired five shots directly into the bunker just off to his right. The shooting from that direction ceased.

Slinging the second bloody trophy over his shoulder, he continued to make the rounds of the nearby tracks. He inspected the damage to Sheridan A-37 but did not climb up on the tank. He talked to every TC within his immediate area. He wandered almost as far as the extreme left-side position of 1st Platoon, turned around, and came back to the command track, and during this extraordinary walk the battle continued to rage all around him. By the time he arrived back for a third reload of his .45, which Dush obliged with again, the cobwebs had started to clear from his brain. The walk had done some good.

It was absolutely clear to him by 1845 that Team Alpha was stalled. Neither side was giving an inch of ground. His tracks and Armer's infantry were so close to the NVA at this juncture they could practically punch each other. Darkness was beginning to fall, and the tracers were glowing brighter. He had made the "one last push" that he had been determined to make. His left was being strung out to avoid an envelopment from that side; his right was dangling against an untraversable ravine and a bomb-scarred wasteland. His rear was only tenuously holding on due to the fatigued status of Charlie Company, his ammunition supply was rapidly dwindling, and he had lost two of his tracks, so far. Should they try one last, ultimate thrust? Or should they call it a day? It was time for one of those so-called command decisions.

He tossed his latest swag onto the rear deck. He noted, with a clinical eye, that he could actually see the deck of the ACAV, which meant they were down to their last level of ammo. The radio for the battalion net was still working—*At least Dush hadn't shot off that antenna yet*, Poindexter observed wryly—so Poindexter asked for, and got, help with hooking himself back up to the radio.

Poindexter concluded he was right at the tipping point, possibly on the verge of being able to deliver a decisive defeat to a normally elusive and mysterious enemy. The morale boost would be felt across the entire battalion, maybe even the whole division. They had paid a price, of course, but the temptation to finish the whole affair was nearly overwhelming. On the other hand, they had achieved the objective for which they had made the trek: Charlie Company had been saved. There were also many wounded, too many good men bleeding and in need of more assistance than the troop's limited medical resources could deliver. It was likely some of these wounded would expire if they weren't evacuated to better facilities—and soon.

With a warrior's reluctance, but a concerned commander's desire to see to the welfare of his men, Poindexter got on the radios with Conrad.

"Stone Mountain, this is Writer. Permission to withdraw, sir."

18

"AND THAT'S ALL SHE WROTE . . ."

1900, MARCH 26, 1970, TEAM ALPHA BATTLEFIELD

Almost as if both sides sensed that the tempo was somehow changing, a lull occurred. The slackening of the rate of fire allowed Poindexter to disconnect from the radio and climb down off the back of A-66 and survey the battlefield one more time. The hiatus also permitted SP5 Craig Wright to get a field dressing on Poindexter's ugly wound. The forearm and wrist were carefully wrapped and treated for potential infection. The broken bones were left as they were. Wright knew that only a qualified doctor could reconnect and reset that mess. At least he was able to stop the bleeding.

"Hey, Captain, how 'bout a shot for the pain?" Wright offered solicitously.

The prospect of a couple of hours of morphine-induced bliss was very tempting.

"No . . . no," Poindexter sighed. "I'll be fine. You go back to treating the men. I'm good."

"Roger that." Wright trotted back to his assigned track, leaving Poindexter alone with his thoughts—and the continuous throbbing of his bandaged arm.

There was more work to do, Poindexter knew, and of all the officers on the field, only he had the requisite knowledge to round up all this equipment, their men, and his and get everything moving back to their previous NDP. There was no guarantee that they could get out of this mess without another serious battle and a lot more casualties. They were still effectively surrounded, after all, and breaking out of the enemy's encirclement would be no picnic. Not the right moment for painkillers. Poindexter needed a clear head, and as ironic as it might seem, the pain kept him awake—and focused.

On ACAV A-33, 3rd Platoon's medic track, Sergeant Vaughan was in serious trouble. While moving his track forward, firing all the way, Vaughan veered to avoid some big trees. He drove through a narrow gap between two of them. He didn't see the sharply pointed stump between them, hidden by tall grass, until it was too late. The ACAV was instantly impaled. No amount of backing and shoving would get the stubborn track dislodged. A-33, which its crew had playfully dubbed *Anti-Maim* because of its primary mission as a fighting medic track, was mortally wounded—and a sitting duck for any and all enemy gunners.

Sure enough, moments later, as Specialist Wright returned to his station, an RPG exploded against one of the trees A-33 was stuck between and sprayed shrapnel everywhere. Sergeant Vaughan got a faceful of the backblast. Wright caught several metal fragments in his left arm.

Wright managed to get most of the large pieces of metal out of Vaughan's face and eyes, but it was clear that the sergeant was done for the day—and that his eyesight was in imminent danger. Wright got help bandaging his own painful lacerations, then helped evacuate Vaughan to the casualty collection point.

––––––––

SP4 Floyd Clark's A-34 got the tough task of trying to haul A-33 off the stump, but they had no tow cables—neither did any of the other nearby tracks. Sergeant McNew radioed that his platoon had a couple. Creating one of the more indelible and remarkable images of the entire battle, Specialist Clark leaped off his track, marched smartly across the battlefield to 1st Platoon, retrieved the coiled, heavy tow cable, and quick-stepped back, bullets flying all around him. The grunts of Alpha Company were plastered to the ground, as flat as they could make themselves, trying to avoid getting shot. Clark, as if he were on a stroll to the mechanic's shop for spare parts, nonchalantly traversed the killing ground and returned unscathed. Just another day in Alpha Troop.

Captain Poindexter started a visual tally of the condition of all his equipment as the troop's field mechanics began swarming over the tracks that had been damaged. Still under fire, although not as intensely as they had been, the technicians worked like demons, field-stripping parts and trying to get every vehicle as functional as possible. It was clear, however, that A-33, *Anti-Maim*, was done.

Sheridan A-18, which had almost caught fire and burned as the troop was busting jungle going in, was, amazingly, back in the thick of it. The crew of A-18 had somehow rallied the beat-up, ancient (it was the oldest in the troop) Sheridan for the fight. A-19, well, that was another matter.

The attempted tow of A-33 did not work. It was permanently affixed to the tree stump, or so it seemed. Poindexter ordered Lieutenant Henderson to get some men and strip it down. They'd salvage anything of value, and after they quit the area they'd call in TACAIR to blast the hulk and prevent it from being used by the enemy.

Henderson and his men got right to work. Using whatever implements they could scrounge from the toolboxes attached to the nearest ACAVs, they quickly pried loose anything from A-33 that could be removed without a blowtorch or a sledgehammer: extra gun barrels, ammo, radios, equipment boxes, gun mounts, medical supplies, map cases, manuals, documents, and the like.

The opposing fire started to pick up again. Poindexter felt Henderson needed a prod to get moving a little faster, so he crouched low and scuttled, crablike, to Henderson's side. Just as he was about to say something, a quizzical look crossed Henderson's face and he sank to the ground. Poindexter could see dark splotches begin to spread underneath Henderson's fatigue trousers. Poindexter used his good hand to quickly yank up Henderson's pant legs. Several deep lacerations were evident, but none were crippling. He had been zinged by pieces of flying shrapnel.

Looking at his own cuts, then the bloody bandages on Poindexter's arm, Henderson, not wishing to be perceived as doing less than he could—and certainly no less than his commanding officer—struggled back to his feet. "I'm OK, sir, really. We should be done quickly." He then hobbled away from Poindexter to carry on the task at hand.

Poindexter shrugged. His young lieutenant seemed to be all right, and he would not deny the man his pride in front of his troops by ordering him to the medics.

Next, Poindexter told McNew to get A-19 rigged and ready for towing. It had blown its power pack, and the engine would not function without it, but at least it was movable. They'd take her back with them if at all possible. The venerable old A-18 got the job.

Poindexter turned once more to assessing the damage. The ground he and his men—and the NVA—had fought over for the past two hours reminded him of the devastation left in the aftermath of a tornado, only worse. Uprooted trees, shattered trunks, torn and twisted vegetation, smashed bunkers, smoking craters, rucksacks, torn clothing, empty ammo cans, twisted chunks of metal, abandoned weapons, the smell of dirt, diesel, and blood—and, just as he looked down, an abandoned candy bar wrapper and two Coke cans.

Who had time to eat a candy bar and drink two hot Cokes in the middle of all this? he wondered, shaking his head in amazement.

1930, MARCH 26, 1970, COMBINED OPERATIONS FIRING LINE

Sunset. Not that anyone in that immediate patch of jungle could see it. The thick stands of trees were starting to block all the ambient light. Slowly, carefully, every functioning track started to back away from the front line. All weapons were still face forward, ready to reengage the enemy if the NVA opposed the withdrawal. One by one, the enemy's guns fell silent. What were they up to? Were they reconsolidating inside the bunkers that had survived? Or were they, more likely, fanning out into the jungle, plunging ahead of the lumbering troop to set up an ambush across the trail?

Poindexter gave the order to get every man, dead or alive, aboard a vehicle. No one was walking out. They would all ride. The worst casualties—and the dead, of course—were put into whatever vehicles were handy by those who could still do the lifting.

Lieutenant Healey's 2nd Platoon had the fewest casualties, the least damage, and the position closest to the avenue back. They were in the best relative shape, so it fell to them to lead the way home. Healey turned his vehicles around, one by one, and got them ready to move back down the makeshift road the troop had created on the way in. Going back out the same way they had come in was risky, especially if the NVA were seeding the path with mines, furiously constructing tank traps of downed trees, or setting up interlocking firing zones with heavy machine guns and RPG teams, all of which was entirely possible. However, there was no time—before darkness or more men started dying from lack of proper medical attention—to carve a newer corridor through the jungle. Would 2nd Platoon's good fortune hold or be short-lived?

Lieutenant Henderson's 3rd Platoon and the command element would follow. They started by loading up as many of the wounded from Alpha and Charlie companies as they could accommodate. Any able-bodied men nearby who could still find a space hopped on after the disabled had been placed aboard.

Sergeant McNew's 1st Platoon would cover the withdrawal from the rear and load the last of the infantrymen. As soon as Poindexter was convinced he had every man accounted for, he radioed Colonel Conrad.

"Stone Mountain Two-Nine, this is Writer Two-Nine. I'm ready to move out the advance element now. Can we get some light for the trip?"

There is no leisurely twilight in the middle of the jungle. It was getting dark—forbiddingly so. Illumination would be critical to a quick trip home and possible survival. The lumbering shapes of the tracks and the amount of machinery noise they made could not be disguised. Darkness would not provide any advantage to the Americans. Light would certainly make them easier targets, but without it they would be nearly blind. The tracks had headlamps, the few that survived the gun battle, that is, but in this inky blackness, they would be of very little value. Stumbling around and feeling the way back would also make their trek incredibly slow—something many of the wounded might not appreciate as their vital fluids poured out onto the floors of the tracks. A full-court press down an illuminated trail might be risky, but it would definitely be quicker. In this instance, the risk was deemed to be more than worth it.

"This is Stone Mountain Two-Nine. Go ahead and move out. Have your point and rear elements identify themselves so that I can put some air on your flanks and rear. The light is coming."

Poindexter was relieved that his immediate boss was agreeing with his decision to quit the area, but that little voice in the back of his head—behind the bigger voice that was battling the fatigue and pain—wanted to know what Conrad meant by "the light is coming." That didn't sound so encouraging.

"Writer Two-Nine, wilco, out," Poindexter radioed back to Conrad.

Poindexter reached for the radio control box, flipped the switch to the one antenna he had left, changed frequencies, and called Healey.

"Two-Six, this is Six. Lead us back down the trail. As you pull out, shoot up the area to your front and be very alert for an ambush. After you've traveled well beyond the old bomb strike, hold up, toss some smoke, and contact me."

"This is Two-Six. On the way."

With that, Healey's lead tracks belched diesel as their drivers lurched forward, anxious to head on out. The troop was under way, to what new fate, no one knew.

SP4 James Cadotte was still nervously manning his M-60 on the right-hand side of A-34. They'd been through a hell of a fight, that was sure. Miraculously, he had somehow avoided getting killed or seriously wounded. His only injuries—so far—were a sprained left wrist, which he had gotten deflecting a falling tree that had been hewn down by .50 caliber fire, and some first- and second-degree burns to his hands that he had endured while changing out a red-hot gun barrel.

They were heading back, or at least that was what he had heard, and it seemed to be true since all the tracks were lining up in column formation again. Cadotte also remembers he and his crewmates helping several extra men aboard, some of them grievously wounded. The normally tight quarters inside an ACAV became incredibly cramped with the extra bodies. Cadotte wondered if he'd be able to work his gun effectively if they got into another fight. He also recalls, to this day, the moans from the wounded men and the coppery smell of blood—too much blood.

———

"Six, this is One-Six. I'm ready to go." This from Sergeant McNew and 1st Platoon.

"Six, this is Three-Six. Me, too," Henderson chimed in.

"Writer, this is Racer," echoed Captain Hobson. "We're all loaded up."

Captain Armer, who was once again riding on the rear deck of Poindexter's A-66, simply reached around and tugged on Poindexter's flak jacket and gave him a thumbs-up signifying that he and his men were also ready to roll.

"One-Six, this is Six. I'm afraid you're last," Poindexter intoned, delivering what was surely less than welcome news to McNew. "Make a lot of racket when the rest of us move out, and throw plenty of smoke for the choppers so they know where you are. Give us a couple of minutes and then come out as fast as you can. Good luck."

There was a short silence before McNew radioed back an "OK" that seemed to Poindexter to be a little less than enthusiastic.

Third Platoon and the command elements pitched forward, trundling off in pursuit of 2nd Platoon. Ever mindful of the tactical scenario, even while battling his own discomfort, Poindexter tried to think ahead. Had the NVA commander sent his minions coursing through the jungle after all, to mine the way out? Were enemy soldiers out there already felling trees to block their path? Had the NVA commander rallied his men, pulled them from the bunkers, and prepared them to charge after the troop while their guns were facing the wrong way? Worst of all, maybe, had the NVA had time to radio for an entirely new battalion blocking force that might be sitting in ambush a klick or two down the trail?

Could they survive an ambush? Probably. Poindexter had at least 150 men who could still fight. They had enough ammunition left for a defense, but certainly not enough for another protracted battle. They had some water, a few medical supplies, and enough C-rations to get most of the men something to eat, but they'd be on their own. There were no reinforcements anywhere in the area.

TACAIR would be useless in the dark, and the artillery no better. Poindexter had made up his mind to circle the wagons where they stood and set up a makeshift NDP if the NVA jumped them. It wouldn't be pretty, and more men would probably die or become casualties, but he was convinced they couldn't be completely overwhelmed.

At least a few of us should survive, he grimly observed to no one in particular.

Painfully cut face, fat purple lip, blistered hands and all, completely soaked in sweat, SP4 Don Dush helped load the wounded into A-66. He had to jostle some of the bodies to make a space near his M-60 to squat down and man his weapon—even though it was virtually useless. Some men were piled on top of one another three deep, and Dush thought at least one guy on the bottom of the pile was probably dead. He was cramped and miserable but had a square foot or two to himself. The thought of having to sit or stand on top of some of those bodies so horrified him he almost forgot about the danger they were still in.

There were several ammo cans in reach, and Dush used one as a footstool and several others to create an islandlike refuge from the carnage all around him. From the squirming mass beside him he noticed the grimy, blood-streaked, but grinning face of one black soldier looking up at him. The smiling grunt managed to wriggle one arm free and give Dush a thumbs-up. Dush smiled back weakly and repeated the hopeful sign.

Topper Hart, still at his station aboard A-66, his left arm swathed in bandages and throbbing, watched four grunts walk by slowly and solemnly carrying a fellow grunt on a stretcher, a poncho loosely covering the body. A puff of hot air from somewhere, maybe exhaust from a nearby track, blew the poncho off. Hart stared at the body.

"I remember thinking to myself, *I don't see any wounds or any-thing*; it looked like he could just get up off the stretcher and start walking. With a closer look, I saw that this brave warrior had taken a shot almost directly between his eyes."

[Author's Note: This was most likely the body of SP4 David Solis from Charlie Company. He had been killed in the first seconds of the battle.]

Hart goes on, "A Troop and Charlie Company continued to load up men and some wounded and some KIA. You could see that we were loaded to the max, with men hanging and sitting just about everywhere. We were taught not to ride with our legs hanging over the side of the track because of the dangers of hitting land mines, but this was one time it wasn't going to matter. There wasn't much said going back, just a lot of staring. Occasionally one of the grunts would smile and give the peace sign or thumbs up. They were glad and so were we to be leaving that contact area."

At just eighteen years of age, Hart was one of the youngest members of Alpha Troop that day. He was growing up in a real hurry.

S. Sgt. Gus Gutierrez had A-27 pointed in the right direction, or at least what he believed was the direction of relative safety. After carefully backing away from his position on the line, firing all the way, he had requested permission from Lieutenant Healey to slew his tank around and get in line. He was still nervous that they were going to be jumped. Nothing had really gone as they had planned that day, so why should they expect to be allowed to just turn around and move out without some serious opposition?

As they inched forward, though, there was no firing. Gutierrez was amazed. Unconsciously, he began to relax, but only a little. He unclenched his hands from the handles of the .50 cal. They were stiff from the tension of his constant grip. The tinkling sounds of empty shell casings rolling around in the bottom of the tank could be heard faintly over the growling diesel. Gutierrez then realized that they must have gone through thousands of rounds of ammunition—there wasn't a full belt left anywhere in the tank. He looked to see how many rounds he had left for the main gun, should they be needed, and was shocked to find he only had a handful of HE rounds remaining. The grenades were nearly gone, too. He glanced at his watch. What had seemed like minutes of furious combat had actually been almost two hours—where had the time gone? He also realized for the first time since the battle had started that he was absolutely drenched, from head to toe, in sweat. He was also slathered in lubricating oil from his biceps to his knees, and he was utterly exhausted.

Twenty-year-old SP4 Kenny Euge, from Dupo, Illinois, was driving ACAV A-10 that day. The former railway switchman had driven a Sheridan for Sergeant McNew when he had first gotten to Alpha Troop, but he disliked both McNew and the stifling, sweltering, claustrophobic driver's position in the Sheridan so had asked for, and gotten, a transfer to an ACAV. As the driver of an ACAV, you could at least stick your head and shoulders above the hatch and get a little fresh air once in a while. He didn't like guns, either, and had refused to handle one. It was not that he was a conscientious objector or anything as unwarlike as that. He had just seen too much of what guns could do to people, so a driver he would be.

Euge had pushed and shoved his track all over the battlefield that day, and he, like everyone else, was spent. Luckily, none of the men on his track had been hit, but they had done plenty of hitting. At that moment, all Euge and his trackmates wanted was to get the hell out of there and get back to the NDP and maybe a little rest and some hot chow.

PFC Tommy Hudspeth, the "long-haired surfer dude" from Riverside, California, was Euge's right M-60 gunner. He had been firing his weapon as fast and as often as ammunition and overheated barrels would allow. He was stunned by the amount of ammunition expended by both sides—and the concomitant noise. Green tracers from the enemy's guns had lit up the battlefield much like a game of laser tag would amuse teenagers today. The red-orange tracers of the American guns were equally as bright and plentiful. Once in a while, seemingly defying the laws of probability and physics, two tracers would actually intersect, and the resultant collision mimicked a star shell burst on the 4th of July. In another improbable defiance of the odds against survival Hudspeth, during one split second in the battle, clearly saw the brute-force, blunt-end, high-speed specter of an RPG coming directly toward his skull. For some reason, he does not know why, he was already in the process of ducking. Had he not done so, the round would have neatly and cleanly taken off his head.

As Euge worked his ACAV into the line of tracks heading back, it was getting very dark. Also worrying him was the vegetation they would have to travel over on the way out. Coming in, they had smashed and pounded the small trees and thick grasses under their tracks and in the direction of their trek. The same broken sticks, shards of bamboo, busted limbs, and small trees had had a few hours to spring back up. Like a bizarre cheval-de-frise, these natural obstacles had become small spears or sharpened stakes pointed directly at the tracks. Each vehicle had to roll over them once more, this time against the grain, trying to flatten them or push them back in the opposite direction. Since it was dark, the drivers would not be able to see anything outside their tracks if they stayed safely inside their compartments. They would have to drive with heads and shoulders exposed.

Navigating this nightmarish and totally impersonal sea of pointed objects in the gloom was not something Euge or any other driver was feeling comfortable about. *Wouldn't it be just wonderful,* Euge mused to himself, *if I survive this fucking battle, then get a pointed stake through the brain?* The phrase "poked in the eye with a sharp stick" inevitably came to mind.

After a grueling week in the jungle and then, this day, eight solid hours of intense combat, there was no telling how exhausted Capt. George Hobson might have been—only adrenaline was keeping him vertical. Amazingly, despite all the risks he had taken that day, all the humping around the battlefield and keeping his men on task and alive, Hobson had not suffered a scratch—until right then. Hobson was rounding up his men and getting them all aboard the various tracks to be evacuated. As he was standing next to a Sheridan—he does not recall which one—talking with his RTO, an RPG came whizzing into the perimeter and smashed into the turret of the tank. The curved configuration of the turret deflected most of the blast up and away, but not all of it. Hobson found himself on the ground, lying on top of his bug-eyed RTO. The RTO had been shielded from the flying metal by both the tank and Hobson, but Hobson was—as he later laughingly called it—"kissing close" and bleeding all over the frightened soldier. Some hot shards had smashed into Hobson's helmet but not penetrated, thereby sparing Hobson's life; however, other bits of lethal metal pierced his unprotected face. His left eye was damaged (he would later lose it), and his left cheek and lips were peppered with stinging metallic nettles.

Though the wounds were uncomfortable, they were more painful and annoying at the time than crippling. Hobson picked himself—and his RTO—up off the ground and continued to round up his troops. He would seek medical assistance later, when there was more time.

The tracks forged ahead and disappeared into the black avenue of withdrawal. The last of Hobson's men were safely aboard the final tracks to leave the scene. The soldiers were still taking small-arms fire as they withdrew, but its volume was far less than before. Appropriately, some of the men of Charlie, who had been first into the firestorm that day, would be the last men out.

Hobson got a scare just as they were leaving the area. He spotted an abandoned and burning track hung up on a stump between some trees. This was Vaughan and Wright's previously wounded and discarded A-33, but Hobson, not knowing if anyone might still be alive in that wreck, decided he had to find out if they were inadvertently leaving anyone—or any bodies—behind.

As painful as it was for him, he jumped off his ride and sprinted over to A-33. He did not find anyone in or near the hulk. Satisfied that he had abided honorably by the dictum of "leave no one behind," Hobson turned to see that his ACAV was the last track in sight. He made record time getting back to the track and urged the driver to make all due haste in catching up with the rapidly disappearing column.

Hobson allowed himself a sigh of relief. What had seemed like certain doom just four hours ago had been turned into a dramatic rescue and a magnificent victory for the human spirit, if not total annihilation of their opponents. All in all, though, he'd sure as hell take it.

2000, MARCH 26, 1970, TEAM ALPHA'S RETIRING COLUMN

The laboring column lurched along in the spreading blackness. Lieutenant Colonel Conrad was still overhead trying to shepherd his battered and fatigued men home, but he was losing sight of some of them. With a touch of irritation and tiredness in his own voice, he radioed down to Poindexter:

"Writer, this is Stone Mountain Two-Nine. I've got your rear in sight, also the point, but where are you? Get out some smoke so we can cover you, OK?"

Poindexter resisted the obvious smart-ass response: "Well, if you can see the front and the rear then I guess I must be in the middle!"

Instead, he said nothing, just directed his driver to toss a couple of olive green cans of smoke over the side of A-66. Yellow tendrils of smoke immediately curled upward, barely visible in the fading twilight. Conrad acknowledged yellow.

Lieutenant Healey's excited voice broke into the radio stream. From his advanced position across the B-52 strike zone and well down the trail they had blazed going in, he announced to Poindexter, "Six, this is Two-Six. You won't believe this! It's clear here. Repeat, clear all the way out!"

Poindexter was not sure he had heard Healey correctly. *Clear? All the way out? How is that possible?*

If Healey's report was accurate, this was a bolt from providence, an incredible piece of good fortune. Poindexter could not help but wonder if the NVA commander hadn't made an incredible blunder. The enemy could have still pressed them and probably caused considerable additional damage and a lot more suffering. Why weren't they doing that? Maybe they were as spent as Team Alpha. Maybe the NVA commander was dead or seriously wounded. Maybe they had simply had enough. It didn't much matter as long as it was true.

Poindexter wanted additional clarification, but as he acknowledged Healey with a quick "Roger," Sergeant McNew, behind him, radioed that he was under fire again. *Damn! Now what?*

Someone on the NVA side had opened up on A-18 with a recoilless rifle as it had A-19 in tow. One round had slammed into the turret of the tank. The crew had bailed out, fearing the tank might explode or catch fire, but it didn't, and the crew remounted.

McNew called Poindexter once more. He reported they were still taking fire, but they had silenced some of it, and then he posed another dilemma to Poindexter's aching brain. "Six, this is One-Six. This tow is going to slow us down—maybe cause more casualties. Can we leave her?"

It was abundantly clear that McNew didn't want to be bothered with the crippled Sheridan, and he was probably correct in that it would likely cost precious time and more casualties. Poindexter, however, was troubled: In addition to the spirit of "no man left behind," it was an ironclad 1st Squadron tradition to leave no vehicle on the field of battle, if at all possible.

Poindexter was also considering the wounded men suffering at the bottom of McNew's various tracks. Could they stand another delay—and another firefight? What if this was a ploy? Maybe the NVA commander was trying to play catch-up. If he could delay and then surround 1st Platoon as they attempted to haul out a worthless hulk for the sake of honor, maybe he could draw the entire troop back into yet another scrap to rescue 1st Platoon.

Poindexter hesitated—but not for long. "Bring it back unless they're trying to surround you."

The sounds of racing engines in his headset told Poindexter that McNew had gotten the message and was hauling ass—and a tank—in an effort to catch up. *Now, back to Healey's hopeful news . . .*

Poindexter wasn't quite sure how Healey knew that the way was clear "all the way out." He couldn't have gotten that far yet, for one thing, but at least he wasn't running into any opposition, and that was good news, indeed. On the other hand, even a clear path, if it was clear, was not going to be of any use unless the drivers of the tracks could see it, and by this time they were all but halted by a lack of usable light.

Poindexter knew that it was fish-or-cut-bait time for Colonel Conrad and any illumination he might have in his back pocket.

"Stone Mountain Two-Nine, this is Writer. Have we got any light?"

"Not yet, Writer. How many more minutes can you move without illumination?"

"This is Writer. Not long. Let's see if our mortars can shoot some for us. We'll keep you advised. And watch out above."

"Give it a try, out."

With that, the rotor blades of Conrad's slick began to churn the air a little faster as he gained altitude and separation from any mortar rounds that might come arcing out of the jungle.

The ball was back in Sgt. Bud Smolich's court. Until, if, and when Conrad could get some airborne or artillery illumination on top of Alpha Troop, the column was dead in its tracks unless the mortar section could come up with some light. Making matters even more dicey, the only parachute flares available were back at the NDP, which was still three klicks away, and in the hands of the remnants of the shattered mortar crew and the equipment that had been left behind.

Poindexter hadn't thought about the men back at the NDP for hours. Were they still there? What if the NVA had sent a splinter force to overwhelm them and wipe them out?

"Writer Control [the M-577 at the NDP] and Eight-Six [the mortar section call sign]. Did you both monitor?" Poindexter radioed, holding his breath.

Sergeant Steege, the radioman at the NDP, came right back with a "Roger" and the welcome news that the mortar crew at the NDP was ready—and still functioning.

Sergeant Smolich was several tracks behind Poindexter. He called in with "This is Eight-Six. Confirm where we are, Six, and I'll handle it."

Reassuring, indeed, sighed Poindexter. He tried to find a chart but quickly realized that if they still existed they were somewhere on the floor of the track and under God-knows-how-many broken, bleeding bodies. He gave up on that.

"Eight-Six, this is Six. We're about four hundred meters south of the contact area, and that's the best I can do. We'll correct your second round after you fire the first one."

"Eight-Six, OK, that's good enough," Smolich replied reassuringly.

Poindexter knew that if anyone could pull this trick off, Smolich was the man. Somehow, Smolich would have to coordinate his position with the lead elements of the troop ahead and the jittery, apprehensive crew he had left at the NDP.

Due to what Smolich would later call "divine intervention," he had, for reasons not known to him to this day, taken the precaution of "laying in" the coordinates of the mortar track he had left behind. What this meant, provided that the track had not moved (and it hadn't), was that he knew the exact position of the only track capable of firing any illuminating rounds to help the troop get back "home." With this position on his plotting board and knowing roughly where the rest of the troop was at that moment, Smolich could radio decent instructions back to the crew at the NDP. They would not be guessing: they would have the right direction, azimuth, fuses, and firing times—thanks to the prescience of Sergeant Smolich.

A-66 continued to crawl ahead while Poindexter waited for something to happen. The track swayed from side to side as it rolled on. Poindexter, in his pain and the darkness, could almost imagine A-66 as a landlocked lifeboat wallowing in a matted jungle sea. It was mostly quiet, except for the groans of the men suffering below.

C'mon, Smolich! Make it happen!

Then, as if on cue, Lieutenant Healey called in: "This is Two-Six. We can't see a damn thing out here. Do you want me to hold up?"

I knew it was too good to be true, Poindexter groused to himself. As he searched his brain for a good answer, he began to realize that he could see a faint glow inside the track. The squirming bodies below him were coming into focus. *How can that be?*

Seconds later it dawned on him—truly dawned on him—that light was starting to flood the interior of the track. *My God! They did it!* Poindexter fairly shouted to himself.

The brilliant glow from a glorious paraflare split the gloom of the night and floated above the jungle and slightly off to the right.

Poindexter pounced on the radio handset. "This is Six. Drop two hundred and fire for effect. Keep one up as long as they last. Outstanding!"

"Eight-Six, thanks. I'll adjust as needed. Out."

Somehow, with a plotting board on his knees, in a cramped space aboard a track jammed full of wounded men, operating in the dark, Smolich had gotten the mortar section functioning and tossing those beautiful beacons of salvation into the night sky. He also managed to keep enough of the flares airborne to guide the entire column straight back down the pathway they had taken just seven hours and several lifetimes earlier that day.

No one could accuse Sgt. Ron Bench of bad timing—at least not on March 26, 1970. Bench had been detailed from Long Binh as a replacement NCO for Alpha Troop's mortar section. He had been scheduled to arrive on March 25, but a logistics SNAFU ("situation normal, all fucked up") delayed him one day. After a mad dash by truck and an unscheduled vertical replenishment by Shit-hook (Chinook) the next day, Bench finally arrived, but the troop had rumbled off to try to rescue Charlie Company three hours prior. Bench reported to Sergeant Holloman, who was the NCOIC (noncommissioned officer in charge) while Captain Poindexter was away and in the field. Holloman told Bench to hang tight and when the troop got back—if they got back—he'd be detailed to Sergeant Smolich.

With not much else to do while the rest of the troop was out in the boonies, Bench wandered over to where the mortar section was stationed. This was where he learned of the unfortunate accident of the evening before, heard the rumors of the missing firing pin, got the gruesome descriptions of what had happened to the three men that had been killed, and collected all the other scuttlebutt that any of the troopers who had been left behind were willing to share. It was not a pretty picture and made for a rather lurid and unsettling introduction to life in the field with Alpha Troop.

As the men sat around swapping their stories, a muffled roar could be heard somewhere off to the north. One of the troopers jumped up and shouted, "There they go!" When Bench inquired what that meant, he was told that what they were hearing was the sounds of Team Alpha letting loose on the NVA. Bench glanced at his watch: 1700, straight up.

The roar had a distinct tenor. Even though the sounds, to an untrained ear, were all jumbled together, the experienced soldiers, who were listening intently, could parse out the individual sections of the deadly symphony.

"That's an M-one-five-two!" one former tank gunner shouted. "There's an RPG!" one veteran grunt determined. The roar seemed to go on and on, punctuated by brief periods of silence. The men sitting around the NDP smoked nervously, popped open a few C-rats, and grew more and more apprehensive as night began to fall. Around 1900, the sounds of battle seemed to abate.

The silence grew long and ominous. Another hour crept by. Then—orders for the mortar section! The crew with the one remaining mortar ACAV was on the net with their section leader, Sergeant Smolich. Bench couldn't catch all the chatter, but he could certainly recognize what the men were being asked to do: get on the four-deuce and start throwing illumination rounds. The mortar crew turned to and started dropping rounds into the tube. The sky out ahead of the NDP seemed to blaze with a light equivalent to the midday sun.

Shit! Bench thought. *If the NVA are around, they'll be all over us like white on rice!*

Thirty minutes or so later, the advance elements of Alpha Troop broke through the jungle and stormed into the NDP. Blowing exhaust and chuffing around like the giant mechanical beasts they were, they seemed like a gaggle of prehistoric monsters returning from a hunt. Each machine seemed to know exactly where it should be in a line around the ragged perimeter. Tracks spun in the red clay earth; men shouted for assistance; ACAVs disgorged their cargos of the living, the dead, and the maimed. It was the seventh circle of Dante's hell brought to the surface and given its own churning, palpitating life.

One Sheridan (A-37) drove right to the middle of the compound and became a scene of frenzied activity. Bench rushed over to see if he could help with whatever was going on. Scraps of shouted conversations indicated the men swarming over the damaged tank were trying to retrieve the body of one of their dead comrades. He stopped short of the track and thought better of his impulse to assist. It might not be the best time to make new acquaintances. Slicks began arriving to dust off the wounded and the dead. The whirling blades, landing lights, blowing dust, and illumination rounds created a macabre dance of shifting shadows and running men. One bird would land, take on its wrecked human cargo, then roar off into the night. In an instant one slick would be replaced by another. Bench was in awe of how these pilots managed to maneuver in all the darkened chaos without smashing into one another.

Later, Sergeant Bench wrote the following to describe his first night with Alpha Troop:

> The sounds and smells and sights, all buffeting my emotions without mercy, combined with the realization that I was really in the thick of it, were almost too much to assimilate. It was just too unreal and unbelievable. It was the first step in conditioning my brain to realize that no matter what kind of perverted hellish universe I had been transported to, I was certainly far from the real world.

A-66 pulled up to the M-577. The driver, Sgt. Dennis Jabbusch, himself painfully punctured in the neck by several metal fragments, dropped the rear ramp, and the men inside slowly unwound themselves. Some went to seek attention from the troop's medics. Others were too shattered and had to be carried off and humped over to one of the waiting slicks and medevaced. Captains Armer and Poindexter sat quietly atop the track for a few moments. In the flickering lights the two men stared at each other, and Armer slowly shook his head. Poindexter understood. Neither one said a word, but they were silently asking one another just how the hell they had managed to pull this off.

Armer finally slid off the track, hooked up to his RTO's replacement radio with his umbilical, and went off to see to the men of Alpha Company. Poindexter watched in detached approval as his own men, without any orders from him, went about the tasks that still needed to be performed. Everyone pitched in to help the wounded. When the stretchers ran out, they grabbed ponchos. The medevacs came and went for over an hour. Poindexter had absolutely no idea how many of his men had been hurt. It was certainly in the dozens and more likely in the scores. He had a vague notion that there were also several that were dead, but he didn't have an exact number. The only one he knew for certain had died was Sergeant Foreman, and that would be a terrible loss for the troop; indeed, for the whole 11th Cavalry.

Those who weren't helping with the casualties were already sweeping the spent brass out of their tracks or, in some cases, mopping up the gore. Weapons were already being broken down and cleaned. Damaged gun barrels, broken equipment, and basic weapons loads were being replaced. Those who had been hardened by combat loss were even heating up some C-rats. Might as well eat.

Poindexter knew the activity was necessary. They could still be jumped by the NVA, if they were in hot pursuit. Mostly, though, he understood that the men were imposing self-discipline, doing what they had been trained to do, and taking all the necessary steps to keep busy and shut out the horrible images of the day. If you couldn't do that, you would sure as hell lose your mind.

Sgt. Donnie Colwell was among the busiest. There were fifty . . . sixty . . . seventy . . . maybe more wounded. He had to stop counting. All the senior officers had been hit, as had most of the NCOs; one, his friend Robert Foreman, fatally. Even several of the medics had been wounded. He was amazed that he himself had escaped serious injury—something you couldn't tell by his uniform. He was soaked in blood, from his chest to his knees, all from helping with the wounded and trying to lend a hand to the medics. He had been doing some triage himself and had even assisted in one emergency tracheotomy. Lacking the proper tools, the medic had opened up the man's throat with a scalpel, then kept it open with the end of a ballpoint pen. It seemed to work; at least the man was still alive when Colwell loaded him aboard one of the medevacs.

Alpha Troop's executive officer, 1st Lt. Paul Baerman, who had been working frantically to marshal the replacement parts, supplies, food, ammunition, medical gear, and fuel the troop would need after today, had caught one of the first slicks out. He was on scene and with the first sergeant, Jerry Holloman, efficiently directing the evacuations and resupplies. It was a welcome break for Poindexter, who was still very weak from loss of blood and suffering excruciating pain from his shattered forearm.

With his remaining good hand, Poindexter unstrapped his CVC helmet and pulled it off. He shakily tried to slide his lanky frame off the top of A-66. If Sergeant Smolich hadn't been standing there to catch him, he would have gone to the ground in a heap. Smolich slid a supporting arm under the captain's shoulders and tried to steer him in the direction of a medevac. Poindexter did not want to go and insisted that Smolich help him to the command track instead. About halfway to the M-577, Colonel Conrad strode from the shadows. Poindexter didn't even know he was anywhere in the vicinity. Conrad walked up to Poindexter and looked him squarely in the face—and bear-hugged him.

Gus Gutierrez at last gave in to his exhaustion. He climbed off of *American Woman* and sat down on an ammo can. The sweat was finally beginning to dry in the cool evening air, but he was too tired to even eat. Another figure slowly shambled up to him in the dark. He looked up and then jumped up. It was Captain Poindexter. The captain looked drawn, haggard, and about ready to collapse.

"Gus, you did a hell of a job today. Just wanted to let you know that. You probably saved our asses when that RPG took out Foreman's tank. Hell of a job. I'm going to write you up for a Silver Star."

"Yes, sir . . . Thank you, sir" was all Gutierrez could reply. With that, Poindexter turned and walked off, disappearing unsteadily into the night. Gutierrez sat back down again. Later, he was able to put his feelings on paper:

I thanked him [Poindexter] and as he left, I sat back down, dumbfounded and not knowing or understanding the magnitude of what just had transpired. The war made a better man of me, more appreciative of life and thankful to be here and now, in this time and place . . . I am proud to be an American, feeling an overwhelming surge deep inside me when I hear a marching band playing the "Star-Spangled Banner." There is no spirit on this earth like the American spirit, a spirit which faces adversity head on, no matter the odds.

Then Gutierrez added a prophetic coda to his thoughts. "Everyone who served in Vietnam has a story, a story that sometimes takes years to be told."

Some after-battle thoughts were decidedly on the darker side. SP5 Gary McCubbin, twenty, from Kansas City, was the TC of A-23. He fought his track bravely all day long, slugging it out with the other men of 2nd Platoon. Unlike on most of the other tracks, however, not a single man on A-23 was even slightly wounded. That singular good fortune did not impress McCubbin, though. As he sat there, relatively safe once more in the troop's NDP, he was still shaken to his core by what he had seen and experienced that day. So much mayhem, so many wounded, several men killed—plus the guys from the night before! He felt the heavy responsibility of his track and the crew he commanded pressing down on him—hard. The desperation of a man who saw no hope of leaving Vietnam alive suddenly overwhelmed him. Why not just get it over with—right then? He stood up and walked to the rear of his track, out of sight of the rest of the crew. He unholstered the .45 he carried and stared at it. He cocked the hammer back and raised the pistol to his head. He felt his right index finger begin to squeeze down on the trigger. He took a deep breath—and thought about home and then his men. These would be his last thoughts—pleasant thoughts with which to exit the prison his life in Vietnam had become.

The men . . . his men . . . his friends. *You don't do this to your friends,* his mind told him. *You don't leave them this way, with your mess to clean up.*

His hand started shaking. He relaxed his trigger finger. He slowly lowered the gun. These men needed him—to help them make it through. Taking the quick and easy way out would make life much harder for them. The desperation passed. McCubbin reholstered the weapon and walked back to the front of the track.

As the chaos started to subside and the dust-offs slackened, XO Baerman had a chance to begin to assess the troop he would be taking over as Poindexter went off to get treatment for his injuries. He was an "old hand" in the 'Nam, having run a platoon in Charlie Troop, gotten a Purple Heart, and then moved up to XO of Alpha Troop. When he had first gotten in country, which seemed like a million years ago, his former first sergeant had given the inexperienced new lieutenant some invaluable advice. Baerman thought it would be a good time to employ it right then.

The veteran NCO had told Baerman, "Put your hand on them. Just reach out and put a hand on each man's shoulder. If they look up into your eyes, they're OK. If they don't react and keep staring at the ground or straight ahead, they're done."

Baerman walked the NDP. He chatted up the men. Most of them were busy, which indicated they had moved on—they were ready for whatever might come next. Those who seemed distracted or not focused on doing something got the "hand test." Baerman was much relieved to find no one who couldn't pass.

SP5 Craig Wright was temporarily "homeless." His track, A-33, was somewhere back in that dreadful jungle, a derelict. There were other, more weighty matters on his mind, though. He was finding it hard to shake the image of Sergeant Foreman lying in the bottom of his Sheridan. Wright had been the first medic to get to Foreman's tank, and it only took one peek to see that his skills were not going to be needed. Foreman had clearly died instantly. The RPG had passed cleanly through his chest, leaving nothing but a giant hole. *At least he felt no pain*, Wright told himself.

Wright had seen plenty of wounds before, some of them even more gruesome, but he was having a hard time shaking this image. It was most likely because he knew the sergeant so well. Just the day before, the two of them had been discussing their plans after their tours in Vietnam were over. Foreman was anxious to get back to Monterey, California, and his wife and kids—and a new assignment, maybe even as an instructor again; anything far away from the war would do. Wright was excited about being so close to finishing his BA through the army's correspondence program with the University of California, Berkeley. He was only two courses short of completing both his degree and the training for his teaching credential. He had, in fact, just received his latest set of textbooks and was anxious to dive in and start studying. Unfortunately, the books were somewhere in the belly of A-33, and he was sure they had been destroyed. It was either that or some NVA soldier was hauling them off, anxious to show them to his superiors as part of the booty from the abandoned hulk. Wright had lost a good friend, his textbooks, and his track and was in severe pain from the shrapnel wounds he had suffered. *All in all, a pretty shitty day*, he thought glumly.

John Poindexter's postaction wanderings of the NDP were finally interrupted about midnight when Conrad insisted that he get on the colonel's helicopter. Conrad had his pilot fly Poindexter to the nearest field hospital, Conrad holding Poindexter up for most of the trip. The flight crew delivered him, nearly insensible from loss of blood and fatigue, to the duty surgeons. A truly memorable day for Alpha Troop and John Poindexter was finally over.

19

BATTLE OF THE SENSES

All the men who fought this battle were pumped full of adrenaline, hyperaware of their surroundings, and expecting to be shot or killed at any moment. A number of the men who survived have been able to describe selected sensory perceptions in vivid detail, even poignancy. For some soldiers, it was a particular sight that they will never forget. For others, it was a particular sound, or even a smell. Some have memories of a touch or tactile sensation they can't shake, and a few have even come away with a taste of the battle they can bring back to their palates nearly a half century later. Here are a few examples, a "sense" of what it was like.

SIGHT Any battle exists on many planes, all at once. The first of these, of course, is sight. Seeing is believing, what one sees stays in the mind's eye. This book is all about the unforgettable things these men saw during their time in Vietnam and, most particularly, in War Zone C during these fateful days. For most, sight was the dominant sense and was part of every experience. These sights are chronicled in every chapter. Of course, war is more than visual. Battle is also the sound of the guns, the touch of war, the smell of victory or the taste of defeat.

SOUND Or sometimes the absence of it. *PFC Ken Woodward*, of Charlie Company, remembers the quiet of jungle patrol.

Despite the movies, with their images of point men hacking their way through the jungles with machetes, that is BS. It did not happen. The simple reason? Noise. And that could be deadly. I can tell you that Charlie Company was *quiet* when moving through jungle. Vines were parted with hands or rifle barrels. All equipment was fastened down on rucksacks and we moved with deathly silence. And movies also show guys chatting away or talking in normal voices. This *never* happened in the field. No one, and I mean no one, ever spoke above a whisper, and most times it was hand signals for communication. At night it was a touch and whisper at most.

The roar of the battle was, of course, the opposite experience. These were still the days when personal sound attenuators were the exception rather than the rule. The military was just beginning to understand the long-term effects of high-decibel machinery or cacophonous events on the human auditory system. *SP4 James Cadotte*, an M-60 gunner on A-34, came up with an effective and novel method for lessening the noise: "I took out a couple of Marlboros and broke off the filters and stuck them in my ears."

S. Sgt. Gus Gutierrez, who received a Silver Star for his bravery on March 26, 1970, clearly recalls several experiences from his Vietnam days related to the other senses. The first involves certain sounds that have stayed with him:

. . . those sharp sounds of the type of explosions which sends shockwaves pounding against your chest at July 4th fireworks shows, the sounds of rolling thunder, which is reminiscent of distant artillery or B-52 sorties, and last but not least of all, that whopping sound from the blades of helicopters—it's easy to pick out Vietnam veterans in a crowd—whenever a helicopter flies overhead, it's those 50–60-year-old guys looking up and just staring into a time gone by.

SMELL *S. Sgt. Gus Gutierrez* again, this time remembering certain odors:

> I first entered [the] country [Vietnam] in the fall of 1969, after flying some 18,000 miles on a Tiger Airlines troop plane, filled with young men—most of which were in our early twenties, all of us strangers to each other and alone in our thoughts for most of the flight. I recall my first images of Vietnam, while looking out of the window, down onto Cam Ranh Bay. As we circled in our descent before landing, I determined that it seemed an innocent enough place, a tropical paradise by all rights except for what I feared awaited us there, and wondered if I would ever be home again for Christmas. The words "nothing to fear but fear itself" kept spinning in my head as we clumsily de-boarded the plane. As we hit the door we were smacked with the combination of stifling heat and humidity, I would forever remember that smell, which is easily triggered today by wet grass after a summer rain.

Gutierrez went on to add, "Even today, after all these years, my senses are touched off by diesel exhaust [and] motor oil carelessly dripped on a hot engine [calling up] the remembrance of PL Special [gun oil] cooling an M-60 or a .50 caliber."

SP4 Burl "Topper" Hart still has crystal-clear recollections of the smell of death. Not that it wasn't common—it was—but the odor of burned human flesh was forever pressed upon his neural pathways the morning after the March 25 mortar incident. As Topper Hart wrote after the war, "We were still finding pieces of those men all morning, and the foul odors were everywhere." They had certainly experienced the nauseatingly offensive stench of their enemies' cooked human flesh—they had blown to bits or burned to death more than a few—but this time it was different. This time it was coming from their own.

SP4 Larry King remembers palpably—and many other troopers say this, too—the smell of expended ammunition: burned powder, like being too close to fireworks. This was especially true in situations like the battle of March 26. It was amplified immensely within the confines of the hot, sweaty metal boxes the cavalrymen rode. The fine particles would drift through the air and combine immediately with the ever-present water droplets of Southeast Asian humidity. The result was like "sucking down an entire pack of smokes at once," King says. "We could barely breathe."

SP4 "Big Fred" Harrison, Alpha 2/8: "The smell of the war that day was overpowering. The air was filled with the scent of blood mixed with gunpowder. Later on there was the unmistakable odor of death hanging over everything."

TOUCH *PFC Stanley Carter*, twenty, from Woodland, California, spent the entire battle of March 26 in the bowels of Sheridan A-27. He was the loader for Sergeant Gutierrez and *American Woman*. Bullets pranged off the sides of the Sheridan constantly, and he could also recognize the deeper blasts from RPGs that hit nearby. The sounds of the American guns seemed to be nonstop. Carter could see nothing from his vantage point in and under the turret, but that was OK with him. At least he wasn't in the direct line of fire. He can't remember how many times he loaded the main gun, but it was a substantial number. He does remember the litany of the sequence, though: Carter would prep and load a round, flip the main gun switch to "on," and yell out, "She's ready"; Gutierrez would then shout back, "On the way," and the gunner would pull the trigger. When he wasn't loading the main gun he was hustling grenades up to Gutierrez.

When it was finally over, Carter got a chance to escape from the furnacelike heat of the Sheridan. As he jumped out of the turret he suddenly realized he was absolutely drenched. It was as if he had been in a bathtub for the last two hours. The sweat and the anxiety had touched his core, and he would never forget that feeling.

Again, *SP4 Topper Hart*: "The rats were everywhere. Big, ugly, nasty, biting rats." The varmints would get into the tracks looking for food, especially C-rations, every time the troop went near a Vietnamese village, and it was hard to dislodge them. Hart took to leaving his boots on after a particularly loathsome brute nudged up against him one night. That touch has stayed with him for the forty years since. True to the psychology of rats everywhere, however, they would seem to abandon the tanks and ACAVs as soon as they got near an honest firefight.

TASTE *SP4 Bryan Cupp* got his first taste of battle, literally, right at the outset of Alpha Troop's charge into the NVA bunker complex. He was driving ACAV A-26, far out on the right of the line, in the B-52 strike zone, when either an RPG or a grenade of some other type smacked into the earth nearby. Shrapnel flew everywhere, but by the time it reached A-26 most of it had spent the majority of its potential force or had bounced off the metallic sides of the ACAV. Nonetheless, a couple of pieces managed to penetrate the driver's narrow view slit, and both of them slammed into the left side of Cupp's face. Fortunately, they were not incapacitating wounds, but Cupp clearly remembers that the first sensation he had of that battle was the coppery taste of blood as it ran from his nose and punctured lip. He can still taste that blood today.

SP4 Jerry Guenthardt recalls that when the troop was safely back at the NDP, he finally had a chance to sit down and have a soda (warm) and a cigarette. After a day like they had just experienced, both the tobacco and the soft drink tasted like burned powder.

SP4 Larry King remembers the taste of "mashed taters." There were a number of times in the field when the kitchens in the rear would send out a hot meal via slick. King remembers that it was always "some kind of meat" with mashed potatoes, and he clearly recalls that, nearly every time, Captain Poindexter would step behind the serving line and scoop out the "mashed taters." He'd accompany every hearty spoonful with the exhortation, "Step on up, men. These mashed potatoes will put hair on your chests." The funny thing was that Captain Poindexter, turned line server, would nearly always be shirtless, as were most of the men, all suffering in the oppressive heat. King can still see Poindexter in his mind's eye today, tossing potatoes, without a hair on his smooth, sweaty, skinny chest.

SP4 Rick Hokenson and "Blink": C-rations, or "C-rats," were both the bane and the salvation of a soldier's sustenance in the field. Originally developed for use in World War II, this type of individual ration was intended to be a self-sufficient, all-encompassing meal for consumption in the field, as opposed to A-rations (fresh food) or B-rations (packaged, unprepared foods made in field kitchens). In actuality, C-rats were discontinued in 1958 and replaced by the MCI (Meal, Combat, Individual), which was virtually identical. Since the Army didn't change much about the meal except its name, soldiers kept calling the MCI a C-ration. There is also one documented case of a marine tank commander in Vietnam in 1968 complaining about the C-rats issued to his troops. All the dates clearly stamped on the cans were from the early 1950s.

The MCI replaced in 1981 by today's MRE (Meal, Ready-to-Eat) was rigidly standardized and consisted of twelve variants grouped in three menus of four different entrees.

The M unit:

- **M-1:** Beefsteak, Chicken or Turkey Loaf, Chopped Ham & Eggs, or Ham Slices (Cooked in Juices or Fried). M-1A: Tuna Fish.
- **M-2:** Meat Chunks with Beans in Tomato Sauce, Ham & Lima Beans, Beef Slices with Potatoes in Gravy, or Beans with Frankfurter Chunks in Tomato Sauce. M-2A: Spaghetti with Meatballs in Tomato Sauce.
- **M-3:** Beef in Spiced Sauce, Boned Chicken or Turkey, Chicken with Noodles in Broth, or Pork Steak Cooked in Juices. M-3A: Meat Loaf.

The B unit:

- **B-1:** 7 Crackers and 2 Chocolate Discs (*Types*: Solid Chocolate, Chocolate Creme, or Chocolate Coconut).
  o Peanut Butter Spread.

- **B-2:** 4 Hardtack Biscuits (often referred to by the troops as "John Wayne cookies") and a Cookie Sandwich or Fudge Disc.
  o Cheese Spread (*Types*: Processed Cheese with Pimentos, or Processed Cheese with Caraway Seeds). Spread Alternate: Plain Cheddar Cheese.
- **B-3:** 4 Cookies and a packet of Cocoa Powder.
  o Jam Spread (*Types*: Apple, Mixed Berry, Seedless Blackberry, Mixed Fruit, Grape, or Strawberry).

The D unit:

- **D-1 (Fruit):** Halved Apricots, Sliced Peaches, Quartered Pears, Fruit Cocktail. D-1A (Fruit): Applesauce.
- **D-2 (Cake):** Pound Cake, Fruitcake, Cinnamon Nut Roll. D-2A (Cake): Date Pudding and Orange Nut Roll.
- **D-3 (Bread):** White Bread. (There were no alternates.)

The prepackaged rations, like almost every other aspect of a grunt's life in Vietnam, had a number of curious superstitions attached to them:

The "Ham & Lima Beans" entree, a perennial unfavorite since World War II and Korea, was detested by U.S. soldiers and marines, who considered even pronouncing the correct name brought bad luck, instead calling it "Ham and Motherfuckers." U.S. Marines, paratroops, infantry soldiers, and armored vehicle crewmen, particularly AMTRAC [amphibious tractor] personnel, believed that halved apricots were bad luck to eat during combat operations. The peanut butter issued in the B-1 unit was unappetizing to some and was often discarded, but was consumed by those with dysentery, as it was certain to stop a case of "the runs." Soldiers in Special Operations units used to hoard B-1 peanut butter in empty ration cans to make improvised smoke candles while on long patrols. Being extremely oily, the peanut butter burned with ease, and could be used to boil water for coffee, although it left a greasy black soot on the bottom of a canteen cup.

Still, the rations did have their fans, i.e., anyone who was very, very hungry. Parts of the packets were even treasured or hoarded. Such was the case with a grunt from Charlie Company everyone knew as "Blink." Tall, skinny, and angular, he wore thick, dark-rimmed glasses behind which his eyes constantly blinked; thus, his moniker. He was a particular devotee of the D-2 pound cake. He would trade any and every other D-ration, especially the fruitcake, for pound cake at any time. Eventually, he amassed quite a stash of pound cake. He carefully squirreled away the pound cake at the bottom of his rucksack. Presumably, he was going to have a pound cake binge session at some point in his future.

After the horrific day Charlie Company had just endured, SP4 Rick Hokenson came across Blink sitting on the ground in the casualty collection area. He was sweaty and dirty just like everyone else, but as he sat cross-legged, arms atop his knees and his head down, he also seemed to be shaking uncontrollably. Hokenson looked to see if he was bleeding or otherwise wounded, but he did not appear to be. Hokenson went over to Blink and stood in front of him.

Blink looked up, and Hokenson immediately noticed his eyes were red-rimmed and full of tears. Hokenson was surprised. Blink was genuinely well regarded in the company and was not known for being a coward; but, hey, who wouldn't be near the breaking point after a day like this?

"Hey, man," Hokenson gently inquired, "you OK?"

"*No!*" Blink shouted. "Just look at this!"

Blink grabbed his rucksack, which was lying on the ground next to him, and spun it around for Hokenson to view. It was shot to pieces, all tattered, a ragged, frazzled mess.

"The fuckers shot my pound cake, man! They shot my fuckin' pound cake!"

All Hokenson could say in commiseration was, "And there it is . . ."

20

RECALL

By the next morning, Alpha Troop was ready to roll again. Fuel, ammunition, spare parts, food, and all the other essentials had kept appearing during the long night and into the early hours of the next day. Lieutenant Baerman was in temporary command, and he was in a powwow with the other officers and NCOs who were not in the hospital. It seemed likely that the troop would be asked to go back to the site of the previous day's battle to police things up (recover any equipment that could still be salvaged and make sure no valuable documents were accidentally left behind) and see if the NVA were still in their bunkers.

SP4 Kenny Euge was sitting around a makeshift cook fire. During the previous day's action one of his responsibilities had been to hand the TC the spare cans of .50 cal ammo that had been stuffed in the track's belly. During one of those ammo transfers the TC had jacked back the handle of his .50 cal to clear a chambered round. The problem was that the gun barrel was still white-hot from all the firing, and when the chambered shell popped out it had been cooked enough that it had exploded in midair just as Euge was wrestling a new ammo can to the top of the track. Slivers of hot brass had snaked down the space between Euge's CVC helmet and the top of his flak jacket. One of Euge's buddies, with a sharpened bayonet, was trying to pry the brass splinters from Euge's neck. Not exactly the preferred image of sitting around the campfire having a leisurely breakfast.

MARCH 27, 1970, 1ST CAVALRY FIELD HOSPITAL, TAY NINH PROVINCE

SP4 Don Dush had been medevaced during the previous night, taken to the closest field hospital to have someone look at his ravaged face. The cuts and bruises were tended to, but he was advised that he'd have to wait a bit, until some of the swelling went down, to have them start digging out the metal fragments. It took another whole day.

Two days [after the battle] I was sitting in the field hospital waiting to have someone take some of the shrapnel out of my face. My lip was still about five times as big as it should be but my hearing was beginning to come back. Back in the NDP the day before, Doc had told me that the hearing loss would be temporary but he thought I should go into the field hospital and have someone look at my face. Doc said it would be good for a Purple Heart. I sat on the makeshift stretcher and watched as the soldier next to me was having shrapnel dug from the back of his legs. It occurred to me then that my face wasn't as bad as I thought it was and that I really wasn't all that interested in the Purple Heart. I don't know if they missed me when I walked out or not. They were busy with men who were wounded worse than I was. I still carry that little piece of shrapnel in my lower lip today and plan to be buried with it.

Topper Hart was another one of the fifty-odd wounded men from Team Alpha that had sustained injuries on March 26. Among all the WIA, some injuries were serious and life-threatening. Many would leave lifelong scars or lingering problems. Other wounds were not at all grave and would not even meet the criteria for a Purple Heart ("wounded in action against an armed enemy and requiring hospitalization for a minimum of twenty-four hours"). Some men even scorned the need to seek treatment. Hart's hand injuries were fairly serious, so he, like Dush, would be evacuated to the rear—and get his Purple Heart. Quite an accomplishment for an eighteen-year-old kid, although Hart did not think so at the time. He was actually more worried about being able to go on R&R, as scheduled, the first week of April. He didn't want to spend his precious week off the line lying on an army cot. As he sat there at a field dressing station, watching a medic probe his hand under local anesthesia, he asked the "doc" how long he'd been doing this type of work.

"Couple of weeks now" was the answer.

That was enough for Hart. He stood up and informed the medic he'd be back and see him again after R&R. He never did, and like Don Dush with his shrapnel-filled lip, Hart has decided he is going to be buried with the shrapnel still imbedded in his hand.

MARCH 27, 1970, WAR ZONE C

The day after the battle with the NVA, Team Alpha and Charlie Company spent most of their energy on refit, resupply, and abandoning their three-day old NDP. Captain Armer was nursing some minor wounds but otherwise making sure his men were getting treatment, food, replacement weapons, and ammunition. Captain Hobson was having his mangled face repaired and, unfortunately, it wasn't looking good at all for saving his left eye. He took the very last medevac out.

Colonel Conrad ordered Baerman to split up his troop: most of them would head over to FSB Illingworth to await further instructions. Alpha Company and all the remaining men of Charlie Company went to Illingworth as well. Lieutenant Healey's 2nd Platoon and Baerman, with a few tracks plucked from the ranks of 1st and 3rd platoons, would head back to the scene of the March 26 engagement. As expected, their orders were to police things up and see if the NVA had stuck around or fled.

MARCH 28, 1970, WAR ZONE C

Baerman's column arrived on the morning of March 28. The stench of death hung in the air. The NVA had fled the bunker complex. Once their former stronghold had been discovered, they had nothing to gain by remaining in place. The Americans, if they wished, could simply pound the area with merciless air strikes—and that's exactly what would have happened if Baerman's men had found the NVA still in position.

There were numerous graves, more than eighty, hastily dug and very shallow. Most were nothing more than mounds of dirt. The men dug through several of them—not out of a ghoulish sense of conquest but simply to see if there was any usable intelligence on their former foes. Most of the corpses were hellishly disfigured, missing heads and limbs, the sure sign of a horrific firefight with powerful explosives, like tank rounds and heavy machine guns. In one particularly macabre tableau the men found a dead NVA soldier literally nailed to a tree. A beehive round, with its dartlike flechettes, had pinned the man to the trunk like a butterfly specimen in a shadow box.

The single Sheridan and one ACAV that had been left behind had been ransacked, but it was doubtful the NVA had retrieved anything of any real value. Perhaps they purloined the textbooks left behind by SP5 Craig Wright, but certainly not much more.

A few of the men poked around the abandoned bunkers. They

also explored several of the interconnecting tunnels. Nothing—except shell casings, a few busted weapons, several bags of rice, miscellaneous body parts, scraps of paper, and lots of bloodstains. They left everything where they found it except for the crumpled pieces of paper. Every scrap bigger than a postage stamp was collected. Baerman stuffed all the bits of paper in a small duffel.

After radioing back what they had found—or not found, as it turned out—the patrol was told to return to Illingworth. TACAIR was called in once they cleared the area, and the airmen blasted the remains of ACAV A-33 and Sheridan A-19 into scrap metal.

When later analyzed by the Division G-2 (Intelligence) staff, the bits of documents recovered clearly indicated that the force Team Alpha had battled with was, indeed, the 272nd NVA regiment. Everyone believed that the regiment had slipped over the border and back into Cambodia.

That was not the case. Four days later, early in the morning of April 1, 1970, the 272nd, at least four hundred to five hundred of them anyway, boiled out of the jungle near FSB Illingworth and brutally assaulted the three hundred or so Americans guarding that flat, exposed, poorly barricaded compound.

It was a near thing. The NVA came within a whisker of overrunning the base. Twenty-five Americans died; fifty-four more were wounded. Three of the dead were from Alpha Troop, seven KIA were from Charlie Company, and one KIA was from Company A—an unlucky soldier waiting to come out and join his unit. The survivors collected the bodies of seventy-one NVA.

MARCH 30, 1970, WAR ZONE C

Four days after the battle of March 26, with memories still vivid, 1st Lt. Mike Healey finally got a chance to sit down and write a quick letter to his parents. Gilded with a bit of the bravado typical of young officers who have just survived a major, life-changing

battle, Healey relates what it was like and what he was feeling—
mercifully leaving out the gory details that would frighten any
parent (he made no mention of his own wounding). Healey's letter
is here reproduced in its entirety as a typical example of letters
home from a war most of the participants simply wanted to forget.
(Thanks to Mike's wife, Patti, for making the letter available.)

Dear Mom & Dad,
Well, we got into a huge contact on 26 Mar up where we are. We
killed about 45-50 and we lost one killed and 11 wounded. An infantry company stumbled into a huge bunker complex and they became
encircled by the dinks. We had to bust jungle up to them and pull
them out, and it resulted in a 2 ½ hour firefight. My CO was wounded
and I had to take command of the troop.

*[Author's Note: Healey is presenting a very liberal interpretation of
events here, undoubtedly meant to impress. His CO—Poindexter—was,
indeed, wounded, but he never relinquished command in the field; had he
done so or had he been too incapacitated, Healey would have been the next
senior officer on the scene. In Healey's defense, however, he was given the
point and the responsibility of leading the column in its return to the NDP
after the battle.]*

It was really shakey! The thing that was so bad was we got into
contact about 4:30 PM and we had to break at 6:30 PM so as to get to
our NDP before it was too dark. As it was, we almost couldn't break
contact as the dinks tried to encircle us also. We fought our way
through them & made it out, however. We went back in on the 28th
to police up any documents we could find so as to determine the unit
but we didn't find much. The bunkers that they had were about 6'
deep 6' by 8' with about 2 ½' to 3' of overhead cover, reinforced with
logs. Really well built.
We are operating northwest of Tay Ninh in War Zone C in an
area known as the "Dog's Head" due to the shape of the Cambodian border here. The border runs on two sides of us (north &
west) and we are working with the 2nd Bn. 8th Cav 1st Air Cav

Div in this area. NO one has ever worked up here & there are beaucoup bunkers & dinks in the area. The rest of the squadron is working north of us on their own. We are still under the operational control of the 1st Air Cav & have been off & on since coming to this area. They seem to like A Troop a lot & don't want to let us go!

As to getting out of the field. I'm now the Senior Plt Ldr in the Troop. Our current XO goes home on June 4 but he might get a 21 day drop; thereby going home on 17 May. If this happens there's a good chance I'll get the job. I plan to go on R&R 22-25 April and when I get back—if I get the job—I'll only have about 15 days left on the line. Couldn't please me better as it's really getting flaky out here in the jungle. It's really hell being scared 24 hours a day 7 days a week! Don't like it much at all!

Be glad to get home—this place is really bad. Did I tell you my platoon got ambushed about 3 weeks ago. Wasn't neat at all! Scared the hell out of us. We were running down a clearing with jungle on each side when we were hit by a big double-sided ambush of RPG & AK47 fire. We managed to get through the kill zone no sweat with no one hurt—mainly because of all the dust we were making (dinks couldn't see where to shoot) but because it wasn't our AO [area of operations] we couldn't do anything about it!

Congrats on making Honor Roll, Mo! Really outstanding! We at last have two scholars in the family!!!

All for now—must go. We had a Chinook helicopter bringing in our re-supply last night hit a tree with his rotor blades and he is sitting here with us securing him & trying to get him fixed to get him out of here.

I'll call you all on my R&R! I'm going to Hawaii!

Love you both,

Mike

Tell everyone hi for me. Sorry about Carol! Glad about Fritz!

M

APRIL 1, 1970, TAY NINH PROVINCE FIELD HOSPITAL

For John Poindexter, the three days immediately after the battle were pretty much lost to a haze of pain, drugs, bed rest, and staring at the roof of a canvas hospital tent at the 1st Cavalry's hospital complex near Tay Ninh City. By day three, he was getting a little stir-crazy and wanted out. The doctors weren't sure he should go just yet, but he signed himself out anyway and found a ride back to his command wearing a cast on his left arm. He'd have that cast for two more months.

Between his four months commanding 1st Squadron's Headquarters Company and five months commanding Alpha Troop, he had managed to get about three to four months more "command time" at his level than most captains. This, combined with his "short-timer" status, put him at the very end of his tenure as a troop commander, and, sure enough, Lieutenant Colonel Reed informed him that he would be handing off to his replacement on May 1. No appeals, no debate. April went by in a blur. Patrols continued, men came and went, equipment malfunctioned and got repaired or replaced; in other words, pretty much business as usual.

Still, there were rumors, bits and pieces of hushed conversations. Only a few of the senior officers knew that May 1 would be the first day of a big push into Cambodia, but the grunts could always seem to tell when something was up, especially if it was going to be a major activity involving significant risk to life and limb.

Poindexter's unit had been transferred back to the 11th and away from 2nd Battalion a couple of weeks after their battle on March 26. Others higher up the food chain would have to determine if the cavalry/infantry experiment had been a success, but it was certainly judged to have been so in Poindexter's mind. In that regard, while the patrols and skirmishes went on, Poindexter sat down at the cramped writing table in his M-577 command track and dictated a number of awards for valor for those men who had done so much to carry the day on March 26. Poindexter, as was common with commanding officers in the field, did not personally write up the citations. Rather, he directed his first sergeant to take his recommendations and get them worked up. Poindexter would trust the army's ponderous but usually efficient paperwork machine, stoutly manned by umpteen REMFs ("rear echelon mother fuckers"), who were thrilled to be shouldering pens and typewriters over rifles and grenade launchers. He counted on the REMFs to get the job done and obtain the decorations he felt his men deserved. He never gave it a second thought.

MAY 2, 1970, WAR ZONE C

On April 29, 1970, over fifty thousand American troops, accompanied by another sixty thousand ARVN, began pouring across the Cambodian border to seek out and destroy a reported forty thousand NVA and their secret stashes of food and materiel. The 11th Armored started pitching in—but John Poindexter would not be going with them. He turned over command of Alpha Troop on May 2, bid his men a fond and heartfelt farewell, and trudged off to 1st Squadron's base camp, behind the front lines, to assume his new "short-timer's" duties as the squadron's assistant S-1, or assistant personnel officer. It was a thankless, boring, paper-pusher's job, but it would give him time to sit down and write out his thoughts on the battle of March 26.

Poindexter's goal in trying to memorialize the battle was to write a treatise on mobile cavalry operations in a hostile jungle environment—something he believed his fellow armor branch officers might be interested in reading. He wrote furiously for days on end and by the time he was done had a twenty-thousand-word paper, complete with photos and diagrams. He submitted the piece to *Armor* magazine, the U.S. Army's official publication for the armor branch. The editors were interested but wrote back that the article was far too long—and could it please be cut down?

JULY 4, 1970, TON SAN NHUT AIRFIELD, REPUBLIC OF VIETNAM

By the 4th of July 1970, Poindexter was packing to leave Vietnam for good. He tossed the manuscript and the letter from *Armor* in his B-4 bag, intending to resurrect the project as soon as he got to New York, which would be his next stop after taking off his uniform. Poindexter was scheduled to fly out of Ton San Nhut on Independence Day but he got "hijacked" by some TACAIR controllers who had seen his name on the flight manifest. The TACAIR guys had been on the back end of the heroics of March 26 and wanted to host Poindexter for a few congratulatory drinks before he left the country. It turned into a full-fledged celebration wherein far too much alcohol was consumed. Poindexter missed the flight. Somewhat sheepishly, and a lot more sober, he managed to snag a flight on the 5th.

JULY 15, 1970, NEW YORK CITY

With Vietnam, the U.S. Army, and all thoughts of the events of March 26 a million miles behind him, regular civilian Mr. John Poindexter began to pursue his graduate studies, and a particular young lady he had been dating at the time, in the heart of the greatest city in the world, New York, New York.

Poindexter would earn his MBA in finance in 1971 and follow that up with a PhD in economics and finance from the Stern School at NYU in 1976. His doctoral dissertation was "a statistical analysis, utilizing a capital asset pricing model, of the venture capital market." He had traded the steaming, treacherous jungles of Vietnam for the sometimes equally tricky and dangerous "jungles" of Wall Street.

JANUARY 1971, TON SAN NHUT, VIETNAM

Field Cook PFC August Whitlock survived his Vietnam experiences and was processed out at the end of his yearlong tour. As part of the procedure, he was handed the decorations he had earned in country, including the Army Commendation Medal, the Vietnamese Cross of Gallantry, the Vietnam Campaign Medal, and the Vietnam Service Medal. The clerk shuffling his papers asked if he had been involved in any major battles—perhaps there was another decoration or two he deserved. Whitlock thought for a moment and mentioned the events of March 26, 1970, and the battle near Tay Ninh. The clerk flipped through all his data and the pages of battle records and reports of engagements.

"Nah . . . nothing here on any battle on that date in War Zone C," the clerk reported.

"Look again, pal, I was there!"

"Nope. Nothing. And if ain't here in these pages, soldier boy, it didn't happen."

"But that's impossible!"

By this time, the exchange had caught the attention of the duty lieutenant, who came over to the table and asked if there was anything wrong. Whitlock told his story again. The lieutenant took a look at the books and came to the same conclusion as his clerk.

"But . . ." Whitlock continued to protest.

"That's enough, soldier! Move along or you'll miss your flight—unless you want to spend some more time in the 'Nam, that is."

"No, sir."

In an instant, the struggles of March 26, 1970, were inexplicably erased from the record of the U.S. Army in Vietnam. It became, as John Poindexter later dubbed it himself, the day of "the Anonymous Battle." Although a small handful of men did receive awards for valor for their actions that day, many other recommendations that Poindexter had personally made somehow disappeared into the ether. John Poindexter didn't know it at the time, the rest of the men who had fought the battle didn't know it, and the world at large was in danger of never knowing it, but this day would mark the beginning of another "battle," one that would take almost forty more years to complete.

21

AFTERWORD

1999, FORT IRWIN, CALIFORNIA
(THIRTY-SEVEN MILES NORTHEAST OF BARSTOW)

Fort Irwin is located in the high desert—specifically, the Mojave Desert area of southeastern California. It is a challenging environment, to say the least. In winter temperatures drop below zero, and in summer they soar to over 120. It is where, in 1979, the U.S. Army decided to locate one of its main armor training bases.

One of the principal tenants at Fort Irwin is the 11th Armored Cavalry, which, since 1994, has been assigned to function as the U.S. Army's primary OPFOR, or "Opposing Force" component. In this role, the 11th ACR mock-fights other brigade-sized units, one a month, twelve months a year, in war game exercises all across the sprawling 1,000 square miles of Fort Irwin's rocks and sand.

In June of 1998, Colonel John D. Rosenberger took over command of the 11th ACR. Rosenberger says the regiment, at that time, was:

renowned as the finest brigade-sized war-fighting unit in the world, and very few of our brigades ever won a battle against the regiment. The army's training philosophy was if you spar against the best, in open force-on-force contest, it would be the best test of a unit's combat readiness and the most effective means of enhancing war-fighting capability in a short period of time. In essence, we were the anvil against which our army hammered its war-fighting brigades into shape to win the first battle of the next war.

As good as they were, though, Rosenberger began to realize that the officers he supervised, especially the younger ones, lacked a sense of history for the regiment and all its experiences. Colonel Rosenberger decided that he would dig deep into the regiment's past and invite back some of the veteran warriors who were still around. He wanted them to talk about what the regiment had been like "in the day."

Among the old-timers that Rosenberger invited to come back to Fort Irwin and speak to his troopers was the legendary "Doc" Bahnsen, West Point Class of '56, former commander of the 11th's 1st Squadron, and a retired brigadier general. Bahnsen arrived at Fort Irwin in the spring of 1999 and regaled the officers and men of the 11th with many tales of derring-do but also imparted a number of valuable lessons on his combat experiences. At the end of his stay, Bahnsen asked Rosenberger if he had invited John Poindexter to come back to Fort Irwin. Rosenberger admitted that he hadn't. In fact, he had not even heard Poindexter's name prior to Bahnsen bringing it up.

Bahnsen told Rosenberger that Poindexter was a "must-have" if he wanted a true picture of what the regiment had been like in Vietnam, and he urged Rosenberger to give Poindexter a call. He assured Rosenberger that Poindexter would have some great stories to tell, including the recollections of one particular firefight in March 1970.

Rosenberger immediately tracked Poindexter down and extended the invitation. Poindexter was both flattered and interested, but, between one schedule conflict and another, he would not be able to make a visit until the fall of 1999. Rosenberger agreed that that would be fine, and Poindexter got some time to think about what he was going to say to the men of his former regiment after being out of uniform for nearly thirty years.

SUMMER 1999, HOUSTON, TEXAS

The first thing that Poindexter did to prepare for his upcoming trip to Fort Irwin was to dig out the long-neglected manuscript he had initially created for *Armor* magazine, way back in 1970. He hadn't touched it for twenty-nine years. As he reread the pages, the memories came flooding back. He determined that this text would be the touchstone of his presentation to the current troopers of the Blackhorse Regiment, but he wanted to brush up on some of the facts, so he began to do a little research.

Poindexter asked around, looking for recommendations on other texts he could read that discussed the conditions in Vietnam during his time there. A friend steered him to a book entitled *Into Cambodia* by the late Keith Nolan. Although Nolan had written a book primarily about the Cambodian Incursion, he had also included pages that described units that took part in the invasion. One of those units was the 11th ACR, specifically, 1st Squadron, Alpha Troop. Poindexter was pleasantly surprised: He had not known that this account of his troop's actions existed. Nolan had somehow gotten hold of one of Poindexter's former troopers, SP4 Angel Pagan, an M-60 gunner on ACAV A-13, and Pagan's stories of March 25 and 26, 1970, were liberally quoted. As he read further into those pages, his amazement soon turned to shock. What had really gotten his attention was one sentence, toward the end of the narrative: "Pagan [had been] recommended for a Bronze Star, which was later disapproved along with many other awards."

How could this be? Poindexter was stunned. He remembered

Pagan, and he also remembered forwarding the recommendation for Pagan's Bronze Star, along with a fistful of other instructions for medals. *What does this mean? He never received the award? Did the other men not receive theirs?*

FALL 1999, HOUSTON, TEXAS

Poindexter trekked to Fort Irwin and made his presentation on his troop's adventures in War Zone C. The men were spellbound by the stories, and Poindexter basked in the glow of old memories, well met. After the euphoria of visiting his old regiment subsided, the uncertainty of what had happened to the awards his men were supposed to have received way back in 1970 started to vex him. Immediately after he had read Nolan's account, he began tracking down men from his former unit, including Angel Pagan, and asking questions. He started to discover, much to his disgust, that nearly all of what Nolan had written was true.

The first place that Poindexter turned to for help was the 11th ACVVAC (11th Armored Cavalry, Veterans of Vietnam and Cambodia). He had begun to attend some of the organization's reunions in 1992. He would call upon the energetic leaders of the group to help track down more of his former men. The 11th ACVVAC had been building a database of former troopers for years, and it seemed clear that the group would be the best resource for contacting long-ago colleagues.

Information began to come back as Poindexter's former men responded, and as the first few were identified, they, in turn, were asked to network with any other former troopers they might know. The word was put out: "If you think you deserved some recognition for your part in the battle and you didn't get it, or if you want to make sure a buddy was recognized, now is the time to speak up." All the requests had to be verified, which meant more networking, one man to another, until solid, verifiable statements could be written up for each query made.

WINTER 1999 TO SEPTEMBER 2003,
HOUSTON, TEXAS

John Poindexter's outrage was echoed by "Doc" Bahnsen, who suggested that it was going to take a real fight to get the army to move on thirty-plus-year-old award recommendations. Bahnsen also knew that in order to get the army's attention and have any hope of cooperation they would have to use the army's system of rules and procedures, no matter how arcane and slow-moving the process might prove to be.

The second critical task, after reconnecting with the veterans, was to resurrect old reports and documents. By Poindexter's calculations, there were nineteen awards that needed to be made to sixteen different individuals (this would later be raised to twenty and seventeen, respectively). Three of the sixteen men had perished during the war (Lieutenant Henderson, Sergeant Foreman, and Specialist Andrews). Their survivors would have to be located. Three had stayed in the military and retired and would be fairly easy to find (Colonel Healey, Sergeant Cupp, and Sergeant McNew). Ten of the men had left the military almost immediately after their Vietnam experiences, returned home, and long since forgotten anything about any intended or promised awards. They were scattered all over the country.

Each intended honoree—or survivor—would need to be personally contacted and agree to be nominated, then provide a detailed statement on the action or actions under consideration for any award. In the case of the KIAs and others whose recollections had been severely compromised, statements would have to be written on their behalf. It was going to be a long, laborious, drawn-out slog.

No one would have blamed John Poindexter for harboring second thoughts about having taken on this burden, but rather than be cowed by the prospects, he actually started to think in an even more ambitious direction. He began to wonder, in pursuing the long-lost awards, if there weren't others in his former unit who had been overlooked—men whose valorous deeds had simply gone unnoticed or unrecorded at the time. If so, how could he make up for these oversights? Then it dawned on him: *Why not just seek an award for the entire unit? Maybe a Valorous Unit Award or possibly even a Presidential Unit Citation? That would cover everyone and every deed.* So the quest was broadened. The 11th ACVVAC jumped in again and began assisting Poindexter. They contacted the men still living plus all former Blackhorse Troopers who were on the roster during the dates that were being bracketed for the possible award of the PUC. That number quickly grew to over two hundred men. Somewhat more than half were actually attached to Alpha Troop during the events of March 25 and 26, 1970.

Like the army's caissons of yore, the wheels kept turning even though they seemed to be moving at a rate more akin to 1901, when the Blackhorse Regiment was originally established, than the hectic pace of 2001.

2005–2006, HOUSTON, TEXAS, AND WASHINGTON, D.C.

Ever so slowly, the requested awards started maturing. By 2005, the first few had come through, some in time to present at the 11th ACVVAC Reunion that year in Colorado Springs.

By early 2006, the remainder of the decisions of the army's Military Awards Branch were released. Of the nineteen original award requests, fifteen had been approved or reaffirmed (two awards had been made previously, unbeknown to Poindexter and his team). Four requested awards were declined, including the highest among them: the recommendation for a Distinguished Service Cross for Sergeant Foreman. Also declined were Silver Stars (in lieu of Bronze Stars with "V") for retired Colonel Healey and retired Sergeant McNew and a Soldier's Medal for Sergeant Smolich (Smolich did, however, receive a Bronze Star with "V" for his valor on March 26, 1970).

The balance of the awards that had been so tenaciously procured were presented to those individuals who desired to receive them personally, at the 11th ACVVAC Reunion in Kansas City, Missouri, in 2006. Adding extra poignancy to that reunion was its featured speaker: former captain John Poindexter. All that remained was to press ahead on the award of the PUC to the entire unit.

DECEMBER 2007 TO JANUARY 2009, HOUSTON, TEXAS, AND WASHINGTON, D.C.

The PUC package went into a black hole, and the communications lines between all parties went silent for many months. For John Poindexter, it was a time of quiet anxiety. For the ponderous inner workings of the Department of the Army, it was business as usual. In the grand scheme of things, such as fighting simultaneous wars in Iraq and Afghanistan, the energy and attention required to properly evaluate a request to make an award to an obscure group of cavalrymen forty years after the fact was not a high-priority item, and understandably so.

On December 18, 2008, Secretary of the Army Preston M. "Pete" Geren sent a letter that read as follows:

> After giving this request careful, personal consideration, I have determined that the Presidential Unit Citation is the appropriate award to recognize Troop A, 1st Squadron, 11th Armored Cavalry Regiment's gallant acts . . . The unit's brave soldiers have clearly distinguished themselves by their courageous actions. The Army and our nation are forever grateful for their heroic service.

Between the 2008 winter holidays and the labyrinthine process of passing correspondence of this type around to the appropriate parties in the correct sequence, Poindexter and his volunteers did not receive hard-copy evidence of this wonderful news until early

January 2009. When they finally did get the first faxes of Secretary Geren's letter, the celebrations began.

JANUARY TO OCTOBER 2009, HOUSTON, TEXAS, AND WASHINGTON, D.C.

The party was on, but there was a lot to be done. The first thing that had to be decided was "Where are we going to have the party?" Since the award was for the 11th Armored Cavalry, the army was expecting to celebrate it at the headquarters for the 11th. Somehow, though, the significance of getting the award seemed to be demanding a larger stage than a windswept parade ground in the middle of the California high desert at Fort Irwin.

Poindexter and his merry band figured they would go for broke: "Let's have the celebration at the White House! It is, after all, the *Presidential* Unit Citation. Shouldn't it be conferred by the president?"

The Army and the 11th ACR graciously stepped aside in terms of insisting on hosting the ceremony. They had nothing to lose: An awards gig at the White House was a very long shot, but Poindexter had already taken a number of very long shots and hit the target. If the White House said yes it would be great public relations for the army, and if they said no, which was nearly certain, the army would end up having the festivities they had originally envisioned, which would be perfectly fine.

Poindexter and his volunteers opened another front, this one in the public eye. The goal would be to apply subtle pressure on all the local members of Congress of the men involved and their various news media markets to gain support for the president accepting the invitation of the 11th ACR. This would be accomplished by spreading around the stories of all the troopers who would be getting this prestigious award. Locale by locale, the story of each individual trooper's bravery and upcoming honor would be carefully targeted to each man's local press. Newspaper articles and even a few local TV reports began to pop up all over.

In one particularly heartwarming piece, the story of Kenny Euge was documented by the *Sunday News-Democrat*, which serves southwestern Illinois. Euge suffers from a documented case of PTSD related to his Vietnam experiences and is 70 percent disabled because of it. Although after Vietnam he worked for many years as a switchman for the Terminal Railroad of St. Louis, his Vietnam nightmares dogged him. He took to living in a genuine red caboose that he moved to his property and started building "interesting" metal sculptures made of abandoned car parts in his front yard. Needless to say, his neighbors thought him a bit odd and wanted him gone. After many years and many wrangles, county eviction papers were made out and signed and were scheduled to be served on Euge—and then the story broke about "Kenny Euge, Vietnam War hero." The neighbors may be silently fuming, but Kenny is still snug in his beloved caboose and the eviction papers were tossed in the shredder. The reporter who wrote the story on Euge later received a regional Pulitzer.

Local stories soon turned to regional stories, and some regional pieces morphed into a few national bits of recognition. A groundswell of support for the president to personally bestow the award was building. All that was left to be done was synchronizing everyone's timetables and keeping interest at as high a level as possible.

The stars finally aligned on all sides, the president agreed to host the ceremony, and a date was chosen: October 20, 2009. Even better, weather permitting, the investiture and celebration would take place in the Rose Garden of the White House itself. The improbable but justifiable quest had finally come to fruition, but more work still lay ahead.

OCTOBER 2009, WASHINGTON, D.C., HOUSTON, TEXAS, AND TOWNS ACROSS THE USA

It was called "the Magic List," the final dossier on who was committed to coming to the Rose Garden, and who would, in fact, have a seat therein. The list contained 119 names (the maximum number of guests allowed by the White House staff): 86 veterans of the events of March 25 and 26, 1970; 14 men who served in Alpha Troop between January 1 and March 24; six men who served after the battle but before the troop was withdrawn from War Zone C; and 13 special guests.

John Poindexter would write the following after the event:

> It is striking that as many as 106 of our troopers and representatives of the deceased committed to travel to Washington four decades after the event for which the troop was being honored. Almost forty years of death, disability, discouragement and disappearance had reduced significantly the population of candidates for an invitation. The final tally represented a high, but not precisely known, proportion of those still present on the planet and physically and psychologically capable of travel further than their mailboxes. Moreover, in an inspiring demonstration of patriotism and goodwill, every one of the 106 veterans and representatives showed up as promised.

For the men of Alpha Troop who were going to go to the White House, and their date with destiny, the prospects gave rise to all sorts of interesting possibilities and even a little intrigue. Raymond Tarr, former Sheridan loader, wrote to John Poindexter:

> We received e-mails reporting that we would be going to the White House, most likely in October, but we had to keep it quiet for security reasons. But it wasn't easy to keep news like that a secret while being interviewed. We bought our plane tickets and I went to a local

men's clothing store to buy a new suit. As I was being fitted, the owner of the store said, "Where are you going—to see the president?" He knows me personally and he knew that something had to be going on for me to buy a new suit. I grinned and said, "Actually, yes, I am going to the White House—but you can't tell anyone." He said to be sure to bring back a photo of myself at the White House in my new suit.

Ray Tarr's new suit wasn't the only one purchased for the occasion. Men's clothing stores across the nation saw a slight uptick in their individual revenues in a bad economy. Even Kenny Euge, the hard-pressed veteran living in a caboose, bought one. "It cost me two hundred and sixty-nine dollars, but I bought it anyway. I'm going to feel funny," he deadpanned.

OCTOBER 19, 2009, WASHINGTON, D.C.

The men, sometimes by themselves but many with special guests or family members, began to arrive in Washington on Monday, October 19.

George Burks made it to D.C. without much physical discomfort, but his anxiety level concerning the trip was very high nevertheless.

I was going to meet the President of the United States of America! But, my mind really was on seeing again a hundred men from my former unit, A Troop. I thought this was the most impossible thing that could happen to me, and especially after almost forty years had come and gone. The past lingers like a strong scent in the air and in some cases, especially war, there is this special recollection that you cannot see but that you can sense.

As my wife and I entered D.C., I felt it. Now the anxiety was even stronger in me. What do I say when I don't recognize someone, or they don't recognize me? Do I stand there like an idiot pretending to feel welcomed and a part of history?

Once at the hotel, I realized that my subconscious knew more than I could possibly have imagined. I recognized many of the troopers and I started to feel a sense of relief and an easing of anxiety. Several of the troopers came up to me and said, "I remember you, but I can't remember your name." The ice had been broken.

The designated headquarters hotel for the reuniting troopers was the Comfort Inn in downtown Alexandria, Virginia. It had been chosen for its location, number of available rooms, and reasonable prices. It had not been chosen for its available public space, which turned out to be woefully inadequate for the growing gathering of the men and their friends and families. The complimentary breakfast area was jam-packed, the hallways were being commandeered, and the smokers, of which there were still many, were on an overflowing sidewalk in front of the building. No one seemed to care very much. Acquaintances of some forty years were being renewed, long-lost pals were reconnecting, and the air was jubilant in anticipation of the celebrations about to take place.

Some, of course, couldn't make it to this happy occasion because they had been lost in battle, but these men could still be represented by their survivors, and several were, including Gudrun Foreman, Sergeant Foreman's widow, and Ann Ragan, sister to 1st Lt. Robert "Robin" Henderson (who was killed in Cambodia). Ann Ragan remembers the D.C. gathering fondly:

When I arrived at the designated Washington area hotel before the PUC ceremony, the men were lingering in the lobby, hungry to see a face they would recognize and sharing photos of themselves and their buddies in Vietnam. "We looked so young then," they exclaimed as they glanced at the white sideburns prevalent among the middle-aged warriors gathered there. Another joked, "That's not hair, that's mud!" when I remarked about his youthful dark curly hair in the photo. Some showed me scars which they wore like badges of courage and told me how they had received them. I truly began to appreciate them like they were my own younger brothers, all of them. It was moments like these that made my memories of the Presidential Unit Citation ceremony precious.

And then there were the men who were in my brother's platoon . . . Lowell [Walburn], fondly referred to as Wally by his Blackhorse brothers, sat down and held my hand as he told me how Robin had died. He had been with Robin on March 26 of 1970 as well as on the day of his death. Robin's ACAV driver made a special effort to visit with me as well. I am so grateful for the kindnesses and consideration of all of Robin's men.

A welcome dinner was scheduled to take place at Old Town's Union Street Public House. With a group the size of this one, it was also guaranteed to be a raucous affair. The party quickly took up almost the entire main room, then spilled into four additional side rooms. Other patrons of the restaurant who were not part of the "gang" could only look on bemusedly, but after a while some of them became involved. They began to hear the stories of these brave men bandied across the restaurant. The PUC ceremony scheduled for the following morning became a hot topic of proud conversation, so much so that perfect strangers quietly and anonymously contributed to the Alpha Troop restaurant tab as they left.

0830, OCTOBER 20, 2009, ALEXANDRIA, VIRGINIA

No one overslept, and all were "present for duty" the following morning. Promptly at "zero-eight-thirty," the regular army rolled in and took command. Impossibly young-looking soldiers in dress uniforms spilled out from a group of idling buses. Clipboards clutched as firmly as their rifles might normally be, these efficient arbiters of protocol began to smoothly parse the group into Rose Garden attendees and Pentagon travelers.

Former command track gunner Don Dush, who was attending

with his son, was favorably impressed by the efficiency of the army team and was more than a bit amused by the similarities between the call to muster he was experiencing then and ones that he had responded to some four decades earlier:

> A young soldier began to call off our names in roll call fashion to board the buses. His "sound off when your name is called" elicited various pronunciations of "here," "yo," or "present." My son, ever observant, told me later that as many of the men left the group, their wives were hugging and clinging to them and openly crying. He said he realized what an honor we were about to receive, but he wondered at the level of emotion and tears on the part of the wives. I reminded him that some of these women had listened to a very similar roll call a little more than forty years earlier. I'm sure being separated again in this way brought those memories and all the emotion that they carry with them to the surface.
>
> Also, for each of us, veteran, spouse, or family member, our roll call brought finality: a welcome home, a vindication, maybe an emotional exuberance, and certainly a level of recognition that was long overdue. It brought closure for those who were able to talk about their actions on that March day in 1970, for those who still struggled with their memories, and for those who were there to honor the fallen. In many ways, this was a healing process for us, veterans and family alike. How fitting that a roll call of names both of the living and the families of the fallen began this final chapter.

Once loaded, the buses smoothly slid away from the hotel: one group of coaches headed for Pennsylvania Avenue, another to the Pentagon. Those who could not be squeezed into the confines of the White House ceremonies would be feted at the Pentagon, including a live simulcast of the Rose Garden speech. Ray Moreno was deep in thought as he stared out the window of his bus, wending its way through early morning traffic toward the White House:

The road leading to this moment of honor wasn't an easy one. I needed some time to gather my composure and my thoughts during the bus ride to the White House. I took a deep breath, as I had way too many emotions running through me at once. I closed my eyes and my thoughts went back more than thirty-nine years, when I was only nineteen and a part of the 11th Armored Calvary Regiment. As the old memories came to me, I saw my close friend Fred Pimentel and guys like Romeo Martin, Pasqual (Gus) Gutierrez, Stan Carter, and William Sizemore. I opened my eyes and saw them again, this time four decades later.

Today, in the Rose Garden of the White House, we will be awarded the Presidential Unit Citation by the president of the United States. No matter how many times I say these words out loud or in my head, it still feels like a dream.

The stories are apocryphal but sadly true: Many soldiers and sailors returning from Vietnam, most in uniform, as required, were shunned or even spat upon by their fellow citizens as they made their way back from honorable battlefields. Scattered through the prism of forty years, though, the light seemed a little different, as expressed by Topper Hart:

Aboard the bus for the White House, I saw a police escort of motorcycles leading the way. The traffic had been completely cleared from the street we were on. As we continued on, it amazed me how many people were standing on the side of the streets, waving and taking pictures. It made us feel really special.

Pasqual Gutierrez added an extra dimension to what seemed surreal to many of the men who would soon be standing next to the president of the United States:

The ride on the buses was phenomenal as we rolled through Constitution and Independence Avenues. Winding our way to the White

House, we were led by a police escort with sirens blaring. It was midmorning and people who were either on their way to work or sightseeing for the day lined the streets as traffic was stopped at every intersection to allow our passage. Some people curiously pointed at our buses and others waved. One who that morning must have read the *Washington Post* or *USA Today* reporting our visit to the White House held high a two-finger peace sign. We were paraded through the streets of the nation's capital representing a generation of men and women who had answered their country's call to duty. A part of my heart wanted to believe that our parents were looking down from heaven with joy knowing that their sons finally had been welcomed home.

1000, OCTOBER 20, 2009, THE WHITE HOUSE

The buses bearing the heroes of Alpha Troop pulled up smoothly to the southeast gate of the White House. As each passenger stepped off, his or her ID was checked against more lists and computer entries. There was a short walk to be made down a service road. The way was lined with brightly attired military aides, all smiling and gently directing the slow-moving throng to its Rose Garden destination.

When the group reached the Rose Garden, they were soon intermingled with the rest of the guests, most of them high-ranking army officers, the current secretary of the army himself, several politicians, and many aides. The day was crisp, cool, and spectacularly beautiful—the chamber of commerce couldn't have dialed up the weather any better. It was just chilly enough to make those men unaccustomed to wearing suits on a regular basis perfectly comfortable. They might have been sweating mentally, but at least they wouldn't have to show the physical signs of any heat-related discomfort.

The conversation was lively but took place in hushed tones. The group was, after all, at the president's home, the most revered building in America. The gardens were already tinged by fall's touch. Much pruning had been done, and the vines and ornamentals were already shrinking away toward winter. A few faded roses remained, but they, too, would soon wither and fall away to make way for next season's spectacular displays.

The president was being delayed, which was not unusual, as these things go. It seemed that there was some high-ranking Mideast dignitary chewing into the available time on the president's schedule. The men gathered in the Rose Garden did not seem to mind. They were in the middle of a fairy tale they knew would not last, and they would savor every moment of it. It was a day to remember and a moment to last a lifetime.

JC Hughes had a memorable conversation with one of the generals:

> We stood around in groups and some of us started talking with today's commander of the 11th ACR, the current A Troop CO, and the sergeant major as well as a few generals. One four-star stepped forward, thrust out his hand, and said, "Hi, I'm Pete Chiarelli [the vice chief of staff of the army]." Cavieux, Sorich, and Forbes all looked at me with "Well, you were the TC, so do something" expressions. I shook hands and introduced the group around me. As we were talking, I told General Chiarelli a story about the current army chief of staff's father [Maj. Gen. George Casey Sr.].
>
> *[Author's Note: this was the story of General Casey's heroic helicopter flight to bring critical supplies to a desperate Charlie Company.]*
>
> General Chiarelli asked that I send that story to him and he'd see that the chief of staff got it. He handed me his card, which has become one of my souvenirs from the trip.

There were unforgettable moments for Ray Tarr as well:

> We went to the [Rose] Garden, dressed in dark suits with our medals on our chests on a beautiful October day. I stood with the guys I

had been in combat with. Nearly forty years after fighting together in a jungle, we were together again, this time talking to high-ranking army officers at the White House, waiting to hear the president speak.

Also present in the Rose Garden were former captains Ray Armer and George Hobson. They hadn't seen each other since the events of forty years ago. There was much to discuss.

Then, at last, a murmur rippled through the crowd. The president would be appearing shortly. The men and all the guests who were not yet in their proper seats began to move toward their assigned stations. Pasqual Gutierrez captured the mood of the moment perfectly when he later wrote:

We carefully moved toward the seating in the center of the garden, the second platoon taking the second and third rows on the left side. A lady who I did not know sat to my left, and I later discovered at the Pentagon reception that she was Mrs. Robert Foreman. At the reception, I introduced myself to her and her daughter and mentioned that she was to my left in the Rose Garden, as Sergeant Foreman was on my left on the 26th of March when he lost his life. She replied that she knew who I was and she said, "Maybe that was Robert's way of being here today."

Ties were straightened, jacket lapels smoothed, and a last look to make sure that shoes were still shined and that their medals were still secure. All was finally in readiness. John Poindexter's thoughts at that moment, after all the hard work and effort, were these:

Soon an unaccustomed quiet overtook the audience and activity was stilled as the imminence and gravity of the ceremony asserted themselves. For just an instant, my mind flicked back, ludicrously, to the unearthly stillness in the seconds before our massive assault began the Anonymous Battle.

A voice from the area of the portico firmly and loudly announced, "Ladies and gentlemen! The president of the United States!"

The Great Mandala, the giant Wheel of Life, completed one more turn at that very moment, and the stark, frightening events that occurred deep in a faraway jungle some forty years before had finally come full circle.

EPILOGUE

The area that was once known as War Zone C has changed dramatically over the last four decades. A significant native population has returned to what was once a no-man's-land of death and destruction. Small farms dot the countryside, including all the area that the men in this story fought over with such tenacity. All that is left of what used to be FSB Illingworth is the very faintest outline of its perimeter, lingering in the dirt. Rubber trees have been replanted in other parts of the region; as might be suspected, the voracious jungle has overtaken everything else. Every once in a while the current citizens of the region will come across the remnants of a long-abandoned bunker or the jagged pieces of an exploded ACAV.

The men who roamed that countryside, on foot or in their armored vehicles, have changed, too. Some did not survive the war. Just five days after the rescue mission described herein, three members of Alpha Troop, seven soldiers from Charlie Company, and one soldier from Alpha Company died on April 1, 1970, during a battle at FSB Illingworth. Seven more from Alpha Troop were killed in June 1970 during the Cambodian Incursion (including 3rd Platoon leader 1st Lt. Robin Henderson).

Of the three hundred men, plus or minus, who were directly involved in the momentous events of March 26, 1970, many did survive, though, and they came home to new beginnings, children, and then grandchildren. A few stayed in the military and completed long stretches of service and retired. Among the rest are at least one senior airline pilot, a judge, a prominent architect, a couple of lawyers, and a scattering of business executives, but for the most part, these brave men simply folded themselves back into the multihued fabric of American society. Some picked up where they had left off, returning to farm the land, make steel, drive trucks, paint houses, deliver the mail, switch rail cars in train yards, and lay pipe, or run wires. Some took up traditional, time-honored skills and became teachers, ministers, dental technicians, firemen, prison guards, coal miners, and repairmen. One veteran oversaw a hydro-electric dam, another shipped missile parts worldwide, two engineered software, and another was a radiologist in Saudi Arabia.

Although illness, accidents, natural causes, and at least one drug overdose have claimed a few more over the intervening years, there would still be enough men today to fill the ranks of a couple of lively companies. Not all the men have been accounted for, as of this date, and some, apparently, wish to keep it that way. Nevertheless, of those men whose names appear in the pages of this book, here is, to the best of our knowledge, a record of what happened to these soldiers and their status as this book goes to print.

Walter "Chip" Andrews Jr., from Garnerville, New York, was born on January 27, 1950, and died in the mortar accident that befell Alpha Troop on March 25, 1970. He had just turned twenty. When the mortar tube exploded, Andrews raced to the scene to assist his buddies. It was too late, and there was imminent danger of exploding ammunition all around. He went anyway. His disregard for his own safety ultimately cost him his life. He was posthumously awarded the Soldier's Medal for his bravery and a Bronze Star for his overall superior performance while in Vietnam.

Ray B. Armer, seventy-one, lives in Columbia, South Carolina. After Vietnam and command of Company A, Ray was transferred back to Fort Benning, Georgia. He was caught up in one of the active duty "reductions in force" after the Vietnam War ended but immediately volunteered for the Army Reserve. After twenty-eight years of active and reserve service, Ray retired with the rank of major. Sometime long after Vietnam (Ray does not recall exactly when) he received, in the mail, a Bronze Star with Combat "V" for his bravery on March 26, 1970. He is certainly grateful for that recognition but notes with some curiosity that John Poindexter had nominated him for a Silver Star instead. His one real regret in regard to his experiences relative to the rescue of Charlie Company is that his own men were not included in the award of the PUC to Alpha Troop. General Conrad regards this as an unfortunate oversight and one that he and John Poindexter are actively trying to correct.

Paul Baerman, sixty-three, was born in Lansing, Michigan, and after a year at the Citadel transferred to West Point, where he graduated with the Class of '68. He served with distinction in Vietnam, earning the Silver Star, Bronze Star, and Purple Heart. Baerman stayed with the army, but ten years after Vietnam he was diagnosed with Type 1 diabetes. Since Baerman was in top shape, and there was no history of diabetes in his family, the best guess as to the cause was Agent Orange exposure. The army doctors treating him wondered whether Baerman should be allowed to remain on active duty or should be medically retired. Baerman issued them a challenge: "Go get your PT clothes and we'll run the obstacle course. If you beat me, I'll retire." None of the doctors took up the challenge, so they approved Baerman for continuation on active duty. Just before Desert Storm, in 1991, Baerman had been given command of the 3rd Battalion, 2nd Armored Division. As the Iraqi

Army rolled over Kuwait, Baerman's battalion was told to deploy. The army doctors were more insistent this time. There was no guarantee that the insulin he was required to take every day could survive the harsh desert environment—and what if he suddenly went into insulin shock in the middle of a battle? Reluctantly, Baerman handed over command. He realized then it was time to move on. He retired from the army, as a full colonel, in 1994. He is an urban planner and lives in Colorado with his wife, Kerry, whom he met at West Point and married shortly after graduation. They have three children and three grandchildren.

John C. "Doc" Bahnsen, seventy-six, is a retired brigadier general who lives as a "gentleman farmer, lecturer, and writer" at his family farm in West Virginia. There are very few army officers who fought in Vietnam who have bigger legends or more lasting combat legacies than Doc Bahnsen. During his wartime service in Southeast Asia he earned a dazzling array of personal decorations, including the Distinguished Service Cross, five Silver Stars, three Distinguished Flying Crosses, four Legions of Merit, four Bronze Stars, fifty-one Air Medals, and two Purple Hearts. His exploits as a helicopter pilot, battalion commander, and cavalry leader are still discussed in classrooms at West Point (Bahnsen was Class of '56, the same class as Mike Conrad). It was as commanding officer, 1st Squadron, 11th ACR that then-Major Bahnsen gave tall, skinny, newly minted Capt. John Poindexter his first field command.

Ronald Bench, sixty-three, is retired and living in Spokane, Washington. He was drafted into the army and sent to mortar training, then to Vietnam. He was immediately detailed to the 11th ACR, but he arrived on scene just a few hours too late to take part in the battle of March 26. Getting an early "drop," he was released from active duty just shy of his two-year obligation and went back to Grand Coulee, Washington, his hometown. He got a job with the Bureau of Land Reclamation, Department of the Interior, working at Grand Coulee Dam and spent the next thirty-five years in the Operations Department. He recently retired from government service. I am grateful to Ron for several excellent photos he supplied for this book.

John Biggs, as far as we were able to determine, is still with us and living—quietly—in Akron, Ohio. He did attend the ceremonies in Washington, D.C., in regard to the PUC.

George Burks, sixty-one, lives in Huntsville, Alabama, with his wife, Elizabeth. They have six children and a growing group of grandkids. Burks grew up in Huntsville, where he was an avid fisherman and hunter. After the battle of March 26, 1970, he was part of the 11th Cavalry detachment that endured the April 1, 1970, "day of hell" at FSB Illingworth. George Burks describes that battle, for him, as an "out-of-body experience." Neither Burks nor the medics knew it at the time, but this was the beginning of a lifelong battle with PTSD. Burks reupped for another tour and was stationed in Germany for three years, but after that decided he was not enamored with the new "Volunteer Army." He decided to get out and return to Huntsville, get a college degree, and enter into the emotional therapy field—perhaps he could help others who had been afflicted like himself. He got that degree and became a therapist but after six years found it too stressful. With a referral from the VA he obtained a job as a logistics manager at the army's Redstone Arsenal near Huntsville. He worked there until his retirement in 2000. He no longer hunts or fishes, having decided that all forms of life are too precious. Besides, as Burks now says, "As long as there are grocery stores, I don't need to hunt."

Jim Cadotte, sixty, lives in Duluth, Minnesota, his original hometown. He enlisted in the army at age eighteen because he felt it was his duty to do so. After serving his three years he returned to Duluth and got a job lumberjacking—and continued in the Army Reserve for another five years. He later found stable work in the steel industry. He spent the rest of his working career in the steel business until his recent disability retirement. He continues to enjoy life in Minnesota but has finally had enough snow. "This year, I'm going to Arizona for the winter!" he says with a laugh.

Stanley Carter, sixty-one, is retired and lives in Port Orchard, Washington. Carter was drafted into the army after dropping out of college and spent twenty-one months on active duty. He was seriously injured while in Vietnam (after the battle of March 26) and was medically retired from the service. After the army, Carter became a car painter and worked in Sacramento, then went to work as a painter for the U.S. government. He and his wife are hoping to spend more time with their first grandchild and are thinking about moving to the Oregon coast, or perhaps back to Sacramento.

George Casey Sr.—Major General Casey—assumed command of the entire 1st Cav in May 1970, as the incursion into Cambodia commenced. The invasion caused a huge uproar of protest back in the States, but President Richard Nixon promised to withdraw all American troops by the end of June. He kept that promise, and at 6:00 P.M. local time, June 29, General Casey stood on the tarmac as the last U.S. soldiers from Cambodia stepped off the helicopters. He greeted them as conquering heroes, and the men loved him for it.

The *Washington Post* printed the following, part of a retrospective on the Vietnam War, on December 20, 2009:

A week after the withdrawal from Cambodia, Casey climbed into the copilot seat of his Huey helicopter at 1st Air Cav headquarters and took off, flying east. He was headed for the U.S. base at Cam Ranh Bay to visit wounded soldiers. It was raining and visibility was so poor that his chief of staff, Col. Edward "Shy" Meyer, had urged him to cancel the trip, but he wanted to see his men before they were transferred to hospitals in Japan. The helicopter's path took it across Vietnam's mountainous central highlands. At about 10:00 A.M. his Huey flew into a dense cloud and disappeared. A second helicopter flying behind crisscrossed over the shrouded peaks, looking for any sign of the general's craft, but finally had to break off when its fuel began running low. The American military headquarters in Saigon ordered a massive search. Not wanting to alert the Vietcong that a high-ranking general was unaccounted for, it held off making a public announcement until a few days later.

General Casey and all aboard his Huey were killed as the aircraft plowed into a mountainside in dense fog and clouds. He was among the highest-ranking American officers to die in the Vietnam War, but he died doing what he was known best for: caring about his troops.

George Casey Jr. was a new second lieutenant at the time his father, General Casey Sr., was killed in Vietnam. Young Casey had graduated from Georgetown, where he had been a member of Army ROTC before receiving his commission. Like his father before him, he had a spectacular rise through the officer ranks of the army. He commanded brigades, served at the Pentagon, and from 2004 to 2007 commanded all U.S. forces in Iraq. He became the army's chief of staff, the "number one" soldier in the army, in 2007, after being nominated for the job by President George W. Bush. He retired from the army in April 2011.

Peter Cavieux, sixty-one, lives in Cortlandt Park, New York, with his wife of thirty-four years ("I'd marry her again tomorrow—it has been a ball!"). Originally from Floral Park, Queens, he enlisted right out of high school in 1968. "I didn't do very well in high school," Cavieux related to me. "I knew I wouldn't get into a good college, so I signed up. I was going to get drafted anyway." Cavieux served his three years honorably, left the service, and enrolled in Westchester Community College, receiving his AA degree two years later. He went on to SUNY, New Paltz, where he received his BA in 1976. He was in the office supply business for twenty-five years. For the last five years, he has been a postal clerk for the U.S. Postal Service. As he told me, jokingly, of course, "Imagine me telling people I went to Vietnam and now I work for the Postal Service. Talk about 'going postal'!"

Dennis Cedarquist, sixty-three, is retired and living in Montague, Michigan, his original hometown. After finishing a two-year agricultural program at Michigan State University, Cedarquist was drafted. He served two years and three months before returning home. The extra three months beyond his requirement was to recover from wounds received on his very last day on the line. After his release from active duty, Cedarquist went back to Michigan, where he married and had three children and has had, as he told me, "about as normal a life as I guess you can have. Vietnam was not a big part of my life, and I have mostly put it far behind me. I don't even think about it very much, and it never bothers me." Cedarquist went on to a career as a heavy equipment operator for Occidental Petroleum, then Consumers Energy. He retired at the age of fifty-nine and now collects and restores antique John Deere tractors.

Floyd Clark, sixty-two, lives in Harrisonburg, Virginia, with his wife, Sherry. They have a son and two grandchildren. Floyd was drafted in May 1969 and spent two years in the army, earning two Army Commendation Medals, one with *V*, a Purple Heart, and a Good Conduct Medal. After his army service Floyd worked in a factory for a short time, then the excavating business, and finally settled into a job as a long-haul truck driver. He's still driving today, but just on local routes. He said in a recent note, "Although I was drafted, I was proud to serve, especially with such an outstanding outfit as the 11th."

Floyd Coates, originally from Culpepper, Virginia, was born on August 15, 1949, and died in the unfortunate mortar incident on the evening of March 25, 1970.

Donnie Colwell, sixty-three, is retired and lives in Brookville, Pennsylvania, with his wife, Stephanie. After his stint in the army he became a coal miner and worked the mines for twenty-five years. I first caught up with Donnie as he was out cutting wood on his property, something he once enjoyed doing just for fun and fitness. Donnie is as tough as they come and never pulls any punches. His candid comments and vivid descriptions of what life was like in Alpha Troop were extremely valuable to me. Unfortunately, Donnie has had a bit of recent misfortune. After surviving the horrifying experiences of Vietnam and twenty-five years in the coal mines, he, of all things, recently tripped over his dog at home and fell in such a fashion that it crushed a portion of his spine just below the neck. He is currently a quadriplegic, but there is some hope that he will eventually regain the use of some if not all his extremities.

I know that there are many of his buddies, including me, who are pulling for him to make a complete recovery.

Michael Conrad, seventy-six, went on, after Vietnam, to a very distinguished career in the U.S. Army, retiring with the rank of major general. He now lives in Arlington, Virginia, and is the president of his West Point Class of '56. His medals from Vietnam include the Silver Star, Distinguished Flying Cross, Purple Heart, and Bronze Star. General Conrad was instrumental in assisting John Poindexter with his quest for both the PUC and making sure Poindexter's men finally received their lost awards. He is now seeking to have Company A honored for their service on March 26, 1970, and is petitioning for them to be included in the award given to Alpha Troop. He classifies Company A's exclusion from the original PUC application as "an oversight. It was my fault and I'm going to fix it." Mike Conrad has been extremely generous with his time and recollections. There is one additional anecdote about General Conrad that bears telling: Before General Casey boarded his fatal flight to visit wounded troops, he invited Mike Conrad to accompany him. Conrad already had his orders to rotate out of Vietnam, however, and he was anxious to go home to see his wife and children. He respectfully declined—a decision he has definitely not regretted.

James Crew, former sergeant and tank commander of A-39, passed away on September 11, 1991.

Bryan Cupp, sixty-one, is a retired sergeant first class who now lives in Washington Court House, Ohio, with his wife, Janet. As Cupp has written to me, "I was drafted in March 1969, and then I just kept reenlisting. I suppose you could say that me and the Army were a good fit, and I enjoyed my twenty-three years of service, until my retirement at the end of March 1992." Cupp's Bronze Star for March 26, 1970, was one of the lost medals but was finally awarded to him at the 11th ACVVAC Reunion in Kansas City, Missouri, in 2006. SFC Cupp was also awarded the Purple Heart and the Vietnamese Cross of Gallantry for his service in Vietnam.

William Daniels, sixty-four, lives in his hometown of Alliance, Ohio, the city from which he enlisted in the army in 1968. He served three years in the army, then returned to Ohio, where he worked for thirty-eight years in a factory making auto parts and fork lift tires. He was forcibly retired when the owners of the factory outsourced all their work to Sri Lanka during the recent recession. Daniels was recommended for a Bronze Star for his bravery on March 26, 1970, but the nomination was lost. He finally received his Bronze Star at the 2005 Colorado Springs reunion of the 11th ACVVAC. Daniels was also wounded in the March 26 battle but, for some reason, did not receive the Purple Heart he deserved. When I learned of this, during my talks with Bill, I contacted Bill's congressman and requested that his staff look into Bill's service jacket, especially his medical records. I'm pleased to report that they were able to locate the proper paperwork and Bill finally got his medal. It became especially important to Bill when he lost his health benefits as his company downsized. Finally having his Purple Heart moved him up near the top of the VA's eligibility list, and Bill now has access to the medical treatment and prescription drugs that he needs, courtesy of the VA.

Preston Dawson, acting platoon leader for Charlie Company on March 26, 1970, stayed in the army, advancing to the rank of sergeant first class before retiring. Unfortunately, he has since passed away.

Don Dush, sixty, is a registered nurse and is still working in the occupational health and education field at Parkland Health Center in Farmington, Missouri.

Kenny Euge, sixty-one, is retired and living in his original hometown of Dupo, Illinois, near St. Louis. Unfortunately, Kenny is typical of far too many Vietnam veterans who went off to the war, survived, and came home but never returned completely. Kenny was drafted and spent a little less than two years on active duty and returned to his job as a railway switchman. Although his time in the 'Nam was very brief, he thinks about Vietnam every day. Kenny lives on his railroad pension and his 70 percent disability rating from the VA for PTSD.

Paul Evans, sixty, former rifleman in Charlie Company, lives in retirement in Copperas Cove, Texas. After spending eight years in the army he resigned and enlisted in the U.S. Navy. He spent twelve years in the navy, retiring as an E-5.

Gary Felthager, sixty-three, is retired and lives in Pueblo, Colorado, with his wife, Cathy. They have one daughter, Jeri. Gary was drafted and entered the army on March 27, 1969. During his time in Vietnam he was awarded the Army Commendation Medal and the Combat Medic Badge. He was nominated for a Bronze Star with *V* for his bravery on March 26, 1970, but his recommendation ended up in the group of so-called lost medals. Fortunately, like several of his fellow troopers, he eventually received his well-deserved decoration after the lobbying done by John Poindexter and his volunteers. After receiving a six-month "early out," Gary settled in Colorado. He was a firefighter with the Pueblo, Colorado, fire department for thirty-one years, retiring as a captain.

Robert Foreman, from Lake Charles, Louisiana, was born October 27, 1938, and was killed in action on March 26, 1970. Every single member of Alpha Troop that I have talked to who knew Sergeant First Class Foreman classified him as a first-rate soldier, a remarkable man, and an exceptional pal if he was your friend. As has been noted in the text, Foreman was an African American in an army that was still uncomfortably racist, but, again, all those who knew him never seemed to see the color of his skin—just the man within. He was well liked, well respected, and fearless. He was awarded a Silver Star for his actions on March 26, 1970, and a Bronze Star for his overall record of superior service in Vietnam—both awards made posthumously. Captain Poindexter later petitioned to have Sergeant Foreman's Silver Star upgraded to a Distinguished Service Cross. Regrettably, the army's Board for the Correction of Military Records declined the petition. Sergeant Foreman is survived by his wife, Gudrun, and their three children.

"Gert" Foreman never remarried. Until recently, she continued to live in Monterey, California, near Fort Ord, where she and Robert Foreman were last stationed. Today, she lives in University Place, Washington, near her grown children. Her son is a manager with UPS, and her two daughters are both nurses—one of whom works at the U.S. Army Hospital at Fort Lewis. I asked her to tell me more about her husband:

"What I most remember is that he was always one hundred percent in everything he did and his men loved him. When he was a drill sergeant his 'boys' would all seek him out after graduation from basic and thank him, all of them glad to have had him as their teacher. Even later, after Robert was killed in Vietnam, I would get letters from the men who knew him, and sometimes they would even come and visit me . . . I guess I never remarried because I felt it would be unfair to whomever I might marry, because I would always be saying "What would Robert do?" Even now, in times of worry or stress, I think of him and ask him for help. He doesn't always answer me, but when I think about him and talk with him a great calm will come over me, even today."

Don Grayson, sixty, is retired and living in Bradenton, Florida. Don comes from a roving air force family and grew up all over, including four years in Okinawa. He joined the army just before Christmas 1968 and served two years and nine months. After his army service he "bounced around and through about twenty jobs" until going to work for SKIL Corporation. After five years at SKIL he moved over to Makita USA, where he became a branch manager in the service department. After ten years at Makita, Don moved to Florida, where he started his own business as "the Tool Doctor." He sold his business in 2008 and now spends the majority of his time riding his Harley, working on old cars, and fishing. He signs all his e-mails "Always remember, fish till ya drop!"

Jerry Guenthardt, sixty-two, is director of facilities at Little River Casino Resort in Manistee, Michigan. Jerry was drafted into the army, served two years, went back home, and got married, and he and his wife raised two children, both girls.

Pasqual "Gus" Gutierrez, sixty-three, is a practicing architect with HMC Architects in Ontario, California. Gus was a student at East Los Angeles Community College when the specter of the draft sent him to the recruiters to volunteer. He was sent to Fort Knox, where he was enrolled in the advanced NCO program colloquially called "shake 'n' bake." Barely a year later, as an E-6 staff sergeant, Gutierrez found himself with the 11th ACR in Vietnam. He served on active duty for one year and eight months before returning home. He came back with an impressive array of decorations, including the Silver Star (for his actions in the March 26, 1970, battle), Bronze Star with *V*, and Purple Heart. He reenrolled at East L.A. Community College, this time in their architecture program. After he graduated, he received a shock, however: a "Letter from the President" recalling him to active duty. Like most other regular army enlistees, he had a combined six years active duty and reserve obligation, but the reserve obligation was rarely exercised. Gutierrez spent a summer at Fort Lewis, in Washington State, training new recruits before being demobilized again. Back home once more, he studied hard as an architectural apprentice and eventually sat for the state licensing exam, passing it on the first try. He worked for an interior design firm before starting his own architectural practice, something he successfully pursued for twenty-three years. In 1999 he sold his firm and joined HCM, an architectural design company that specializes in schools and medical buildings. He plans to keep working for "at least a while" and also enjoys spending time with his children and grandchildren. Gus Gutierrez contributed much to the story of Alpha Troop, both through his deeds and later his words. One of his many eloquent observations came right after the White House PUC Ceremony. Gus said, "When all of us who served came back from Vietnam we had to reenter society through the back door. Now, forty years later, in a different world, there we were, walking through the front door and right into the Rose Garden of the most famous building in America. What a difference!"

Fred Harrison grew up in Riverside, California, and was boyhood friends with Tom Hudspeth, who ended up in Alpha Troop at the very same time Harrison was in Company A. Harrison was an avid football player in high school and was even contacted by a scout for the Minnesota Vikings; but, knowing his draft notice was probably "in the mail," he went down to his local recruiting office and enlisted. He told the Vikings he'd be back in touch when he got out of the service. While in Vietnam "Big Fred," as he was called, garnered an impressive two Bronze Stars with the *V*, two Army Commendation Medals with the *V*, two Purple Hearts, five Air Medals, and a Vietnamese Cross of Gallantry. Sadly, when he returned home, the Vikings were no longer interested, so Fred became, as he described it, a "Viking of the Road" instead, driving 18-wheelers. He also tried heavy construction, several other hands-on jobs, and spent many years as a dental technician. Unfortunately, Harrison died on January 23, 2011, from systemic failures brought about by exposure to Agent Orange.

Burl "Topper" Hart, sixty, is the maintenance supervisor of the Fountain Inn First Baptist Church in Fountain Inn, South Carolina. Originally from Quincy, Illinois, along the Mississippi River, Burl Hart was working for an extermination company when, at eighteen years of age, in 1969, he decided to enlist. His lifelong nickname of "Topper" was given to him, as a young boy, in honor of the early 1950s television show *Hopalong Cassidy*. Topper was Cassidy's horse and a much easier name for a young lad to sport than the rather formal "Burl." He served in the army for two and a half years, earning, among other decorations, the Purple Heart and the Combat Infantryman's Badge. After his army service Topper became a steelworker, and when that industry crashed in 1980 he moved his family to South Carolina and went to work for TV Guide Publishing. He worked for TV Guide for twenty years and has just recently taken up his duties at First Baptist. Hart and his wife of forty years, Becky, have three children. He has no thoughts about retiring—at least not anytime soon.

Michael Healey, sixty-five, lives in retirement in Williamsburg, Virginia. After Vietnam, Mike Healey elected to stay in the army and completed twenty-three years of service. He retired with the rank of lieutenant colonel in 1991. For his actions on March 26, 1970, Mike was awarded a Bronze Star with the Combat *V* (his second award) and the Purple Heart. Captain Poindexter had originally intended for Mike Healey to receive the Silver Star, but that paperwork was lost and a Bronze Star awarded instead. A petition to change the record and award the Silver Star was forwarded to the army's Board for Correction of Military Records but was declined. Colonel Healey did receive his PUC, however, in a private ceremony, at his local Veterans Home. I am indebted to Mike and his wife, Patti, for allowing me to use his enlightening letter concerning the battle, written to his parents within four days of March 26.

Robert K. "Robin" Henderson (March 2, 1946–June 19, 1970): was killed in action in Cambodia while leading a ground assault against another suspected NVA bunker complex. As the leader of 3rd Platoon on March 26, 1970, he distinguished himself in the face of the enemy, and Captain Poindexter recommended him for a Silver Star, an award that was originally lost. Henderson's family would finally receive his Silver Star in a moving ceremony thirty-five years after his death.

George C. Hobson, sixty-nine, was born in Hinton, West Virginia, and was drafted into the army in 1965. At the completion of basic training, he was selected for Officer Candidate School, and upon completion of OCS, was commissioned a second lieutenant of infantry. After finishing Airborne and Special Forces schools, he was assigned to the 8th Special Forces Group in Panama. In 1969, he was sent to Vietnam. He spent a year as a military adviser and then, from January to August 1970, was Commander of Company C. He continued in the army after Vietnam, serving at various posts in Europe and the United States. His last assignment was as inspector general at Fort Leonard Wood, Missouri. He retired with the rank of lieutenant colonel in 1990. Colonel Hobson lives in Columbia, Missouri, where he owns and operates Eastwood Kennel and Farm.

Jerry Holloman, former first sergeant of Alpha Troop, retired from the army as a command sergeant major (E-9, the highest enlisted rank). Although a grizzled veteran of many years in the regular army, Holloman was much loved by the men of Alpha Troop. He received both a Bronze Star and a Purple Heart for his service in Vietnam and was also decorated with a slew of other service and campaign medals. Unfortunately, he passed away on August 13, 2007.

Rick Hokenson, sixty-three, is retired and lives in Cotton Lake, Minnesota, with his wife, Gail, and their Weimaraner, Heather. Rick, originally from Detroit Lakes, Minnesota, was attending Fergus Falls Junior College when he got his draft notice. He remembers looking at the clock on a nearby desk as he signed his induction papers. It read "10:00, 26 November 1968." When he got out of the army, he signed his discharge papers at 10:10, so he likes to joke that he was in the army one year, nine months, nineteen days—and ten minutes. Rick volunteered to be a sniper. He proved to be very good at it, earning a Bronze Star with a *V*, an Air Medal, a Purple Heart, his Combat Infantryman's Badge, and Expert Rifle status as a Sharpshooter and Machine Gun specialist. After the army, Rick got into steel construction, then heating and air-conditioning fabrication. He signed on with Northwest Bell, which changed to US West and finally Qwest. He worked at the phone company for twenty-six years before retiring out of the Qwest branch in Fargo, North Dakota. He and his wife now enjoy, as he says, "the laid-back life on the lake." In one of Rick's e-mails, he mentioned that he was sending me some pictures (which he did). "I looked for some pictures of the soldiers from Charlie Company during March 26th, but we had such a high turnover rate that we were getting new 'bodies' all the time. I was told at the Replacement Center that they called Charlie Company 'the Company of the Living Dead' and you did not want to be sent to that company. If I remember right, George Hobson is [another one] who told us that when he was sent out to our company. I would like to tell you that I feel very lucky to have survived all the battles we were in and I feel honored to have served with such a great bunch of soldiers and the great leadership skills of George Hobson."

Thomas Hudspeth, sixty-one, is a Superior Court judge in Riverside County, California. On the day he was drafted, July 21, 1969, Neil Armstrong became the first native of earth to walk on the moon. Hudspeth served in the army for two years and then four years in the army reserve. He returned from Vietnam with two Army Commendation Medals, a Purple Heart, the Vietnamese Cross of Gallantry, and the Combat Infantryman's Badge. He believes he also had a nomination for a Bronze Star with a "V," but he never received the award. He used the GI Bill to go to law school. He became a successful trial lawyer and has been a judge for the past twelve years and a law school professor for a quarter century. In one of the many subplots to this story, Hudspeth grew up with Fred Harrison, who was drafted a few months before Hudspeth, went off to war in Vietnam, and ended up in Alpha Company. Hudspeth rode off to battle on March 26, 1970, with his childhood friend. The two men remained lifelong friends until "Big Fred" Harrison passed away in early 2011.

JC (Joseph Colan) Hughes, sixty-two, is a senior captain with American Airlines and is still flying passenger jets, mainly in the Caribbean. He enlisted in the army at age eighteen and served three years. After his stint in the army he went to flight school, earned his commercial pilot's license, and has been flying ever since. He was on R&R the day of the March 26 battle. For his service in Vietnam he earned two Bronze Stars with a "V," the Army Commendation Medal, his Combat Infantryman's badge, and now the PUC. Although he missed the events of March 25 and 26, he has been a tireless supporter of his former comrades in Alpha Troop and was instrumental in helping John Poindexter not only gain the records he needed for the lost medals but also rallying the troops for the PUC ceremony in Washington, D.C. JC Hughes lives in Delray Beach, Florida, with his wife, Carolyn Parker.

Dennis Jabbusch, former sergeant and track commander of John

Poindexter's command track, A-66, passed away in November 2008; too soon, unfortunately, to participate in the PUC award ceremony. Sergeant Jabbusch was also one of the men whose original award for valor for March 26, 1970, was lost. On a happier note, his Bronze Star with a Combat "V" medal was finally approved and awarded to him at the 11th ACVVAC Reunion in Kansas City in 2006.

Larry King, sixty, is retired and lives in Smithville, Missouri. Originally from Pine Knot, Kentucky, Larry was drifting around as an eighteen-year old, looking for something to do but he also knew the draft would catch up with him soon, so he joined the army on the promise from the local recruiter that he'd be sent to Germany. "I guess he was lying," Larry says now, with a laugh. Larry served for two and a half years, and when he came back to the United States, he ended up in Missouri and started sharecropping. Subsequently, he landed a job as a prison guard at Kansas State Penitentiary and served there for twenty-one years, retiring in 2005. Larry now spends his time hunting and fishing and waiting for his wife, Linda, to retire. He and Linda have a son and a daughter.

Rod Lorenz, sixty-four, is still farming grain in Iowa, something his family has been doing for several generations. He was drafted into the army, served one year and nine months, and returned to his roots, literally.

Romeo Martin, sixty-two, works for the U.S. Postal Service as a route mailman and lives in Plainville, Connecticut, with his wife. They have two sons. He is contemplating retiring, "maybe in a year." Romeo was drafted into the army out of his hometown of New Britain, Connecticut, and served two years, earning a Bronze Star for Meritorious Service and his Combat Infantryman's Badge and now, of course, the PUC. His one overriding memory of March 26, 1970, is, after the battle, "hoping to never experience a day like this again and I never did, thank God."

Gary McCubbin, sixty-one, is retired and living in Kansas City, Kansas. A house painter before he enlisted in the army in 1969, he served three years, came home, and spent the rest of his professional life working for General Motors. He and his wife have one daughter and two granddaughters. Gary, as the TC of A-23, has the following comment about March 26, 1970: "I did not receive a medal for that day and ask for none. Because you see, in my heart, I take pride in the fact that not one of the fine men on my track got wounded or killed in that fierce firefight. That is my reward."

Willie McNew stayed in the army and retired as a platoon sergeant (E-7). He lives in retirement in Copperas Cove, Texas.

Ray Moreno, sixty-one, is the superintendent for the Tulare, California, Road Department. After enlisting in the army in 1969, he served almost two years. He says the hardest part of his army service was leaving his pregnant wife to go off to Vietnam. His daughter was born four days before the battle of March 26, 1970. He and his wife (of forty-two years), Angie, also have a son and four grandchildren.

Dave Nicholson, sixty-seven, is a retired attorney who lives in South Burlington, Vermont, with his wife of thirty-six years, Deidre, and a "few cats." They have one son, Zack. After returning from Vietnam, Nicholson went to law school, graduated, passed the bar exam, and began a long and successful practice in family law, bankruptcy, and civil matters. In 1993 he became quite ill. After exhaustive tests it was determined that he had hepatitis C, contracted from the blood transfusions he had been given while hospitalized for wounds in Cam Ranh Bay in 1970. Nicholson struggled with the disease, a failing liver, and finally liver cancer, which was diagnosed in 2004. The VA classified him as 100 percent disabled due to combat-related illness. Miraculously, a donor liver came through for Nicholson in 2005. Today, Nicholson spends his time gardening, contacting old army buddies, and writing. He completed a book about his Vietnam experiences in 2007—a manuscript he was kind enough to share with me.

John Norton, former commanding officer of 1st Squadron, 11th ACR at the time of John Poindexter's assumption of command of Alpha Troop, has unfortunately passed away.

Angel Pagan, sixty-one, is retired and living in Orlando, Florida. He enlisted in the army in January 1969 and served two years. Since his army days he has worked as a U.S. government investigator at several different agencies and is also a nondenominational ordained minister. Now that he is retired he spends a great deal of his time working on behalf of disabled children and disadvantaged veterans. He is married with one son. He told me, concerning the men of the 11th ACR, "They are my brothers, part of my family. Alpha Troop did an outstanding rescue mission on March 26, 1970. They show[ed] a lot of courage, determination, and valor. God bless." Angel was one of the men whose recognition for bravery was long delayed. He finally received his Bronze Star with a "V" at the 11th ACVVAC Reunion in Kansas City in 2006. We could also say, with certainty, that it was a remark he made to the late Keith Nolan, author of *Into Cambodia*, about medals that were not received that started the whole incredible ball rolling in regard to Alpha Troop's PUC.

Fred Pimental, sixty, from Lynnfield, Massachusetts, enlisted soon after his eighteenth birthday. He had left school and was an ironworker but decided he wanted to give the military a try. They'd soon be looking for him anyway, he figured. He served for two and a half years and then returned to Lynnfield. He started his own HVAC and refrigeration business and continues as president of the company today—although he is looking forward to turning the business over to one of his two sons and spending more time with his family, including four grandchildren.

John B. Poindexter, sixty-six, maintains homes in Houston, Texas, where he is the chairman and CEO of J. B. Poindexter & Co. Inc., and at Cibolo Creek Ranch in the Big Bend country of West Texas. After he completed his army service in 1970, John returned to NYU, where he obtained both an MBA and a PhD in economics and finance. He joined Salomon Brothers as an investment banker in 1971 and later transitioned to private equity investment services with Smith Barney. Today, he is the sole owner of his namesake firm, a diversified manufacturing company with four subsidiaries.

Through his love of Texas history and his stalwart stewardship of the lands of West Texas, John has transformed Cibolo Creek Ranch and its almost 30,000 acres of the Big Bend region into a model for land preservation and historical interpretation. He has restored three nineteenth-century private forts on the land. One fort has been left in its original state, as it was when it served as a refuge against marauding Indians and bandits. The other two forts have been transformed into magnificent museums of Texas history from that era, as well as five-star accommodations for guests who visit the ranch. John's goal is to continue to acquire as much acreage in the region as possible, and he is striving to return the land he acquires to its original and natural condition. Cibolo Creek Ranch has been awarded three listings in the National Register of Historic Places, displays five Texas State Historical Markers, and has received three national and state awards for architecture. The ranch is used by local and statewide cultural, academic, business, and civic organizations for conventions, meetings, and other purposes.

John Poindexter has had a long and distinguished career, starting with the U.S. Army and then the business world, but there is one more honor that has been proposed. John was decorated with the Silver Star, the Soldier's Medal, two Bronze Stars, the Air Medal, two Purple Hearts, the Vietnamese Cross of Gallantry, the National Defense Service Medal, the Vietnam Service Medal, and the Vietnam Campaign Medal for his services in Vietnam. He has added to those awards the Presidential Unit Citation, which he was instrumental in obtaining for Alpha Troop. Through all of his service to the nation and in his quest for delayed and overdue recognition for his men, John never once sought any recognition for himself. In fact, he was not decorated for the battle on March 26, 1970, except for a second award of the Purple Heart. His Silver Star and his two Bronze Stars were for other actions.

Several of John's former army comrades, including Mike Conrad and Doc Bahnsen, have long felt that the lack of a personal decoration for John's actions on March 26, 1970, was a terrible oversight. As the paperwork for the PUC for Alpha Troop was grinding along, these men brought forward a separate petition for John to be awarded the Distinguished Service Cross, a high personal honor second only to the Medal of Honor, the U.S. military's ultimate decoration for bravery. As this book goes to print, that petition is working its way through the system.

Larry Roberts, sixty-three, is still farming in Shelbins, Missouri. After being drafted in 1968 he served his two years, earning the Army Commendation Medal and the Bronze Star with a "V." He has two sons and four grandchildren.

Irwin Rutchik, sixty, lives in Uncasville, Connecticut. We know (from Tom Hudspeth) that Irwin was able to hitchhike from Connecticut to Washington, D.C., for the PUC ceremonies and that he is in tenuous circumstances due to PTSD, but we were, unfortunately, not able to learn more.

Francis "Bud" Smolich, sixty-eight, from Chaney, Illinois, is now retired after a long career in the insulated piping business. He and his wife, Cheri, live in Lockport, Illinois, and enjoy traveling and going to the 11th ACR reunions wherever they are held. Bud was not drafted until relatively late in his youth. He did not receive his "Letter from the President" until age twenty-seven, after he'd already been married to Cheri for five years. Bud was quick to point out to me that he did not serve the required two years: He served two years "and three days." The extra three days were required because he was mistakenly reported AWOL. Almost immediately after the battle of March 26, 1970, Smolich contracted a very rare form of malaria. It was so rare, in fact, that only about eighteen other cases of its type had ever been reported—and twelve of those patients died. Smolich was medevaced to an army hospital in Taiwan for special treatment. Miraculously, he recovered and was sent back to Bien Hoa. It was there that he learned someone had reported him as AWOL instead of marking his records as being in the hospital. In order to get all the paperwork straightened out, he had to go back out into the field, to Alpha Troop, where John Poindexter's successor could officially sign him out. By the time he caught a flight out of Vietnam and got back to Fort Ord for final outprocessing, the army owed him three extra days of pay. "At least they paid me," Smolich quipped. Smolich was nominated for a Bronze Star with the Combat "V" for his actions on March 26. His was one of the lost awards and he finally received his Bronze Star (his second) at the 11th ACVVAC Reunion at Colorado Springs in 2005. He also tells another poignant story about his days since Vietnam: Juan Vargas was Smolich's driver during the time of the events highlighted in this book. The two men became very close, as sometimes only army buddies can become. Both men made it through March 26, 1970, without a scratch, but on April 1, 1970, at FSB Illingworth, Vargas was struck in the head by a large piece of shrapnel and severely wounded. He was medevaced, and Smolich tried for days to find out what had happened to his buddy. He heard nothing and presumed Vargas must have died, but, on the off-chance he had survived, Smolich kept looking for his old pal. All he knew for certain was that Vargas had originally been from Albuquerque, New Mexico. One time when Smolich and his wife traveled through Albuquerque they picked up a phone book only to find hundreds of "Juan Vargas" listings. When it came time to attend the PUC ceremony in Washington, Bud and Cheri decided to take along their eight-year-old grandson, Austin. After the presentation at the White House came the ceremony at the Pentagon. It was a long day and the Smoliches were hungry, but Austin wanted to take the Pentagon tour that was being offered. Reluctantly, Bud gave up his place in the buffet line and went off on the tour. When they got to the next elevator, there stood a man Bud thought he recognized. Could it be? It was: Juan Vargas. Forty years of searching were finally over.

Curtis Sorenson, sixty-three, is still farming wheat, soybeans, corn, and sugar beets in Minnesota. After being drafted in 1968, he served two years, earning the Combat Infantryman's Badge, the

Vietnamese Cross of Gallantry, the Purple Heart, and the usual Vietnam service and campaign decorations. He is married with one son. In his last communication with me he said, "We have tried to put everything behind us, but certain memories are etched in our heads forever." How true, Curtis, how true . . .

Greg Steege, sixty-four, is vice president of Hayden-Murphy Equipment Company, Minneapolis, Minnesota, a construction supply company that specializes in large cranes. Greg was in and out of college in 1969, which attracted the interest of his local draft board, and he was inducted in March of that year. He served two years, reaching the rank of E-5, sergeant, before getting out and returning to his hometown of Denver, Iowa—where he still lives today, with his wife, Susan. They have two sons. Greg was the steadfast radio operator in John Poindexter's command track during the events of March 25 and 26, 1970. For his service in Vietnam he earned a Bronze Star and a Purple Heart for wounds received April 1, 1970, at FSB Illingworth. He is best friends with Donnie Colwell. Greg has no immediate plans to retire.

Raymond Tarr, sixty-one, lives in retirement with his wife, Susan, in his original hometown of Kittanning, Pennsylvania. After the events of March 26, 1970, Ray Tarr soldiered on with Alpha Troop through April, May, and June. He was with the 11th ACR during the Cambodian Incursion, and on June 12, 1970, his tank was ambushed as it patrolled down a Cambodian highway. SP4 Danny Schmidt, twenty, from Evansville, Indiana, was sitting next to Tarr and killed instantly by an enemy rifleman who shot him through the head. The Sheridan was simultaneously hit by a rifle grenade, which ignited a quantity of .50 caliber machine gun ammunition in the turret where Tarr and Schmidt were sitting. Tarr was blown out of the turret and landed on the back of the tank. His injuries were massive and life-threatening. His right eye was gone, his left arm and leg were shredded masses of tangled flesh, and his lower back was punctured by shrapnel that went straight through his colon. Tarr's platoon leader, 1st Lt. Robin

Henderson, and one of the Alpha Troop medics acted quickly and with great skill to get Tarr off the tank and out of the line of fire. The two men managed to haul Tarr to safety and get him aboard an APC (armored personnel carrier). The APC tore back down the road to get to the troop's NDP. The medic got Tarr stabilized but knew he needed more and better treatment—and quickly. They managed to get him aboard a medevac where he was airlifted to the aid station at Quan Loi then further airlifted to the larger 24th Evacuation Hospital in Long Binh. Another month followed at the 249th General Hospital in Japan, then a final ride home to Walter Reed Army Medical Center in Washington, D.C. Tarr had planned to marry Susan, his fiancée, as soon as he left active duty, but as he lay at Walter Reed shattered and disfigured for life, he feared the beautiful young woman he loved so much would no longer want him. That worry proved to be unfounded. Susan kept coming to visit, and as Ray Tarr got stronger, the talk about marriage resumed. They finally set a date: June 12, 1971, exactly one year to the day since Tarr had been wounded. As Susan has put it: "When I told Ray I wanted to get married on Saturday, June 12, he wasn't so sure that was a good idea. After all, that was the date he had been wounded. But I said it was the perfect date to begin our lives together. Instead of remembering June 12 in a negative way, we would celebrate it as our wedding anniversary. God would make something good out of something bad that had happened."

They were married that June 12 and have been married ever since and have two children. However, there was more in store for Tarr: In May 1971, he was going to the VA Hospital in Butler, Pennsylvania, for physical therapy. On one visit he was sent to the dental clinic for a routine checkup. He casually told the dentist his story, that he was getting married soon, and that he was worried that he didn't have a job. He certainly couldn't go back to his old job of apprentice bricklayer. A few days later the dentist called him at home. The clinic had a temporary job available, and would Tarr be interested? He was, he took the job, one thing led to another, and Tarr stayed at the clinic for thirty years, recently retiring as the lead dental technician. Ray Tarr sums it up this way:

"Well, that is the way it was. I'm not exaggerating, and I don't need to be patted on the back. I don't consider myself any kind of hero. I just reacted the same way as anyone else in the same situation. Lots of fine men served with me and went through the same things I did. Thirteen of them didn't come home. A few of them really had their minds messed up over their experience in Vietnam. All in all, it was a traumatic experience for a boy who was twenty years old and who had never been out of Pennsylvania. I give God complete credit for sparing my life and returning me without any major emotional trauma. He sustained me and provided me with a good job, a good wife, and two good children."

Larry Toole, sixty-two, was a farmer in his hometown of Gideon, Missouri, before he was drafted at age nineteen. He served two years and went back to work for Procter & Gamble Paper for twenty-six years, mostly in utilities maintenance as an HVAC specialist. He is retired now and living in Millersville, Missouri. He has been married for forty-three years and has one son who is working as a federal police officer at the Pentagon. Larry loves to fish and ride his Harley.

Ronald Vaughan, sixty-one, is retired and living in Pensacola, Florida, his original hometown. As a nineteen-year-old kid driving trucks for a living, he decided to give the army a try and enlisted in 1969. By March 1970, he was no longer driving trucks but ACAVs in War Zone C. He was severely wounded in the battle of March 26, 1970, and later lost his right eye. But he served bravely, earning a Bronze Star with a "V," a Vietnamese Cross of Gallantry, a Purple Heart, and, as one of the soldiers in the lost medals group, ultimately a Soldier's Medal for his actions on March 25, 1970, during Alpha Troop's tragic mortar incident. Ronald served a total of two years and nine months. After the army, he went back to driving trucks in Florida but also got caught up in the pain of his wounds and his memories of Vietnam. For a while, he turned to drugs, but with the help of the VA and his own determination finally got himself back on his feet. He started a housepainting company, which kept him occupied for many years. Ronald has a son, also named Ronald, who lives in Ohio. In a recent note to me Ronald senior wrote: "Sally Garza sent [my son] a copy of the PUC and he is more proud of his dad than any son could be and after I talked to you I told him about the book that is coming out. And with all this it has brought a father and son closer together than before. And I would like to say thank you all for this." Ronald enjoys attending reunions with his old army buddies and telling great stories; and, as he says, "I'm still fishing!"

Joseph Wakefield Jr., originally from Cincinnati, Ohio, was born on December 22, 1946, and died during the tragic mortar incident that occurred on March 25, 1970, at Alpha Troop's NDP. Wakefield was on his second Vietnam tour.

Lowell Walburn, as far as we were able to determine, is alive and well and living in Faribault, Minnesota.

August Whitlock, sixty-one, originally from Oklahoma City, is now retired and living in St. Paul, Minnesota. He served a total of ten years in the U.S. Army. The first hitch was from July 1969 to July 1972 and the second from January 1974 to December 1980. For his Vietnam service he was awarded an Army Commendation Medal and a Vietnamese Cross of Gallantry along with his Combat Infantryman's Badge and Expert Rifle Badge. It was Whitlock who first learned, when checking out of Vietnam, that the army had somehow lost track of the battle the 11th ACR had fought in Tay Ninh Province on March 26, 1970. After his army service Whitlock worked as a short-order cook, taxi driver, newspaper reseller, security guard, store clerk, desk clerk, bus driver, and bus cleaner.

Ken "Mississippi" Woodward, sixty-one, is now retired and living in Pachute, Mississippi. For his services in Vietnam, Woodward was awarded the Air Medal, Purple Heart, Army Commendation Medal with the Combat "V," Paratroop wings, and Expert Medals for both the M-14 and M-16. After his army service he returned home and entered radiology training. For thirty-two years, until his retirement in 2005, Woodward was a radiology administrator, including twenty-two years with the Saudi Aramco Medical Services Organization in Riyadh, Saudi Arabia. Ken was an invaluable resource for me. He provided crucial and fascinating background information on life as an infantryman in Vietnam, particularly with Charlie Company.

Craig Wright, sixty-five, is now retired and living in Whittier, California. As a college student in 1968, Craig took a course on Southeast Asian history, which led him to further investigate what was happening in Vietnam. His research sent him in a direction that fueled a personal opposition to the war, and he decided to become a conscientious objector. When the army drafted him in December 1968, they did not oppose his claiming CO status. He was sent to medic training and by the time he was assigned to Alpha Troop, 11th ACR, he was a specialist 5th class and a senior medic. Craig served his two years and got out of the army in December 1970, having won a Soldier's Medal, a Bronze Star with a "V," the Purple Heart, and now, of course, a PUC. For the next thirty-seven years, Craig was a public educator, first as a fifth-grade teacher and then teaching high school math. He has recently retired from the teaching profession but is still substitute teaching, playing the piano, and instructing Bible classes at his local Baptist church. He and his wife, Judy, have two children and four grandchildren.

ACKNOWLEDGMENTS

First and foremost, I must acknowledge the men who directly participated in the events described in this book. There are approximately three hundred of them, not all of whom made it, by name, into these pages. Still, collectively it was their bravery and sacrifice that made this remarkable story come to life. As they themselves have said on numerous occasions, they were "only doing their jobs." That is, indeed, true, and yet in so doing, and telling this story, they have come to represent the very best efforts of all the two-and-a-half-million men and women who served during the Vietnam War. These warriors speak for all Vietnam veterans, and they will always have my admiration and utmost respect.

Chief among this "band of brothers" is their former troop commander, John Poindexter, a gentleman I have come to know and respect greatly. I hope he will do me the honor of allowing me to call him "my friend." John is a self-made man of great accomplishment and keen intelligence. In Vietnam, he proved his courage and his dedication to his country and his men. He has never wavered from the principles he showed while in his army greens, and he has lived his life as an example of hard work, dedication, integrity, and perseverance. I could not have written this story without his help.

Anytime I needed a question answered, a point clarified, a door opened, or a record searched, John was ready and willing to help. There were times, I swear, when he answered my e-mails within microseconds of the electrons reaching his mailbox. My debt of gratitude to John will be hard to pay, but I will keep trying.

Of the thousands of possible permutations and combinations of experiences, written statements, interviews, e-mails, phone calls, documents, and photographs provided by the men who were at the center of the events in this book, some made it into the text and some did not. If I skipped anything that should have been included or missed details that some will feel are too important to have been left on my desk, I can only say this: I simply had to draw the line somewhere or this book would still be in draft form without any prospect of completion anytime soon. In trying to decide what would be included I tried very hard to stick with those details that best described the core actions. Beyond that single, most demanding criterion, the second important filter was capturing the feelings and emotions that most clearly represented what these men were experiencing.

In that regard, I am particularly indebted to the following individuals through whose eyes I saw what happened.

2ND BATTALION, 8TH CAVALRY

Mike Conrad was the senior officer on scene during the momentous events that form the core of this book. His perspective, looking at events from the top down, literally and figuratively, was of enormous benefit to this text, and I am grateful for his willingness to share so much of his experience with me. Mike also took on the chore of giving the draft a critical eye in regard to the technical terms, correct use of army terminology, and proper sequencing of the events. His comments were extremely valuable and certainly made the book more accurate.

11TH ARMORED CAVALRY

Retired Col. John Rosenberger, in a sense, started this whole ball rolling. "Rosey" was the one who invited John Poindexter back to the 11th ACR to share his Vietnam experiences, which in turn caused John to dust off his old "Anonymous Battle" manuscript, which led John to do the brush-up research that uncovered the fact that some of his men didn't get the medals they deserved, and so on and so on. If we need to pin this tale on anyone, it should be Rosey, and for that alone I owe him, but he's also a great guy and provided me with important background and some very fine photos.

ALPHA COMPANY

Ray Armer, the quiet, unassuming commander of Alpha Company, was always willing to help me sort through the details. Ray is the complete opposite of John Poindexter; he was then, and he still is now, but that personality was probably exactly what John needed on March 26, 1970. As John tried to hold together the threads of so much action and make the critical decisions that would decide the fates of many, Ray was racing around in the background plugging holes, shoring up weak positions, directing his men to fill in for the cavalrymen who were being taken out of action, and generally providing the solid, experienced presence of a fearless professional. I personally believe that Ray has not been credited sufficiently for the actions he performed. Ray is not the kind of guy to make a big deal out of it. Yes, he received a Bronze Star with a "V" for his courage that day, but frankly, from my research and also my personal experiences in Vietnam, I believe he deserved more: a Silver Star, at least. I also believe that Ray and his men are equally deserving of a Presidential Unit Citation. The fact that they do not have one is a great injustice, but it's also pretty clear that not receiving the PUC was not intentional. I am hopeful that the effort being made to correct this oversight will be successful—it certainly deserves to be.

"Big Fred" Harrison came late to the party, but I was particularly touched by his addition to the list. Fred, you see, represents a whole class of Vietnam veterans who are rapidly fading into the background but should not be. Fred was a young man with great ambitions when the draft called him to the army. He left those dreams behind, never to be recaptured, and off he went, without complaint, to do his duty. He returned wounded, unappreciated, and aimless. He drifted from one career to the next, and although he did all right, he probably never achieved the potential he had before he served. Now, because of his service, and his exposure to Agent Orange in Vietnam, he is no longer among us, gone way before his time. There are thousands like Fred, and it is a shame we cannot do more for them.

CHARLIE COMPANY

Ken "Mississippi" Woodward, the former rifleman and RTO, provided me with many important details about what life was like in the jungle for the grunts of Charlie Company. When I needed to understand what was in a 90-pound pack or how a patrol actually proceeded through the bush (quietly!) or set up on point, all I had to do was ask Ken. He also helped me understand what the men were feeling and thinking as they waited for the next ambush to be sprung or a firefight initiated.

Dave Nicholson offered another unique perspective. The college-graduate point man filled me in on how "Lucky Charlie" turned into "Hard-Luck Charlie" and the "Company of the Living Dead" as they soldiered through the weeks and months leading up to their experiences in that bunker complex in Tay Ninh Province. Whereas Ken Woodward's viewpoint of Charlie was factual and poignant, Dave Nicholson's view was often sardonic and sometimes a bit irreverent. Both perspectives were incredibly valuable to me.

Rick Hokenson, the sniper from Charlie Company, was the fatalistic one. Growing up a hunter and always being around guns, it was natural for him to make the transition to impartial stalker of the enemy; yet he always knew that if the tables were turned, he'd receive no mercy. For Rick, it was a job, and one he took pride in. I needed to see this side of Charlie Company, too, and thanks to Rick, I did.

ALPHA TROOP

Donnie Colwell, the tough, no-nonsense former sergeant and Pennsylvania coal miner, pulls no punches. He told it to me like it was and provided very valuable insight, from the ground level, on what the grunts were thinking as their officers decided their fates.

Bryan Cupp, as a young soldier, seems oddly incongruous in his Vietnam photos. His movie-star good looks, boyish, blond-haired stare, and quick smile belie his tough combat sangfroid and readiness to pop a frag and blow away the NVA. Bryan sent me a thick packet of marvelous photos, detailed descriptions, maps, diagrams, and other items that helped me in my research tremendously.

Pasqual "Gus" Gutierrez pulled himself up by his own bootstraps, out of the anonymity and poverty of his roots in East L.A. The army made him an "instant NCO," then shipped him off to Vietnam with little experience yet great responsibility. Gus, like many of his peers, was forged into a tougher instrument and became, in his own words, "a better man" because of his combat service. He came back, taught himself to be an outstanding architect, did very well for himself, raised kids and now grandchildren, and has become a pillar of his community. I am also indebted to Gus for the many eloquent observations he provided relating to his army days and his time in Alpha Troop.

Mike Healey, who retired from the army as a lieutenant colonel after twenty-three honorable years of service, unfortunately suffered some debilitating complications from a supposedly routine surgery a few years back. His memories of his Vietnam experiences come and go, but, through his devoted wife, Patti, he provided me with some wonderful background pieces and, of course, the striking letter he wrote to his parents a few days after the battle of March 26, 1970.

Ann Ragan, sister of Robin Henderson, was so kind as to share with me her feelings about her brother, his Vietnam days, his death, and her family. This perspective, representing the many who think of Vietnam as a grieving experience, added an important dimension to this work.

Bud Smolich, or "Sergeant Smo" to his army pals, was the key to my unraveling the mystery of what occurred during the tragic mortar incident of March 25, 1970 (along with Donnie Colwell). Bud also provided valuable background for the story of the battle itself, and his ever-ready willingness to provide information and contacts made my job easier.

Ray Tarr, who left so much on the battlefields of Tay Ninh Province and Cambodia, was an inspiration to me for his fortitude and perseverance—and the triumph of true love over adversity. I gained much from his battlefield recollections, particularly the remarkable story of his life after the war.

AND THE REST, WITHOUT WHOM I WOULD HAVE BEEN LOST . . .

My friend and fellow author, the supremely talented and hardworking Tom Clavin, deserves a special note of thanks. Without Tom, this book would not have happened, at least not authored by me. Tom has been a role model and mentor for several years. I took a number of his writing classes, which helped me become a better author, and he has been unstinting in his advice, tips, ideas, and constructive criticism. At one of our regular lunches, Tom gave me the necessary and well-deserved kick in the butt that propelled me down the road toward the nonfiction he thought I should be writing. When I asked him what he thought I should tackle, he simply said, "Write what you know. And one thing you know is Vietnam." Two days later, when the *New York Times* published its piece on Alpha Troop and the pending PUC ceremony at the White House, I knew instantly that this was the story I needed to write. If it hadn't been for Tom, I might have missed this marvelous opportunity.

Another dear friend and fellow author deserves a word here, too: Nelson DeMille. Nelson's string of bestselling works of fiction is truly impressive. Year after year he turns out masterful tales from his fertile brain, spun in part from his own experiences but also from his intense interest in current events and the world around us. He is always busy and seemingly always crunching one deadline or another, yet he has never been too busy to respond to my (often desperate!) pleas for advice and guidance. Everything he has ever told me has been "right on." These are hallmarks of a true friend, and I am lucky to have him in my corner, too.

My agent is Nat Sobel, and I could not have been more fortunate than to have this marvelous man backing me up. I was a complete mystery to Nat, at first, and the last thing he needed was yet another untested, unknown author competing for his invaluable attention (again, I have to thank Tom Clavin for this introduction). I am sure I tried his patience, and I am sure I pestered him to the point of complete rejection, but, somehow, we kept coming back to each other, and if he wasn't quite sure of me, he was sure that the topic was a winner. He beat the you-know-what out of me in regard to the book proposal, and I was ready to have apoplexy over his constant demands for changes and revisions; but, you know what? He was absolutely right, and I can never thank him enough for his persistence, his ultimate belief in me, and his velvet hammer. He knew exactly what to do, precisely what shape the book proposal needed to take, and how to get me to produce for him what he needed to sell the project to the right publisher. Nat, you are the best!

My editor, Marc Resnick, is the consummate professional. He

has an extraordinary ability to see right to the heart of a manuscript and parse out quickly and expertly where all the parts and pieces really need to be. He is also a gentleman, a possessor of great patience, a maintainer of positive outlooks, and just a really nice guy. From the moment I handed over my draft manuscript, with baited breath and great trepidation, he made the process of getting this book done and out the door fun. No author could ask for more than that from a good editor—and I got it. Thanks, Marc.

John Poindexter's personal assistant, Sally Garza, was always willing and able to help me, and her skill at sorting through the reams of materials to get to the facts I needed was a godsend.

Last and certainly not least, profound thanks and gratitude to "the Muse," my wonderful partner in life, Laura Lyons. She gave me the encouragement I needed to pursue this dream once it was formulated and patiently supported my trials and tribulations while I labored on the book. She also sat and listened while I read each chapter to her, as I finished them, one at a time. This is a tradition for us, and it gives me valuable insight into how my work is being perceived by the reader. She sits there listening quietly, taking notes, then lets me know what she thinks. It's instant feedback, and I get lots of great ideas from her. Mostly, though, it's the genuine love and incredible patience from her that nurtures me.

APPENDIX 1

Text of President Obama's Speech on October 20, 2009

REMARKS BY THE PRESIDENT
IN AWARDING THE PRESIDENTIAL UNIT CITATION TO ALPHA
TROOP, 1ST SQUADRON,
11TH ARMORED CAVALRY

Rose Garden

12:24 P.M. EDT, October 20, 2009

THE PRESIDENT: Good afternoon, everybody, and welcome to the White House. And welcome to a moment nearly 40 years in the making.

Last month, I was privileged to present the parents of an American soldier, Sergeant First Class Jared Monti, with our nation's highest decoration for valor—the Medal of Honor. Today, we celebrate the awarding of our nation's highest honor for a military unit—the Presidential Unit Citation.

The Presidential Unit Citation is awarded for "gallantry, determination, and esprit de corps in accomplishing its mission under extremely difficult and hazardous conditions." Since its creation during the Second World War, it has only been bestowed about 100 times.

Today, another unit assumes its rightful place in these ranks—Alpha Troop, 1st Squadron, 11th Armored Cavalry, the legendary Blackhorse Regiment.

To mark this occasion we're joined by Congressman—and Vietnam veteran—Leonard Boswell; Vice Chairman of the Joint Chiefs of Staff, General Jim "Hoss" Cartwright; John McHugh, our Army Secretary; and Vice Chief of Staff Peter Chiarelli; from Fort Irwin, California, leaders of today's 11th Armored Cavalry—Colonel Paul Laughlin and Command Sergeant Major Martin Wilcox; and most of all, the men of Alpha Troop—those behind me and some 100 here today.

Now, these men might be a little bit older, a little bit grayer. But make no mistake—these soldiers define the meaning of bravery and heroism.

It was March 1970, deep in the jungles of Vietnam. And through the static and crackle of their radios Alpha Troop heard that another unit was in trouble. Charlie Company, from the 1st Cavalry Division, had stumbled upon a massive underground bunker of North Vietnamese troops. A hundred Americans were facing some 400 enemy fighters. Outnumbered and outgunned, Charlie Company was at risk of being overrun.

That's when Alpha Troop's captain gave the order: "Saddle up and move out."

As these men will tell you themselves, this isn't the story of a battle that changed the course of a war. It never had a name, like Tet or

Hue or Khe Sanh. It never made the papers back home. But like countless battles, known and unknown, it is a proud chapter in the story of the American soldier.

It's the story of men who came together, from every corner of America, of different colors and creeds. Some young—just 18, 19 years old, and just weeks in the jungle; some older—veterans hardened by the ugliness of war. Noncommissioned officers who held the unit together and the officers assigned to lead them.

It's the story of how this team of some 200 men set out to save their fellow Americans. With no roads to speak of, they plowed their tanks and armored vehicles through the thick jungle, smashing a path through bamboo and underbrush, mile after mile, risking ambush and land mines every step of the way, and finally emerging from the jungle to the rescue—what one member of Charlie Company called "a miracle."

It's a story of resolve. For Alpha Troop could have simply evacuated their comrades and left that enemy bunker for another day—to ambush another American unit. But as their captain said, "That's not what the 11th Cavalry does."

And so, ultimately, this is a story of what soldiers do—not only for their country, but for each other: the troopers who put themselves in the line of fire, using their tanks and vehicles to shield those trapped Americans; the loaders who kept the ammunition coming, and the gunners who never let up; and when one of those gunners went down, the soldier who jumped up to take his place.

It's about the men who rushed out to drag their wounded buddies to safety; the medics who raced to save so many; the injured who kept fighting hour after hour. And finally, with dark falling, as the convoy made the daring escape back through the jungle, these soldiers remained vigilant, protecting the wounded who lay at their feet.

The fog of war makes a full accounting impossible. But this much we know. Among the many casualties that day, some 20 members of Alpha Troop were wounded. And at least two made the ultimate sacrifice—their names now among the many etched in that black granite wall not far from here. But because of that service, that sacrifice, Alpha Troop completed its mission. It rescued Charlie Company. It saved those 100 American soldiers, some of who join us today. And those soldiers went on to have families—children and grandchildren who also owe their lives to Alpha Troop.

Now, some may wonder: After all these years, why honor this heroism now? The answer is simple. Because we must. Because we have a sacred obligation. As a nation, we have an obligation to this troop. Their actions that day went largely unnoticed—for decades—until their old captain, John Poindexter, realized that their service had been overlooked. He felt that he had a wrong to right. And so he spent years tracking down his troopers and gathering their stories, filing reports, fighting for the Silver Stars and Bronze Stars they deserved and bringing us to this day.

Thank you, John.

We have an obligation to all who served in the jungles of Vietnam. Our Vietnam vets answered their country's call and served with honor. But one of the saddest episodes in American history was the fact that these vets were often shunned and neglected, even demonized when they came home. That was a national disgrace. And on days such as this, we resolve to never let it happen again.

Many of our Vietnam vets put away their medals, rarely spoke of their service and moved on. They started families and careers.

Some rose through the ranks, like the decorated Vietnam veteran that I rely on every day, my National Security Adviser, Jim Jones.

Indeed, I'm told that today is the first time in thirty-nine years that many from Alpha Troop have pulled out their medals and joined their old troop. Some of you still carry the shrapnel and the scars of that day. All of you carry the memories. And so I say, it's never too late, we can never say it enough. To you and all those who served in Vietnam, we thank you. We honor your service. And America is forever grateful.

Today also reminds us of our obligations to all our veterans, whether they took off the uniform decades ago or days ago—to make sure that they and their families receive the respect they deserve, and the health care and treatment they need, the benefits they have earned and all the opportunities to live out their dreams.

And finally, if that day in the jungle, if that war long ago, teaches us anything, then surely it is this. If we send our men and women in uniform into harm's way, then it must be only when it is absolutely necessary. And when we do, we must back them up with the strategy and the resources and the support they need to get the job done.

This includes always showing our troops the respect and dignity they deserve, whether one agrees with the mission or not. For if this troop and our men and women in uniform can come together—from so many different backgrounds and beliefs—to serve together, and to succeed together, then so can we. So can America.

I cannot imagine a more fitting tribute to these men, who fought in what came to be called The Anonymous Battle. Troopers, you are not anonymous anymore. And with America's overdue recognition also comes responsibility—our responsibility as citizens and as a nation, to always remain worthy of your service.

God bless Alpha Troop and the 11th Armored Cavalry. God bless all those who wear this nation's uniform. And God bless the United States of America.

Thank you very much, everybody.

[Author's Note: The entire ceremony is available for viewing on YouTube at the following URL: http://www.youtube.com/watch?v=ghNQ8qr F3GA.*]*

APPENDIX 2

The Blackhorse Regiment, the 11th Armored Cavalry

The 11th Armored Cavalry Regiment today is a unit of the United States Army garrisoned at Fort Irwin, California. The following is taken from the unit's current mission statement:

> The 11th Armored Cavalry Regiment's unique mission is vital to the readiness of our army. That mission is to provide the US Army the most capable and lethal combined arms opposing force in the world. The 11th ACR is the Army's premier maneuver unit, the opposing force at the National Training Center at Fort Irwin, California. There, the Blackhorse trains the United States Army, one unit at a time in the brutally harsh climate of the Mojave Desert. Consequently, the tough and uncompromising standards of the 11th ACR have become the yardstick against which the rest of the Army measures itself.

The regiment served in the Philippine-American War, World War II, the Vietnam War, the Cold War, Operation Desert Storm, and Operation Iraqi Freedom. From June to December 2003, members of the 11th ACR deployed to Afghanistan, where they helped to develop and train the armor and mechanized infantry battalions of the Afghan National Army.

In January 2005, the 11th ACR redeployed to Iraq and, with the permission of the former Alpha Troopers from Vietnam, carried into battle with them several of the old Vietnam-era guidons (troop flags) that fluttered through the jungles of Southeast Asia.

Among the 11th's illustrious past commanders have been George S. Patton IV and former secretary of the army Thomas E. White Jr.

Although order-of-battle and regimental organization are always in a state of flux and subject to the needs of the service, the 11th from World War II through today has typically consisted of either three (as in War Zone C, 1970) or four squadrons of battalion size and a support squadron. First Squadron ("Ironhorse") is an armored battalion of four troops. The "Alpha Troopers" in this tale are the first of the four troops in 1st Squadron. Second Squadron ("Eaglehorse") is also an armored cavalry battalion but has for many years operated as the U.S. Army's primary OPFOR (Opposing Forces) training battalion. Third Squadron ("Workhorse") is an armored battalion with attached engineers and a howitzer company and typically operates in small-unit-sized detachments to support the other armored cavalry operations of the regiment. Fourth Squadron ("Thunderhorse") was traditionally the 11th's aviation unit and was used for medevac (medical evacuation), troop airlift, and electronic warfare. It was inactivated in 1994. The Support Squadron is aptly named "Packhorse" and is responsible for supply, training, maintenance, and medical operations.

For a complete history and description of the 11th ACR the following Web site is highly recommended: http://www.irwin.army .mil/Command GroupUnits/Units/11acr/Pages/default.aspx.

APPENDIX 3
The M-551 Sheridan Tank

If, as the old saying goes, "the camel was originally a racehorse designed by a committee," one modern mechanical descendant of the camel might, indeed, be the M-551 Sheridan. U.S. Army planners of the late 1960s, working out the feverish theories of then–Defense Secretary Robert McNamara, decided they needed a new breed of tank to tackle the exigencies of modern warfare. Unlike the hedgerow-smashing main battle tanks that came out of World War II, the Army wanted something lighter, more maneuverable, and "air-drop capable"; that is, a whole lot of firepower that could be deployed from an aircraft big enough to haul and drop a tank. On top of these daunting requirements, this new gun platform would also have to swim across rivers, travel at speeds in excess of 40 miles per hour, and fire a new breed of ground-attack missile from the same gun tube that fired the tank's conventional rounds.

The bastardization of all these requirements resulted in what became the Sheridan. In reality, the Sheridan did not become a true tank at all, and was designated instead an ARAAV, or "armored reconnaissance airborne assault vehicle." The M-551 was named after General Phil Sheridan of Civil War and Indian-fighting fame. The actual general was known for his lightning-quick maneuvers on the battlefield and his exceptional skill at directing firepower where it was needed most. His namesake armored vehicle would also be known for delivering a lot of firepower with exceptional maneuverability, but its other limitations would nearly prove its undoing—at least in the warfare typical of Vietnam.

"Airborne" it proved to be, but only in limited fashion. Air drops from any appreciable height, even with a gaggle of parachutes, generally proved disastrous. The best chance the Sheridan had of arriving by air in one piece was safely in the belly of a giant C-5 Galaxy cargo plane. This behemoth could lift three or four Sheridans, but it needed a 10,000-foot runway to land them again safely. Some limited success was also achieved with the reliable C-130 Hercules cargo plane. The C-130 could deliver one Sheridan at a time and "drop" it, but only with the rear cargo door open and the plane executing a touch-and-go landing. While the Hercules was rolling along the runway the Sheridan—lashed to a giant skid— would be hydraulically pushed to the ramp, then dragged out of the aircraft by a large set of parachutes.

"Armored" was another misnomer that had dire consequences for some of the Sheridan's crews. Although its main gun turret was steel, its hull was made of aluminum. This allowed the Sheridan to be light and fast, but it could not absorb anything like the punishment the M-48 Patton tank, its predecessor, could take. Mines and RPGs often proved deadly to the Sheridan in Vietnam, and heavy-caliber machine gun bullets could penetrate the thin aluminum skin. After the Sheridan's initial forays in Vietnam, a "mine plate" of one-inch-thick steel was welded to the chassis. This added a significant measure of survivability to the Sheridan, at least from mines, but it also added—literally—a ton of weight, thereby cutting back on some of its speed and maneuverability.

Former Sheridan driver and 11th Armored Vietnam veteran SFC Terry Sperry recalled his time in the Sheridan this way:

Yes, I remember them, I was a driver in 1970 when we got them. Nice new tank that ran well as long as . . . you didn't get your ass shot off. In the base camps, we talked about the merits of driving or being in the turret. As the driver, at any given minute, I expected a blinding flash followed by sailing through the air as a mine went off under my ass . . . but most of the drivers I knew survived . . . For the TC and loader, sitting high in the turret . . . well, that's where the RPGs always hit and I saw a lot of those guys end up in pretty rough shape.

"Reconnaissance" as a descriptor for the Sheridan was about a draw: It was, without question, maneuverable and reliable. It could traverse rough open terrain and scramble through arroyos and river-beds with ease. It also hardly ever lost a track. Retired army colonel Clint Ancker rode the Sheridans with the 11th Armored Cavalry in Vietnam in 1971. He reports:

The best part of the Sheridan was its suspension. It could go places that the ACAV couldn't. It had a very low ground pressure, was very rugged, and almost never threw track. While the M-113 threw track not infrequently, the Sheridan rarely threw track. I only saw one thrown track on a Sheridan in Vietnam. This happened in an old trench line where the Sheridan slipped into one of the trenches and threw a track to the inside.

The other part of the recon equation, getting through the jungle, was much more problematic. The Sheridan was deployed to armored cavalry units in a basic ratio of 3:1; that is, one Sheridan to three M-113 ACAVs. The Sheridan, as the bigger of the two types of vehicles, most often got the lead in busting jungle. However, the Sheridan, as has been noted, was not a Patton or a main battle tank, and as such, being lighter, it actually had some difficulty smashing thick vegetation. The Sheridan was also prone to overheating rapidly in this type of work environment.

It was definitely a top-notch "Vehicle": The 300 hp Allison diesel engine could drive the machine all day at speeds in excess of its top-rated 43 mph. It ran through mud even better than the older Pattons. It plowed through dust and dirt with few mechanical breakdowns. Later in its service life—which lasted a remarkable twenty-seven years—it served as the main Opposing Force battle tank at the U.S. Army's tank training center in the high desert at Fort Irwin, California. Running across desert sands or down a lane in the middle of a forest it just couldn't be beat. The problem was, it was sent to Vietnam, where speed and agility were not determining factors in the warfare mix.

"Assault" was another good news/bad news scenario for the Sheridan. The infantry loved the Sheridan. It could deliver a lot of firepower at the point of attack, and when used as a complement or backup to ground infantry operations it was like having your own mobile artillery.

The developers of the Sheridan had decided to equip it with an outsized main gun—a whopping 152 mm cannon. This was much bigger than the 90 mm main guns on the M-48 Patton. It was such a powerful gun that, when fired, it was typical for the Sheridan's front wheels (or running gear) to come off the ground. It was also known to have such a bruising recoil that TCs, if they weren't hanging on, could be bounced around the turret. More than a few TCs suffered cracked or broken ribs before learning this valuable lesson.

The Sheridan fired either the M-657 HE (high-explosive) shell or the M-625 canister round. The HE shells were more like long-range artillery. The canister rounds were used primarily for anti-personnel. A single canister shell contained ten thousand flechettes, or steel darts with fins. When this round was fired, an enormous cloud of tiny metal arrows fanned out over a range of up to 400 meters. One round could shred anything and everything—foliage or flesh—in its path. This munition was sometimes called the "beehive" round because, after firing, the mass of darts seemed to zing through the air like a hive of angry bees. U.S. Army Lt. Col. (Ret.) Burton Boudinot described an experience with the beehive round this way:

> In January of 1969 the first Sheridans and the new equipment training team arrived in Vietnam. The reception of the 11th ACR was cool, but then on January 29, two Sheridans were on picket duty along the Long Binh highway. At about 0230, the crewmen were alerted to movement to their front. The Sheridan searchlights were turned on and enemy troops spotted crossing a dirt road. Two 152 mm "Bee Hive" antipersonnel rounds were fired. The next day, over 125 bodies were found.

The ammunition the Sheridan used was caseless; that is, the projectile and its gunpowder propellant charge were not surrounded by a solid shell or case, as was most other ammunition. Caseless ammunition was designed both to lighten the ammunition load by dispensing with the heavy brass or steel casings and to cut costs. In general, as a munitions breakthrough, it has not found wide acceptance for a myriad of reasons. Most of them are related to safety, heat sensitivity, and fragility.

Nevertheless, all Sheridan rounds were caseless. The warhead, or "bullet," was attached to the propellant at the factory and sleeved in a nine-ply nylon bag. Each round had to be loaded carefully so as not to separate one component from the other. Rough handling in combat operations where the tempo often called for rapid fire under stressful conditions made for many instances when the propellant became detached from the warhead. If this happened, loaders were instructed not to use the round. As a result, there were countless times when highly flammable propellant sacks were left to roll around in the belly of a Sheridan while combat continued. The potential for disaster from an errant spark—inherent in just about all combat evolutions—was fairly predictable and sometimes proved deadly.

In March 1971, five Sheridans from the 11th ACR were lost in one day to RPG fire; all five vehicles burst into flames and were totally destroyed. It became a common scene to observe melted Sheridan hulls with their sunken steel turrets sitting at odd angles with their gun tubes pointing toward the sky in various parts of the country, either awaiting final disposition or simply forgotten.*

It was suspected, but never confirmed, that all five of these tank hulls were penetrated by RPGs that then set off secondary explosions from discarded ammunition.

The Sheridan was also capable of firing the MGM-51 Shillelagh. The Shillelagh was a surface-to-surface, antitank missile with a range of 2,000 to 3,000 meters. It was intended to fire from the same gun tube on the Sheridan as the standard ammunition, and it did work, but not consistently or reliably. It was, therefore, depleted from the inventory of all the Sheridans deployed to Vietnam.

The Sheridan was equipped with two smaller, supporting guns: a faithful and powerful Browning automatic .50 caliber machine gun was mounted in the TC's turret, and a secondary 7.62 mm machine gun was placed in the belly of the tank and was to be used by the loader when not otherwise serving the main gun. The .50 caliber was in a very exposed position, however, so a modification made for Vietnam was to weld a gun shield to a ring on the top of the turret that surrounded the .50 cal.

The Sheridan and the warfare mission for cavalry in Vietnam were not very compatible; but, as the troops were fond of saying, "And there it is," which meant, of course, there wasn't much that could be done about it. The troopers had little choice in the matter, so they took what was given to them and, like soldiers since time immemorial, did the best they could with what they had.

---

* http://en.wikipedia.org/wiki/M551_Sheridan

APPENDIX 4

The M-113 Armored Cavalry Assault Vehicle (ACAV)

The Vietcong called them "Green Dragons." Among the Allied armed forces who bought and used them they had a number of amusing sobriquets. The Australians called them "Buckets"; the Swiss, "Elephant Roller Skates"; the Germans, "Pig Cubes"; and the Norwegians, "Vietnam Dumpsters." The U.S. Army, who commissioned them and had them built starting in the early 1960s, initially called them armored personnel carriers, or APCs. As the M-113 morphed into more of a fighting vehicle than a simple troop carrier, the term Armored Cavalry Assault Vehicle, or ACAV, became more common. The ACAV was the ubiquitous U.S. Army fighting vehicle in Vietnam. Here is its brief history.

The M-113 was equipped with interior benches for ten fully armed combat troops, plus a driver and a TC. Its function, as designed, was to drive troops to the front while laying down covering fire with its .50 caliber machine gun, if required. When the troops arrived where they were needed, the TC would drop the rear ramp, the infantrymen would race out to take up their assigned positions, and the M-113 would scoot to the rear to pick up another load of troops and repeat the cycle. The M-113's could swim through 40 inches of water, crawl over all but the steepest gullies, and, with their reliable diesel engines, run all day. They were air-drop capable (via the C-130 and C-141), like the Sheridans, but proved to be much better at flying than their bigger brothers.

The first batches of M-113s arrived in Vietnam in early 1962. They were immediately turned over to the ARVN, who promptly reconfigured them as light tanks or assault vehicles capable of carrying a few troops *and* blasting away at the enemy. The ARVN added additional light machine guns and reinforced turrets for the TC and bolted extra shielding to the chassis to protect against mines. U.S. Army commanders were furious and accused the ARVN of changing battle doctrine and bastardizing the M-113 into a role for which it was not suited—but it worked. Even with its relatively thin aluminum skin the repurposed tracks proved adequate at protecting troops from small-arms fire, fighting a generally unmechanized enemy, and punching holes in the thick brush and jungle.

Grudgingly, the U.S. Army came around and by 1965 was deploying its own version of the M-113 with belly armor, a shielded turret for the .50 cal, and two M-60 machine guns mounted internally, with shields, in left and right rear positions. The M-113 had become a fighting vehicle, and so it would remain for the rest of the war.

This caused a change in U.S. Army doctrine, of course, and brought the cavalry, with its thousands of tracks, into the fight in a more direct way. What had been an infantry, artillery, and aviation (helicopter) war became a contest supported by all the fighting branches.

GLOSSARY

A   Letter designator for all vehicles in Alpha Troop, followed by two numbers; therefore, "A-66" was "Alpha Troop vehicle number sixty-six."

A-66   ACAV (see next entry) assigned to the Alpha Troop commander.

ACAV   Armored cavalry assault vehicle: a modified M-113 tracked vehicle armed with one .50 caliber heavy machine gun and two M-60 light machine guns (see appendix 4 for a complete description).

AK-47   The AK-47 is a selective-fire, gas-operated 7.62 mm assault rifle, developed in the Soviet Union by Mikhail Kalashnikov. The designation AK-47 stands for "Kalashnikov automatic rifle, model of 1947." Even after six decades, due to its durability, low production cost, and ease of use, the basic model and its variants remain the most widely used and popular assault rifles in the world. The AK-47 was the standard operating rifle for the NVA and usually supplied in quantity by the Soviet Union.

"AND THERE IT IS" One of the most popular phrases used in the war, it was a ubiquitous comment on whatever happened that no one could explain or understand. ("Why did Smith have to get blown away the day before his DEROS?" Answer: "And there it is.") Also: "There it is" and "There it is, man."

AO   Area of operations.

ARVN   Army of the Republic of Vietnam or an individual South Vietnamese regular army soldier.

AWOL   Absent without leave: going off without authorization—a very serious offense, especially in a war zone.

BLACKHORSE   As in "Blackhorse Regiment," the popular designation for the 11th Armored Cavalry Regiment, featuring its distinctive rearing black stallion logo superimposed on a shield of half crimson, half white (see appendix 2).

BLOWN AWAY   Killed: usually in a gruesome manner.

BOONIES   Colloquial expression for the jungle or any area of action out and away from the cities, towns, or fortified bases; short for "the boondocks."

BUSTING   As in "busting jungle": a slang term to define the act of transiting through thick vegetation by using brute force to smash through the greenery. Sometimes it was done by infantry as they pushed through the jungle; in this book, the term is most often used in context of the mechanized tracks smashing down the jungle.

C-4   A composition plastic explosive that usually came in foot-long bars 1 inch thick and 3 inches wide. It was perfectly safe when carried around, dropped, cut, or even molded, like putty or plasticene. It only exploded when set off by a blasting cap. It only burned when ignited by a match or other incendiary device. It was used for everything from blowing ammo dumps to heating coffee or C-rats (see next entry).

CANISTER Antipersonnel ammunition used by the Sheridan main gun: consists of a single round packed with ten thousand dart-like flechettes.

CHERRIES New, untested, untried soldiers or replacements.

CHINOOK CH-47 helicopter manufactured by Boeing and first deployed in 1962. It became a workhorse helicopter in the Vietnam era, lifting and resupplying everything from troops to tanks, beans to bullets. The grunts of Vietnam sarcastically referred to it as the "Shit-hook."

CHOPPER Army slang for helicopter.

CLAYMORE An antipersonnel mine containing 700 small ball bearings that become shrapnel when the mine explodes. The mine is shaped and meant to throw its large volume of metal bits across a 60-degree arc. Effective range is about 100 meters. The mine can be control detonated, set with a timer, or detonated by trip wire, step plate, or (today) laser.

CLOVERLEAF A patrol routine whose sweep, out-and-back, resembles a four-leaf-clover pattern.

COBRA AH-1 helicopter gunship.

COOK-OFF Explode spontaneously, usually as a result of its proximity to a high heat source.

CP Command post: the official headquarters location of a unit's commanding officer.

C-RATION Commonly called "C-rats," these were the standard-issue field meals. They came in three basic types and were packaged inside a thin cardboard container. They could be eaten cold since all the food was precooked or pre-packaged; or, they could be heated by any local means, most often by placing a can on a warm engine or by taking a small Chiclet-sized piece of C-4 (see above) and using it as a heat source. Ham and lima beans was the most despised ration; spaghetti and meatballs, the favorite. Each C-ration came with a plastic spoon, salt and pepper packets, instant coffee, sugar, nondairy creamer, two real Chiclets, and a small pack of four cigarettes.

CVC   Combat vehicle crewman.

DEROS   Acronym for "date estimated return overseas," the day every soldier lived for, literally: the day the Vietnam tour was officially over and the "freedom bird" would fly him home.

DI DI MAU   Vietnamese for leaving quickly or running away.

DINK   Derogatory term for a North Vietnamese (regular) or Vietcong (irregular) soldier: could refer to a person of Asian origin or someone "desperately in need of knowledge."

DUST OFF   A helicopter-borne medical evacuation.

ELEPHANT GRASS   Very tall, tough grass: much like bamboo, with sharp edges that could slice flesh and draw blood easily.

F-4   The F-4 Phantom II was a tandem two-seat, twin-engine, all-weather, long-range supersonic jet interceptor fighter/ fighter-bomber originally developed for the U.S. Navy by McDonnell Douglas Aircraft. It was introduced into the U.S. Navy inventory in 1960. Proving highly adaptable, it became a major part of the air combat strategy of not only the navy but also the Marine Corps and the U.S. Air Force. It was used extensively by all three services during the Vietnam War, primarily as an air superiority fighter but also for ground-attack and reconnaissance operations.

FLAK JACKET   A sleeveless jacket with collar designed to provide protection from shrapnel and other indirect, low-velocity projectiles. It was made of a nylon material into which small steel plates were sewn.

FO   Forward observer.

FRAG Fragmentation grenade or hand grenade: a small, metal, handheld munition primarily used as an antipersonnel weapon. "Frag" could also mean "to frag," as in using a grenade or other explosive device to "blow away" an officer or NCO who was not liked by the troops (230 documented cases in Vietnam).

FRIENDLY FIRE Being fired upon by one's own troops: an occurrence all too frequent in Vietnam.

FSB Fire support base: a military encampment designed to provide artillery support to infantry operating beyond the normal range of direct fire support from their own base camps. FSBs were originally used by South Korean troops during the Vietnam War, and the United States adopted the practice after South Korean troops proved its usefulness. Most FSBs were temporary encampments, but some became famous—or infamous, as the case may be—such as FSB Illingworth, in this story.

GOOK Derogatory term for a North or South Vietnamese soldier or civilian; etymology suggests the word is originally Korean and refers to a "country" or "rural" person.

GRUNT Slang term for an American infantryman; a regular "GI."

HE High-explosive ammunition used by the Sheridan main gun. As opposed to canister (see above), these munitions were mostly long-range, artillery-type rounds.

HOOCH Slang for a native hut or home.

HUEY UH-1 basic utility helicopter: transports eight to ten soldiers; used as gunships and medevacs; also called "slicks," "birds," or "choppers."

HUMP To pack up and carry all of one's gear, as in "saddle up and hump the boonies."

IN COUNTRY Army slang for being in Vietnam. The standard tour for a

U.S. soldier during this period was twelve months "in country" (thirteen months for the marines).

JUNGLE PENETRATOR   A device that could be deployed from a hovering helicopter and used to vertically extract troops, especially wounded troops, from thickly forested or dense jungle environments. Torpedo shaped in its folded position, it would be dropped down through the canopy. When its anchorlike flukes were unfolded on the ground, it became a seat to vertically lift personnel back up to the helo.

KC   Kit Carson Scout (*Hồi Chánh Viên* in Vietnamese). Named after the famous American frontiersman, the KCs were almost exclusively former NVA or Vietcong who had, for one reason or another, defected and agreed to work for the ARVN or American forces as scouts or sometimes as interpreters.

KIA   Killed in action (see also MIA and WIA).

KIT CARSON   See KC, above.

KLICK   Slang for "kilometer," or .625 miles.

LAAGER   A defensive formation of tracks, mostly used at night (see NDP, below).

LIGHT UP/LIT UP   To place/have placed the enemy under fire.

LOACH   Nickname for the OH-6 light observation helicopter.

LZ   Helicopter landing zone.

M-16   The M-16 entered U.S. Army service as the XM-16E1 and was put into áction for jungle warfare in South Vietnam in 1963, becoming the standard U.S. rifle of the Vietnam War by 1969. Initially, it was poorly suited to the conditions of jungle warfare and often jammed or malfunctioned in the heat, high humidity, and dirt-filled environment of Southeast Asia. The main problems centered on the powder used in the cartridges and dirt accumulating in the rifle barrels. The ammunition problem was solved quickly, and rifle barrels were lined with chrome to make them smoother and less susceptible to collecting dirt. Once these changes were made, the M-16 performed better, and soldiers started preferring the M-16 to any other standard-issue rifle. The M-16 became, in fact, the second most widely adopted infantry firearm in the world after the rugged AK-47 (the M-16 being more accurate, however).

M-60   The M-60 was a standard, widely used machine gun in Vietnam. It fired 7.62 mm ammunition fed into the gun via disintegrating-link belts. It was first accepted into the U.S. Army in 1957. The M-60 could fire 500–600 rounds per minute. It was carried by infantry squads, deployed on river patrol boats of the U.S. Navy, and mounted on M-113 ACAVs and the Sheridan tank. Because of its large size and substantial weight, compared to prior personal machine guns like the Thompson and Browning models, the grunts in Vietnam called it "the Big Pig."

M-79   A shoulder-fired 40 mm grenade launcher: capable of firing about six rounds per minute and effective to about 350 meters. Sometimes called a "Dooper" for the loud, hollow *doop* sound it makes when fired.

M-113   Army designation for the ACAV (see appendix 4 for a complete description).

M-551   Army designation for the Sheridan tank: a lightweight, air-drop-capable tracked vehicle with a 152 mm main gun (see appendix 3 for a complete description).

M-577   Army designation for the mobile command post tracked vehicle, a variant of the M-113 ACAV. The M-577 typically acted as a mobile office and radio center.

MAD MINUTE   Prearranged, simultaneous discharge of a cavalry or artillery unit's main weapons, often used as a nighttime deterrent to surprise attacks. The infantry alone would not do this—it would be suicidal.

MEDEVAC   Medical evacuation, which in Vietnam was often carried out by helicopter. Only used for nonambulatory cases, as a general rule.

MIA   Missing in action (see also KIA and WIA).

MORTAR   An indirect-fire weapon that launches several types of munitions at low velocities, short ranges, and high-arcing ballistic trajectories. It is typically muzzle-loading and has a barrel length less than fifteen times its caliber.

MORTAR TRACK   A variant of the M-113 ACAV used to transport and fire mortars.

NAPALM   A jellied gasoline that is thick and syrupy and used in flamethrowers and incendiary bombs. It burns at a temperature of about 800°F. In Vietnam, napalm was often used as an antipersonnel weapon and was greatly feared by the NVA.

NCO   Noncommissioned officer: typically, an enlisted sergeant ranked E-5 or above (to E-9).

NCOIC   Noncommissioned officer in charge; on occasion, senior NCOs were designated as unit commanders in the absence of any commissioned officers.

NDP   Night defensive position (the cavalry also called it a laager): overnight defensive formation wherein all forces were arranged in a circle, weapons pointing outward. Support and noncombat tracks were placed in the circle's interior.

NEWBIE   Slang term for a new replacement soldier, officer, or enlisted.

NVA   North Vietnamese Army or an NVA regular soldier.

OCS   Officer Candidate School.

OH-6   Numerical designator for the Loach light observation helicopter.

ONE-SIX   Radio call sign of Alpha Troop's 1st Platoon leader (SFC William McNew).

POINT   The first soldier at the head of a line or column on patrol; also, "point man." It is an extremely dangerous but critical function. The point man is the eyes and ears of the patrolling unit and usually the first to contact the enemy or get targeted by them. Probably the only member of the unit who moved with his weapon off safety.

PRC-25   The PRC-25 is a back-pack, portable, VHF FM combat-net radio transceiver used to provide short-range, two-way radiotelephone voice communication.

PUC   Presidential Unit Citation, the highest U.S. military award for valor given to a unit (as opposed to an individual soldier).

QRF   Quick Reaction Force—a group assigned to be the "next up" if something happens that requires the immediate deployment of manpower.

R&R   Rest and relaxation. During a typical in-country tour in Vietnam, each soldier was guaranteed between five and ten days off the line on R&R, usually in Thailand, Hawaii, Australia, or some other close-by but exotic location designed to get their minds off the madness of combat.

RACER   Radio call sign of Charlie Company (Capt. George Hobson was Racer Two-Nine).

REMF   Rear echelon motherfucker: pejorative term for a soldier in the rear or not on the front lines.

ROGER   Radio jargon for "I understand."

ROME PLOWS   Large, armored, specially modified bulldozers used to clear jungle vegetation. During the American incursion into Cambodia, Rome plows cleared over 1,700 acres of jungle near the Fishhook region and destroyed over 1,100 enemy positions. The plows took their name from the city of Rome, Georgia, where they were made by the Rome Plow Company (now located in Cedartown, Georgia). The plows were equipped with a very sharp "stinger blade," which weighed more than two tons and was able to cut down even fairly large trees.

ROUND   A single projectile of any type.

RPG   Rocket-propelled grenade: a shoulder-launched, shaped-charge grenade and a staple of the NVA, mostly manufactured in the former USSR, although by 1969–70 many were being made in China.

RTO   Radio telephone operator: typically a unit's radioman.

SAPPER   Infiltrator: a soldier-specialist whose principal mission was to infiltrate defensive positions, usually at night, using explosives and/or wire-cutting tools.

SHIT SANDWICH   A very tough spot: a bad place to be in.

SHRAPNEL   Metal fragments produced by the explosion of a round.

SIX   Radio call sign for Capt. John Poindexter, CO, Alpha Troop.

SKS   Semiautomatic rifle used by the Vietcong or the NVA: it fired the same 7.62 round as the AK-47. It was not automatic but it was longer, making it more accurate.

SLICK   Army jargon for a small unarmed helicopter, typically the UH-1 Huey, used mostly for transport, dust-off, resupply, and extraction of troops (noncombat evolutions).

SMOKE   A colored smoke grenade used for marking positions.

SNAFU   Acronym for "situation normal, all fucked up."

STONE MOUNTAIN   As used in this book, the radio call sign assigned to the battalion commander of the 2nd Battalion, 8th Cavalry (Lt. Col. Mike Conrad).

STRAIGHT-LEG   Army slang for an unmechanized unit, i.e., pure infantry.

TACAIR   Tactical air support: airborne assets, typically fixed-wing fighters, bombers, fighter-bombers, and helicopters.

TC   Track commander: the individual in charge of a tracked vehicle, usually a sergeant (E-5) or above.

TEAM ALPHA   A tactical-arms combined force. In this book, Alpha Troop and Alpha Company are operating together as a combined unit called Team Alpha.

THREE-SIX   Radio call sign of Alpha Troop's 3rd Platoon leader (1st Lt. Robert Henderson).

THROW TRACK   When the mechanical treads that linked the drive wheels of a Sheridan or ACAV came off, it was said to have "thrown track."

THUMP GUN   Slang for M-79 grenade launcher (see above).

TRACK   Slang for a tracked vehicle such as the M-113 or M-551 Sheridan.

TROTTER   A trail in the jungle wide enough for two men to march along side by side.

TWO-SIX   Radio call sign of Alpha Troop's 2nd Platoon leader (1st Lt. Mike Healey).

VVAC   Veterans of Vietnam and Cambodia: a special fraternal group of veterans who had served in both Vietnam and Cambodia, especially during the Cambodian Incursion in 1970. The 11th Cavalry VVAC is one subset of these men and is particularly active in veterans' affairs.

WIA   Wounded in action (see also KIA and MIA).

WILCO Radio jargon for "I will comply."

WORD (THE) The "word" could either be a rumor of what was about to happen or official notification on what was going to happen.

WORLD (THE) Anywhere but Vietnam, mostly where a soldier came from or wanted to go to, as in "back in the World . . ."

WRITER Battalion call sign for Capt. John Poindexter.

XO Executive officer: typically the second in command of a unit.

SELECTED BIBLIOGRAPHY

Atkinson, Rick. *The Long Gray Line: The American Journey of West Point's Class of 1966*. Boston: Houghton Mifflin, 1989.

Bahnsen, John C. "Doc," Jr. *American Warrior: A Combat Memoir of Vietnam*. New York: Citadel, 2007.

Bowden, Mark. *Black Hawk Down*. Reissue ed. New York: Grove Press, 2010.

Caputo, Philip. *A Rumor of War: With a Twentieth-Anniversary Postscript by the Author*. New York: Henry Holt, 1996.

Halberstam, David. *The Best and the Brightest*. New York: Random House, 1972.

Jacobs, Jack. *If Not Now, When?* New York: Berkeley Caliber, 2008.

Marlantes, Karl. *Matterhorn*. New York: Atlantic Monthly Press. 2010.

Moore, Harold. *We Were Soldiers Once . . . and Young*. New York: Random House, 1992.

Nicholson, David A. *Tales from the 'Nam*. Manchester, NH: Oak Manor Publishing, 2008.

Nolan, Keith. *Into Cambodia*. Novato, CA: Presidio Press, 1990.

Nolan, Keith. *Search and Destroy*. Minneapolis: Zenith Press, 2010.

Olds, Robin. *Fighter Pilot*. New York: St. Martin's Press, 2010.

Poindexter, John. *The Anonymous Battle, Parts I and II.* Houston, TX: published by the author, 2004 and 2011.

Sheehan, Neil. *A Bright Shining Lie.* New York: Modern Library, 2009.

Stanton, Shelby L. *The Rise and Fall of an American Army: U.S. Ground Forces in Vietnam, 1965–1975.* Novato, CA: Presidio Press, 1985.

INDEX

Military units are listed numerically. American units are cited in reverse hierarchical order. Example: 1st Platoon, Alpha Troop, 1st Squadron, 11th Armored Regiment. North Vietnamese units appear under the heading NVA.